MW01174021

Reinventing
PATIENT
CENTRICITY

Advance Praise

"Improving patient health outcomes starts with embracing the rise of consumerism in healthcare and adopting a patient-centric approach. Healthcare leaders must marry the science with the human being and their everyday behavior and expectations to meet patients where they are. This book adeptly showcases why a patient-centric healthcare approach can achieve improved healthcare outcomes. It is full of extensive examples and case studies of innovators who truly adopt a patient-centric model."

– **Amy West**, Head of Digital Transformation and Innovation, Novo Nordisk

"ZS presents an impactful and introspective book that navigates the intricate landscape of patient centricity, shifting from a moment to a movement. You vividly see and hear the lived experience of diverse patients and their care partners, who are at the heart of the book's curiosity, scientific evidence and comprehensive insights. While making the case for patient centricity, it does not assume omniscience. The book welcomes us all as mere mortals to search our blind spots, working toward a more equitable and inclusive healthcare ecosystem that improves not just the patient experience but the humans experiencing it. An ah-ha! moment is available for every stakeholder."

– **Monique C. Gore-Massy**, Global Lupus Patient Advocate

"Patient centricity is a comprehensive approach relevant for everyone in pharma. It ensures that we ask 'what is the best thing for the patient?' throughout product development and all the way to post-approval to ensure we are meeting patient needs beyond the medicine. This book poses proactive ideas for pharma and examples of what 'great' can and should look like in patient centricity—a must read for the industry!"

– **Kris Flynn**, Global Commercial Lead, Hemophilia Gene Therapy, Spark Therapeutics

Reinventing
PATIENT
CENTRICITY

Bringing patient-led
business models to life

By Sharon Suchotliff & Hensley Evans

Copyright © 2022 ZS Associates, Inc.
All rights reserved.

No part of this publication may be reproduced, copied, or transmitted in any form without the prior permission of the publisher. Request for permission should be directed to: publications@zsassociates.com.

This publication is designed to provide accurate and authoritative information and opinions in regard to the subject matter covered. It is sold with the understanding that through this publication the publisher and authors are not engaged in rendering legal, accounting, or other professional services. If legal, accounting, or other professional advice or assistance is required, the services of a competent professional should be sought.

Trademark Notice: Product or corporate names may be trademarks or registered trademarks and are used only for identification and explanation without intent to infringe.

Published by ZS Associates, Inc.
1800 Sherman Avenue, Suite 700
Evanston, Illinois 60201

www.zsassociates.com

ISBN: 978-0-578-29379-0 (Hardcover)
ISBN: 978-0-578-29881-8 (eBook)

Table of Contents

Acknowledgments

Writing and editing this book has been an epic journey and a humbling and sincere honor. While ZS has been engaging in patient-centricity-related work for as long as the industry has talked about the topic, this is the first time we are bringing all of the various pieces together to show patient centricity's true impact and what it takes to make lasting changes—to reinvent and give new meaning to patient centricity. The enormity of this undertaking is certainly not lost on us, and it would not have been possible without the determined team that helped make this idea a reality.

This book was created with the catchphrase one often hears patient advocates repeating at conferences and other public events—"nothing about me, without me"—in mind, so we owe a big thanks to the patients who came forward to share their stories, who provided their endorsements and who helped us think about what we should include in this book and figure out the title. To the patients who so generously offered their perspectives to us, we hope that we have done a good job capturing and integrating your ideas and suggestions.

We are also so very grateful to the 12 authors who dedicated time and thought to crafting the stories in each chapter. As senior leaders at ZS, they all carry many other responsibilities to their clients, the firm and their families, and yet they made the time and commitment to share their wisdom with us, write, rewrite and rewrite again. Their relentless dedication to imparting the stories, examples and collection of best practices contained in the book has helped shed light on the patient-centric transformations that are possible and that we hope the industry will adopt and advance.

Part of what makes ZS such a special place to work is the sense of curiosity and intra-preneurialism that is so fundamental to who we are as a company. We have been so lucky to work with individuals who have, from the very start, supported this endeavor and helped us flush out the idea of what a book on patient centricity might look like. Many thanks to Jeff Gold, Nan Gu, Kurt Kessler, Pratap Khedkar, Judith Kulich, Pete Mehr, Aaron Mitchell and Maria Whitman for their suggestions, challenging questions and support along the way.

None of this would be possible without the collaboration of our clients, who, as leaders and trailblazers in their respective organizations, have worked with us to develop, pressure test and activate many of the ideas we highlight in the book. Due to confidentiality agreements, many of the companies and individuals who contributed must remain anonymous, and we owe a great deal of thanks to each and every one of them. A special thanks to our early advisors on the project who helped shape the idea, including Andrew Benzie, Katie Mazuk, Laurie Meyers, Nancy Phelan, Bharat Tewarie, Keri Yale and several other members of the ZS Patient Centricity Advisory Board.

There are many other colleagues at ZS that contributed to the creation of the book you have in your hands today. Our core team, Lauren Goldenberg, David Thai, Teun van der Loo, and Cecilia Zvosec was instrumental in building out the initial book outline and helping to onboard authors; they worked tirelessly to help corral a (sometimes unwieldy) group of busy and distracted authors through drafts, updates, legal reviews and communication among the various parties involved in the book development. Thank you to our researcher, Jyoti Sardana, who helped track down case studies and fact check our stories, as well as our legal team, including Kyra Flores, Leslie Jackson and Cem Kuru.

We would like to thank our incredible marketing team who supported the idea from the outset and helped us every step of the way—Lena Bent, Ann Marie Gray, Elizabeth Torp and Megan Wolfe. Thank you to Elliot Langerman for naming the book and to Adrianne Schoen and Neil Warner for the cover design and guidance on interior graphics. We also want to thank Dr. Allen Roda and the editing team at Dissertation Editor for their guidance and collaboration.

There are additional acknowledgments at the end of each chapter to recognize the many other individuals who contributed to bring that individual piece of the larger book to life.

And, as a final close, a tremendous thanks to our families, who inspire us daily to be our very best and kindly gave us countless evenings and quiet weekend mornings to pursue this endeavor. We both particularly owe a debt to our partners and co-parents—Todd Suchotliff and Jason Adams respectively—for keeping the kids occupied, fed and in the right places while we were working on the book.

– Sharon Suchotliff and Hensley Evans

Foreword

Bharat Tewarie, M.D., MBA

Helping people living with diseases live the life they desire has been a constant theme throughout my career. That's why I became an M.D. and started my professional life working in a hospital. But then I decided to give the business world a try. So, I got a job at a multinational pharma company, fell in love with this world and began dreaming about how my efforts could turbocharge a greater impact. I traveled through several medical and commercial roles in pharma companies at Boehringer Ingelheim, Roche and Merck Serono to become the executive V.P. and chief marketing officer at UCB. My own journey didn't stop there, as I subsequently started my own advisory company, Boston BioPharma Consultants; joined boards; and simultaneously became the CEO of ViroCarb, a start-up with an antiviral drug platform. This journey allowed me to not only observe first-hand the rise of patient centricity in the pharma space but also to lead many of these efforts.

Through this all, I could choose the life I wanted for myself. I know I owe my ability to pursue my dreams and ambitions at least in part to my good health. For people living with diseases, there are often times when their aspirations have to take a backseat to the more immediate demands of their health.

Pharma companies are trying to help facilitate better experiences and outcomes for these patients by continuously rolling out patient support programs and services. A prerequisite for all who desire to bring bold changes to the patient experience is state-of-the-art knowledge about the frontiers of patient centricity and, most importantly, the patient journey—or should I say patient odyssey? This book provides a comprehensive and thought-provoking account of how patient centricity evolved but also shares actionable insights into the why and what-next.

Through careful selection and rigorous discussion of key examples drawn from the industry, the authors offer the reader a valuable window into pharma's hits and misses related to patient support programs and services. Pharma companies are investing a lot of energy in developing new programs each day, pushing forward enthusiastically with tenacity and dedication, believing themselves to be on the right track. But, when we consider impact, not just effort, the question arises: Are we really achieving what we set out to achieve? Can we demonstrate a measurable win-win for both patients and the business?

Maybe. Maybe not.

As the authors will explore in detail, the ZS Patient Centricity Maturity Index highlights the fact that no pharma company is transformational on any dimension of patient centricity. Many in the industry agree. Patients too. The patient stories shared in this book are a vivid reminder that we still have a very long way to go to reach the kind of patient centricity for which the ZS authors powerfully advocate.

Which brings me to the matter of definitions. ZS's definition of patient centricity encompasses four elements: insight, integration, improvement and impact. Not only is patient centricity about getting the right patient insight but also about the company culture and its capacity to integrate this insight into day-to-day decision making. From there, patient centricity is about having the capability to improve the patient experience and about achieving meaningful impact for both the patient and the business. It's easy to see why no company has reached the transformational level yet, as all four elements, from insight to impact, need to be in place to truly move the needle on patient centricity. No easy task!

There are many other definitions of patient centricity out there, as we somehow have not yet landed on a common understanding among all healthcare stakeholders. It will be imperative to do this. If we cannot align on one definition, how can we work together to measure and maximize patient centricity?

This is why patient support programs and services have become a patchwork of great intent, but with limited impact in the eyes of people living with diseases. Who wants to guess what our patients will tell us if we solicit their feedback and ask, "Do we get you?" or "Do we make you feel smart and respected?" or "Do we put you first?" Considering that, as reflected in a recent Harris poll, only 9% of Americans indicated that they think pharma puts patients over profit, we have to assume that the answers to the questions I just posed would not be good either.

The challenges involved in providing a true and measurable impact for both patients and the businesses are both difficult and interesting. Many healthcare stakeholders simply assume that targeted actions to improve patient centricity will provide patients with the experience they seek. Actions alone, however, will not be sufficient.

"Begin with the end in mind" is an often-heard mantra. But what is the end we have in mind for patient centricity? If we cannot answer these questions, we are spinning our wheels and wasting valuable time. After many stops and starts, we are at a crossroads now. So, what is next?

If actions drive outcomes, then bold actions will drive bold outcomes.

So what produces bold actions?

Bold thinking.

Are we thinking boldly?

Here is where this book is also helpful, as the authors make you aware of which current assumptions, beliefs, learnings and experiences are preventing our current thinking from evolving into bold thinking. One such belief is that patients' unmet needs are largely medical, meaning they're related to symptoms, treatment specifics and curing the disease.

A publication I co-authored in the January 2019 edition of NEJM Catalyst details a study using natural language processing and machine learning to analyze more than half a million patient posts online to learn about their unmet needs in their own words.[1] Only two out of the eight top unmet needs were medical. Six of the top eight dealt with long-term emotional concerns, with the top two focusing on how to live on a daily basis with the disease.

This is an example of the kind of thinking that we need to change in order to design, develop and deliver both a transformational patient experience and business impact. We all know that simply wanting things to be different never gets us very far. Not only do we need good intentions and "bricks of action" but also bold thinking to shift the horizon of what we see as possible.

What would happen right now if we could shift our thinking away from acting *for* patients to acting *with* patients? What if we could see them as people who live day-to-day with their disease, see them as consumers who expect convenience and choice, and see them as individuals?

Maybe then our patients would tell us, "you speak my language" or "you meet my needs like no other can" or "you see it my way."

Will we be there? Is that the impact we seek?

After reading this book, you may be emboldened to move away from putting the patients at the center and instead put them in front of you.

Maybe it's time to stop becoming patient-centric and instead become patient-led.

– Bharat Tewarie, M.D., MBA

Endnotes

1. Bharat Tewarie et al., "Unmet Needs: Hearing the Challenges of Chronic Patients with Artificial Intelligence," in NEJM Catalyst, January 30, 2019, https://catalyst.nejm.org/doi/full/10.1056/cat.19.0018.

Introduction

Hensley Evans

Three years ago, a colleague of mine (Albert Whangbo, one of the co-authors of this book) and I were in Pune, India, working with our real-world data (RWD) and insights team there. We felt that RWD was an underutilized resource for understanding the patient experience and were exploring different ways to leverage data sets to gain new insights. One of our experiments was inspired by a primary market research project I had done a few months earlier with people suffering from non-alcoholic steatohepatitis (NASH).

Our client on that project had asked us to interview several dozen NASH patients to understand their experience, but we had struggled to find patients that met the criteria the client was looking for: diagnosed NASH patients with the typical co-morbidities (e.g., obesity, type 2 diabetes, heart disease). We kept finding patients who were, in the words of the client, "really sick." They had a much wider variety of other illnesses and conditions than the client expected, such as fibromyalgia and auto-immune conditions like Crohn's disease or psoriatic arthritis. In our conversations with patient after patient, we discovered that NASH wasn't a key priority for them. This wasn't necessarily because they didn't understand their diagnosis but because they had so many other health issues to manage—many of which were much more urgent. Our client was frustrated that we weren't finding "regular" NASH patients, who didn't have a lot of other chronic conditions—but I suspected that the "regular" NASH patients the client was looking for weren't the norm at all!

So, now in Pune with several enormous real-world data sets at our fingertips, we decided to do what we dubbed a "virtual chart audit." We used diagnosis codes to find confirmed NASH patients in the data set and then selected 100 patients at random from that group to evaluate. For many of these (anonymized) patients, we were able to see a decade or more of their healthcare data, and what we found was staggering. One example (not even an outlier) was a man in his 50s who we named "Bob" and who had seen 42 separate physicians for seven distinct chronic disease diagnoses over the course of the previous five years! He had experienced a heart attack, multiple serious complications from his type 2 diabetes, and a cancer diagnosis. His NASH diagnosis followed on the heels of almost a decade of constant, escalating and life-threatening health issues. Looking at the data, it became clear to Albert and me that there was no such thing as a "regular" NASH patient—all of these patients were people who had a huge range of health and other concerns. Conducting a research project that entailed zooming in on only one aspect of the patients' lives—their NASH diagnosis—while trying to hold all other variables constant essentially ignored the humanity of the people we were trying to understand.

After that, Bob became a recurring figure in my thoughts as I worked with various clients on patient centricity initiatives. One morning, on a run around my neighborhood, I was (as usual) contemplating the day or week ahead and doing a mental audit of some of the projects I was focused on. We had just read out some early findings from our Patient Experience Index (PXi) study, and while some of the data was unsurprising other pieces were interesting and even confusing. For example, why did female respondents report lower overall experience scores than male respondents in every therapeutic category except diabetes? As I pored through the quantitative research, I remembered Bob and thought about all the other factors outside his NASH diagnosis that were impacting his experience. While the Patient Experience Index showed one side of the picture—how four key factors impact the overall patient experience with a medication—it didn't address some of the qualitative aspects of the patient experience. Most notably, while the Index showed us that social determinants of health (SDOH) impact experience, it didn't answer specifically how or why. A question formed in my mind: How could we bring together all the different perspectives we had gained in the past three years—qualitative and quantitative, R&D and commercial, patient and HCP—to paint a more complete picture of the patient experience and illuminate what patient-centered healthcare can and should look like?

Meanwhile, on the TED Radio Hour podcast I was listening to, the host introduced the author of a new book … Suddenly, the answer was clear: We could pull together all of these perspectives, white papers, POVs, research studies and professional experiences into a book—*the* book—on patient centricity.

The idea quickly gained momentum as I talked with more and more of my colleagues at ZS. One of the unique aspects of patient centricity is that it is relevant to everyone who works in healthcare. Or at least it should be! Colleagues around the globe who were working on SDOH and health equity, rare diseases and oncology, clinical development, value and access, medical devices, digital health, product marketing and many more issues—they had all been working on various aspects of patient-centered care and were enthusiastic about contributing their perspectives. We quickly realized that, by bringing together all of these different lenses, we could offer a broader and hopefully more integrated view encompassing what patient centricity is, why it's important (both to patients, pharmaceutical manufacturers and other healthcare providers) and how we might accelerate our progress toward more patient-centered care.

At ZS, we do much of our work with pharmaceutical manufacturers, and thus this book primarily offers a discussion on how and why pharma can play an important role in moving the healthcare system toward a more patient-centered future. For those in pharma who are in roles specifically focused on patient engagement, patient centricity or the patient experience—this book is definitely for you! But we believe that every function within pharma has a role to play, so the book also contains a wealth of information for people working in early research, clinical development, medical, commercial, enterprise or operational roles. And we're confident that the stories, lessons and examples we present will pique the interest of people outside pharma too: patient advocates, providers, payers and even just "regular" people who are interested in understanding more about patient centricity. Finally, while many of the individual patient stories come from the U.S., the majority of the companies with which we work are taking a global approach to patient centricity initiatives, so most of the information here will be broadly relevant across geographies.

We have organized the book into three sections: loosely, the why, what and how of patient centricity. The first section addresses what patient centricity is and why it is important. We outline the current challenges in today's healthcare experience that lead us to believe patient-centered care is a better alternative, define what exactly we mean by patient centricity and discuss all of the reasons why we are now seeing more and more organizations focus on patient centricity. We then wrap up the section with a bit of perspective on why—given all of the compelling reasons to make the shift toward patient centricity—we haven't seen more meaningful change (yet). The second section examines how pharmaceutical organizations are pulling patient-centric thinking into their work and decision-making at the functional level. We explore how organizations can build a strong foundation for patient centricity through a deep understanding of the patient experience, identify ways to remove barriers to patient participation in clinical trials, contemplate how to address unmet patient needs in new and emerging therapeutic areas, detail what pharma can do to help patients find and select the most appropriate treatment options and, finally, describe how companies are beginning to transform the post-Rx patient treatment experience. Lastly, we conclude with ideas about how to make this vision a reality at the enterprise level. What organizational structures and change initiatives are required, and what might patient centricity look like in terms of both the patient outcomes and business impact?

We wouldn't have been able to write this book without the generous contributions of stories from dozens of patients as well as the examples, case studies, lessons learned and a few cautionary tales from many of our friends and clients who are working tirelessly to make patient centricity a reality within their organizations. It's our hope that their stories and experiences will be valuable to all of our readers and will provide some inspiration for each of you as you seek to make your work more patient centered. Achieving patient centricity will require commitment and coordination across the industry and the larger healthcare ecosystem, but it's within our reach. Let's work together to help all of our patients—people like Bob all around the world—to live better and healthier lives.

SECTION ONE INTRODUCTION:
Is Pharma Finally Ready to Embrace Patient Centricity?

First, thanks for reading! We're guessing that, if you've picked up this book, then you probably already have some ideas about why patient centricity is important, particularly now. If you work in pharma, you may already be pursuing patient-centric initiatives within your organization. If so, great! But regardless of where you are on your patient centricity journey, we believe that, as an industry, we can and must do even better. Why do we say that?

First, because it's clear from the many patient stories we collected for this book that we have a long way to go to get to true, patient-centered healthcare. In Chapter 1, we zoom in on one patient's journey that unfortunately illustrates many of the challenges and barriers that exist in the system today. While A.C.'s experience may be very different from that of the patients you or your organization seek to support, her story contains an important takeaway that applies to every single one of us: We have to listen to our patients. Earlier. With more frequency. And more deeply.

Second, there is a lot of evidence that we are still missing many opportunities to integrate what we hear from a diverse and representative set of patients into our work. Early on in our patient centricity work at ZS, we shared our (then) new Patient Centricity Index (PCI) with a group of thought leaders from across the pharmaceutical industry. We wanted their feedback and input. About 20 minutes into the discussion, one of them asked a simple question: "Have you showed this framework to patients? What do they think?" We were mortified. Here we were talking about patient centricity and how to measure where an organization was in terms of its capabilities to integrate the patient perspective … and we hadn't asked any patients what they thought! It was a great lesson for us—that we can always do more to listen to and integrate the patient voice into our work.

The good news is, we believe that the time is right to make some meaningful changes that have the potential to vastly improve the patient experience. Chapter 2 explores some of the internal and external drivers prompting many organizations to renew their efforts or rethink their organizational structures in order to put patients at the center. Part of that requires that pharma reflect on and take accountability for some of the inequities of the past that have impacted marginalized patients. Even organizations that remain product-focused are thinking about how to deeply embed diverse patient perspectives into their work. It's so encouraging to see the amount of focus patient centricity is receiving increase in so many companies.

One of the first things organizations are doing as they seek to increase their focus on patients and drive a more patient-centered culture is to align on what exactly they mean by patient centricity, patient engagement, patient experience and patient focus. In Chapter 3, we share what we believe is the emerging consensus definition of patient centricity and how it differs from other buzzwords we frequently hear (and use).

While we want to acknowledge the groundswell of activity, we'd be remiss if we didn't point out that those of us working in pharma have been talking about patient centricity for more than a decade. While we've made incremental progress here and there, we haven't yet delivered on the promise that we will hold the patient's needs at the center of all our decisions. Will today's surge of interest turn into "all talk, no action?" As the authors of this book, we obviously don't think so. But, in order to understand why this moment might be different, we take a look in Chapter 4 at why pharma has been slow to change to date. We hope that, at the end of this section, you too will believe that we are on the cusp of meaningful change and will be eager to dive into Section 2 to hear about how organizations are starting to tip the scales decisively in the direction of patient centricity.

Chapter 1:
The Healthcare Journey

Fiona Taylor and Michael Thomas

A.C.'s Story

In 2011, A.C.[1] was a manager at a large consumer goods company in the Midwest, focused on her career aspirations and her passion for fitness, including training for a marathon she planned to conquer. After catching the flu, she developed terrible chest pains. She rested for a few days, and the pain subsided, allowing her to get back to work and to her marathon preparation. But when the pain returned, she followed up with her primary care physician, who at first suspected an issue with her gall bladder before ruling that out. This was the beginning of A.C.'s long, wearying search for answers. Another doctor reading her chest x-ray picked up a mass on her lung and referred her to a pulmonologist. A follow-up MRI showed something on her sternum that raised concerns. This led to more doctors, a thoracic surgeon, tests and scans, ideas about what it was and what it wasn't, yet no diagnosis. Frustrated but determined, A.C. picked up her race training again, even as she continued scheduling periodic appointments for all the tests needed to understand her condition and ensure the mass wasn't growing. At the end of the year, her MRI showed the mass was gone. What a relief!

But this wasn't the end of A.C.'s healthcare journey. Over the next two years, she and her doctors followed up with MRIs to confirm that everything was okay, even considering the possibility of it being a false alarm. A.C. was living well, training hard for more sporting events, but then found that she was unexpectedly (and oddly, given her training regimen) gaining weight. She considered that this may have been due to general aging, or perhaps perimenopause. It never occurred to her that the weight gain was connected to a broader issue with her body until it became significant. A.C.'s physical trainer noticed one of her arms was bigger than the other. A.C. herself noticed her face was swelling; she hoped it wasn't so obvious to other people, but even an Uber driver commented. He suggested she might be allergic to mold in the Pacific Ocean—imagine being so desperate for answers that you consider that diagnosis, and from your Uber driver!

A.C.'s brother could immediately tell something was wrong when she visited him in Iowa. He watched his typically articulate and athletic sister stumble for words and literally stumble, unable to keep her balance. They packed up and drove to the Mayo Clinic. A.C. saw a 31-year veteran ER doctor at Mayo who started at the beginning of her medical history. By taking the time to talk with her and truly see her as an individual sitting in front of him, he noticed something only her trainer had noticed before—A.C. had one arm that was bigger than the other. This was the "eureka!" moment. The ER doctor said something that marked this moment as the turning point in A.C.'s journey: "Before you leave here, I promise you will have an accurate diagnosis."

Unfortunately for A.C., that accurate diagnosis was a rare stage 4 thymic cancer; she had a tumor the size of an orange behind her sternum—the same tumor discovered five years earlier, which had seemingly disappeared, was now back and larger than ever. The tumor was causing fluid to become trapped and unable to get to her heart, thus the swelling in her arm and face. As someone who had worked so tirelessly on her health and fitness, she was now a patient, navigating what seemed like an endless series of hospitals, oncologists and treatments, steps that for many patients are intimidating or even paralyzing. For A.C., the experience prompted a sobering realization: "If I had been diagnosed early, I would probably have been cured in the early stages. Now I am fighting for my life."

Her experience also gave her a new outlook on what it means to be a patient, and she began to draw connections to what other patients were going through. She realized that she knew how to navigate the healthcare system better than many patients who either did not have the right medical knowledge or who had financial constraints and could not get the care they needed and deserved. As she made her way from the first to the fourteenth cancer center, she reflected on her personal journey. Inspired to connect with other patients, she learned how to leverage social media and patient advocacy organizations, and, perhaps most importantly, she learned the difficulty for patients who have to advocate for themselves. A.C. used her advocacy efforts to create a task force of patients with the same cancer, who are committed to seeking a cure. Today that task force has become a platform for identifying treatment options and providing advocacy and awareness for much-needed research.

We Are All on a Journey

It's easy to forget, when in good health, just how fragile and precarious our well-being really is. While many of us may never experience an ordeal like A.C.'s, delays on the road to a diagnosis and the anxiety of living with uncertainty are common realities for many patients and their families. For some of us, our healthcare journey has so far mostly involved regular appointments with our family doctor and the occasional trip to our neighborhood pharmacy to pick up a prescription. For others, this journey has unfortunately been much more onerous. This is especially pronounced for those contending with complicated and rare conditions. A.C.'s story about living with agonizing uncertainty for years is not uncommon, despite how rare her specific diagnosis might be. Each step a patient must take, from first experiencing symptoms and sensing that something is wrong up to the point of receiving proper care (either short-term or long-term), can be arduous. Add to that the stress of wondering "what is wrong with me?" or "am I ok?" or "is my child or loved one going to be ok?" Even for those who face more common ailments, the ups and downs can be emotionally taxing. If only everyone's healthcare journey were as simple as quickly identifying the condition, finding the right treatment and then going "back to normal."

So how can pharma help? Developing an understanding of the patient journey is critical for identifying where there are opportunities to improve the patient experience and overall patient care. After all, isn't the whole point of healthcare and medicine to help patients? Of course, all patients are unique, and the spectrum of known diseases is vast and variable. Healthcare professionals, from doctors and nurses to pharma executives, need to strike a balance between understanding individual patient experiences and understanding the patient experience in the aggregate. We also need to remember that context matters and do our best to understand patients' experiences holistically, as their illnesses are only part of their lives and identities.

We can contextualize the patient experience across four primary aspects of the journey:

- Experiencing symptoms and seeking medical care

- Undergoing testing and navigating diagnosis

- Selecting and starting treatment, if available

- Continuing treatment and monitoring disease progression

Each of these steps is an experience in and of itself, and one that's even more pronounced for historically marginalized communities and those impacted by social determinants of health (SDOH). A step can be quick or quite slow, simple or complex, and it may result in success, painful disappointment or more questions. In this chapter, we will explore each of these steps in the patient journey in more detail. Many of the subsequent chapters in this book will discuss not just the importance of the patient journey but its connection across the healthcare value chain and how various stakeholders, most notably pharmaceutical manufacturers, need to understand the journey and create opportunities that provide meaningful benefit to the patient, family and caregiver alike.

Figure 1-1: The Healthcare Journey

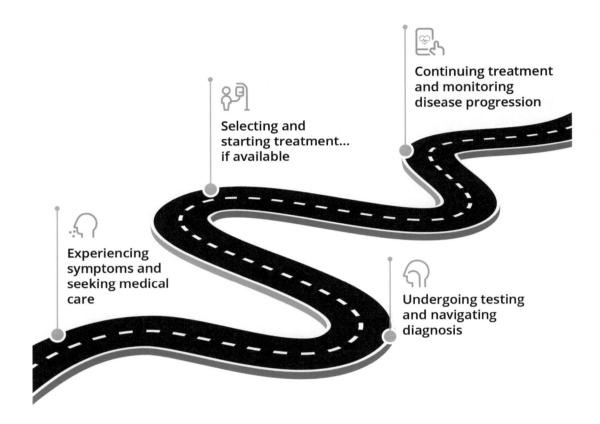

Experiencing Symptoms and Seeking Medical Care

We all hope to wake up each day feeling good and ready to tackle the day's challenges, whether they involve work, family life, hobbies or whatever else we might have ahead of us. Sometimes we experience symptoms of the common cold or flu, sometimes a pain here or there, sometimes worse. Many patient journeys start off with a rough morning, when we don't quite feel ourselves. Depending on the type and severity of our symptoms, we may choose to wait and see how we're feeling the next day; employ a traditional remedy, like applying a heating pad or having a cup of herbal tea; or try over-the-counter thera-pies, like Ibuprofen or antacids. We often hope the symptoms will go away on their own or attribute them to something else—aging, an over-active weekend, stress. We might even acknowledge that the symptoms are disruptive but avoid seeking care immediately because money is tight or because we have other more pressing priorities—finding a job, paying the rent, caring for children. But the symptoms may become more severe and disruptive to our daily activities or, worse, cause an undeniable emergency that requires immediate medical intervention. As our symptoms evolve or worsen (some-times they even improve and then worsen again at a later point, such as in A.C.'s case), we eventually need to focus attention on "figuring it out." Sometimes, this process is straightforward and leads quickly through the other steps of the journey. Unfortunately, for many patients, this initial step marks the beginning of what will become a lengthy, arduous and uncertain path.

Undergoing Testing and Navigating Diagnosis

Doctors are quite good at uncovering and diagnosing common disorders using clear-cut and standardized tools. They might take your blood, make you pee in a cup or send you for a scan of some sort. There's a saying in medicine, attributed to Dr. Theodore Woodward, a physician in Baltimore in the 1940s: "When you hear hoofbeats, think of horses, not zebras." His point was that physicians should focus first on identifying and diagnosing the more usual conditions rather than putting patients through more extensive, invasive and costly testing to seek low probability conditions.[2]

But it's not always that simple. Sometimes, the cause of the hoofbeats *is* a zebra. This has become a bit of a rallying cry for people living with uncommon or rare diseases, for whom it can feel like they're not even zebras—they're more like elusive okapis! Rare diseases and other complex conditions, including many types of cancer, aren't necessarily easy to diagnose. This creates challenges for patients and clinicians alike. To get to an accurate diagnosis may require a variety of specialized doctors, specialized tests and an inordinate amount of being poked and prodded, plus the accompanying flurry of bills. The impact for the patient goes beyond the physical toll of all the testing; it also includes the emotional toll of seeking an obscure answer, and often the financial toll stemming from the cost of various tests and therapies as well as the loss of income due to missed work. Outside the U.S., while medical bills may not always be the primary driver of anxiety due to national and regional payer systems, the time, effort and emotional toll are still major hurdles for patients. Lengthy processing of referrals, waiting lines for diagnostic tests and the difficulty of scheduling appointments to review results with a physician can all be obstacles that even the most adept and knowledgeable patients and families may still struggle to navigate.

Ongoing advances in technology and genetic testing, as well as a growing awareness of rare diseases and other complex conditions, have helped improve doctors' ability to diagnose many illnesses sooner. But there are still enormous hurdles to overcome. An often-quoted 2013 study by Shire Pharmaceuticals (now Takeda Pharmaceuticals) indicated that it can take, on average, five to seven years for a patient with a rare disease to receive the proper diagnosis![3] Even conditions that are considered more "common" because they afflict a larger population (e.g., Parkinson's, lung cancer, multiple sclerosis) can be challenging to diagnose, as symptoms may take time to reveal themselves and co-morbid conditions may exist.

Sometimes diagnosis is complex not because of the disease, but because of access to care. Health inequities exist worldwide. People of color, transgender people and other marginalized communities often have more limited access to care, especially specialty care, which amplifies the challenges associated with diagnosis. These factors don't act in isolation; rather, they compound and magnify one another. This is why some patients describe their experience as an odyssey when trying to answer the seemingly simple question: "What is wrong with me?"

During a recent ZS project, a 49-year-old patient, Aisha,[4] described how she felt when she received a definitive diagnosis after encountering delay after delay: "I always knew in my gut that something was wrong, as I was always sick. I knew something was going on but never knew what. So, to finally be able to put a label on it: 'Yahoo, finally!'"[5] This feeling is consistent with many people's diagnostic odyssey—there is a huge sense of relief in knowing that what they are going through has been validated by the medical community. For some patients, a diagnosis brings hope that it will now be possible to address the symptoms and potentially even resolve the underlying cause of their condition.

Selecting and Starting Treatment ... If Available

It's surely every patient's hope that, having found an accurate diagnosis, it will be possible to treat the identified condition and then get back to normal. For some patients, treatment may be as simple as their doctor prescribing an available drug that is approved, in stock and can be picked up at a local pharmacy or even shipped directly to their home. For other patients, treatment may be complex and intimidating. Cancer treatments, for example, often include a combination of surgery, radiation and chemotherapy; specialty therapies administered via injection or IV; or navigating enrollment in a clinical trial. For many people, drug therapies offer critical benefits that put the patient on the way to recovery. For the most unfortunate patients, such as those diagnosed with Huntington's disease, amyotrophic lateral sclerosis (ALS, perhaps better known as Lou Gehrig's disease) or Niemann-Pick disease, there is (as of the time of writing) no viable treatment. Rather, there is only a path from diagnosis to declining function and, sometimes, end of life. That said, the increasingly collaborative nature of research, between scientists, patients, pharmaceutical manufacturers and numerous other stakeholders, continues to create hope. Between recent advancements in technology (cell and gene therapies, for example) and greater awareness of many conditions, there are abundant innovative treatments and potentially even cures that are currently under development.

Where viable treatments exist, the experience of choosing and beginning drug therapy can be quite complex, overwhelming and scary. The experience of starting a new therapy can raise a whole host of concerns for patients: fear of (and sometimes real) pain associated with more complicated therapies that involve injections or infusions, logistical concerns associated with where and how often treatments may need to be administered, anxiety over possible side effects and, of course, financial concerns about potential out-of-pocket costs.

Jeremy,[6] a patient beginning therapy for a complex inflammatory bowel disorder, reflected on the early stages of his treatment:

> I was nervous about initiating therapy, mostly because of a fear of nee-dles and also the challenges with getting through insurance approval. But I was willing to do anything to find ways to relieve my symptoms. At first, the nurse walked me through the injection, which was great. But I still had to learn how to inject myself at home for the long term. She showed me what to do, and, while I was doing everything as I was shown, I was still really nervous, even hiding alone when I first tried. Over time, I realized that this wasn't that difficult, and the tradeoffs with my condition and the severity of those symptoms made this an easy choice.[7]

Jeremy felt grateful that he was able to navigate the financial process and start his treat-ment in a timely manner, and fortunate that he had help learning how to do the injections. He is still grappling with the emotional burden of both his disease and of administering his treatment, but the early support provided to overcome his fears has allowed him to inject himself as needed and stay on a therapy that, while a little intimidating at the outset, offers substantial relief from his symptoms.

Financial concerns tend to dominate the mindshare of many patients and families facing high-cost therapeutics, especially given the complex insurance landscape in the U.S. and many other countries around the world. Often, patients are left to navigate the autho-rization or approval process on their own, and many face rejections from insurance companies or health systems as well as requirements that aren't always clear or easy to overcome. For patients who have just received a diagnosis of a potentially serious, life-altering condition, financial fears combined with the stress of navigating the complex processes necessary to ensure approval or insurance coverage make an already devas-tating, frightening and exhausting experience even more so.

Despite efforts by pharma in many markets, especially the U.S., to offset out-of-pocket costs for patients through co-pay support, rebates and other financial support services, many patient communities face additional costs associated with disease treatment and management. Understanding the true overall cost of living with and managing a disease is critical to determining how patients need to be supported through and beyond the pill.

Let's take an example from the spinal muscular atrophy (SMA) community. SMA is the number one genetic cause of death for infants due to a mutation in the survival motor neuron gene 1, a protein "critical to the function of the nerves that control our muscles."[8] SMA only affects a very small population of babies born each year and causes significant difficulties in the development of basic functioning, often leading to death in the first two to three years. A 2018 study by the Cure SMA Industry Collaboration, which was established to address scientific, clinical and regulatory challenges associated with SMA therapeutic development and evaluation, highlighted the costs involved in treating SMA, beyond the price of the drug itself:

> There are also many other associated costs that must be paid out-of-pocket to help people with SMA type II and III lead as independent a life as possible. When asked about the estimated annual SMA-related expenses or costs that patients or their families pay directly—including out-of-pocket costs for prescriptions, medical supplies, adaptive vehicles and mobility devices—more than one third of the respondents said that they spent $5,000 to $15,000 [...]. A small percentage paid close to or more than $100,000 per year in out-of-pocket costs. One mother to a daughter with SMA type II described how these costs can accrue. First, her family decided that they needed to build a new fully handicapped-accessible house with an elevator: "Just to add the elevator to our house is an extra $50,000." Then, they realized that the child also needed a power chair but that they would be unable to afford both the power chair and a vehicle that could transport the chair between home and school.[9]

Understanding the financial burden placed on families beyond the cost of the therapy alone helps create awareness and opportunities for various stakeholders across the ecosystem to provide better support. These stakeholders include patient advocacy organizations, healthcare institutions and even (maybe especially) pharmaceutical manufacturers.

While beginning available treatment is a major milestone for many patients and families along their lengthy journeys, it is clearly not the end of the road. Additional solutions are needed to improve the overall experience and provide truly holistic patient-focused care. Patients and families or non-profit patient advocacy organizations, which typically have numerous priorities but limited funds, can't be left to try to drive this change alone. If patient centricity means anything in practice, it is about the broader set of stakeholders (doctors, institutions, pharmaceutical and other healthcare companies, and many others) determining how best to understand patients, their conditions and the whole of their challenges ... and then doing something about it.

At ZS, we have seen many companies across the healthcare spectrum lean into the challenge of providing better support for patient communities. There are many examples of pharmaceutical manufacturers creating reimbursement teams to help guide patients and families through the difficulties and red tape associated with gaining access to an available therapy. We have also seen other healthcare organizations and governments around the world develop programs to help patients managing challenging care situations. For example, in Queensland, Australia, the Patient Travel Subsidiary Scheme (PTSS) is designed to aid patients who have been referred to specialist medical services that are not readily available within the local public hospital. This assistance includes travel, accommodation and even escort subsidies to support patients who need to seek care far from their homes.[10]

Another recent example in the pharmaceutical world points to the opportunity to more broadly support families dealing with the challenge of understanding and caring for sick loved ones. In 2021, Zogenix, a global pharmaceutical company, partnered with 10 patient advocacy organizations, each focused on different forms of rare epilepsy, to create resources to address one of the key unmet needs in the community: "the experiences and emotions of well siblings in rare epilepsy families."[11] Zogenix took to heart a sentiment heard across many patient communities: "Show up. Listen to families. Listen to their stories."[12] So the company did. And the outcome, while in its early stages, has been the development of various age-appropriate resource and communication guides to help children understand the experiences of their siblings with epileptic conditions and to provide a reminder of "how important and loved they are."[13]

For many conditions, the reality is that there still aren't available therapies. Or, there may be therapies that treat symptoms, but nothing is available that addresses the underlying cause of the disease. As science continues to evolve, and as patient communities work collaboratively with both scientific boards and pharmaceutical researchers and manufacturers, hope does sometimes sit on the horizon. Pharmaceutical pipelines are ripe with new technologies, including curative cell and gene therapies, vaccines and other advanced therapeutics that may reduce many of the burdens that patients and families still currently carry.

Continuing Treatment and Monitoring Disease Progression

The hope, of course, is that a treatment will either cure an acute disease or provide substantial relief to patients' symptoms, allowing them to return to a "normal" life. For many medical conditions, there are numerous effective treatments available that offer a good chance for success and possibly even a rapid recovery. But any type of treatment brings with it a variety of new challenges. Many patients will need to try a host of therapies or different dosing regimens in order to get it right. And sometimes available therapies and interventions will only slow the progression of debilitating or even fatal diseases. There are also cases in which the financial challenges associated with chronic drug therapy create serious hardship for patients or cause them to drop off of therapy.

We often see this in the case of diabetes patients who are "rationing" insulin, using less than is needed/prescribed in order to make their supply last longer. When describing the financial burden associated with managing his type 1 diabetes, Joaquin[14] shared a deeply intimate and scary memory: "I went through a period of unemployment […]. At one point, I was choosing between insulin for myself or a meal for my son."[15] In some cases, these types of tradeoffs can lead to terrible consequences. Alec was a 26-year-old diabetes patient who had just aged out of his mother's insurance plan. His yearly salary as a restaurant manager was about $35,000, too high to qualify for Medicaid or state health insurance subsidies. Alec's own insurance plan carried a monthly premium of $450 on top of an annual deductible of $7,600, and so, "Alec decided going uninsured would be more manageable [...]. He died less than one month after going off of his mother's insurance. His family thinks he was rationing his insulin. He died alone in his apartment three days before payday. The insulin pen he used to give himself shots was empty."[16]

While some people may (often rightfully) point to the complexities and barriers within the U.S. healthcare system as a primary cause of such struggles, similar situations arise in healthcare markets across the globe. In fact, the Prescription Charges Coalition in the UK conducted a study in 2017, finding, among other insights, that nearly a third of study participants living with long-term chronic conditions, such as lupus, Parkinson's and rheumatoid arthritis, "admitted that they are skipping or reducing medication doses, with cost concerns a key factor." Further, and due to this shift in behavior among such patients, "nearly three in five (59%) became more ill, with half of these needing to take time off work."[17] Understanding patients' perspectives, fears, and needs creates opportunity. As described earlier, this opportunity may come from such programs as co-pay offsets or vouchers, supporting the reimbursement process to make it easier on patients trying to navigate the system, or even emotional support to overcome the myriad challenges associated with complex diseases and their impact on individuals and their families.

Health Equity and Patient Centricity

Sadly, Alec's situation is not unique, although the consequences are not always as dire. Many people struggle to manage their health, and we often see that those in marginalized communities struggle more than others. Why is that? Over many decades, we have learned that inequities in health outcomes are strongly tied to social determinants of health (SDOH)—drivers of health beyond genetics that are rooted in our everyday lives. These factors include subjection to racism and discrimination as well as access to housing, transportation, nutritious foods and opportunities for physical activity, among others.[18] In fact, about 50 to 90%[19] of our aggregate health outcomes are due to social conditions, living conditions and individual behavior, with poverty and discrimination as the causes of many barriers. Health disparities due to SDOH are well documented and range from high-level aggregates, such as life expectancy and infant mortality differences by race,[20] to a list of more than 250 detailed metrics (e.g., deaths per 1,000 hospital admissions, obesity rates, cancer rates by geography) tracked by governments around the world.[21]

A related concept that has gained momentum in the past decade is health *equity*, the idea that everyone should have a fair and just opportunity to be as healthy as possible.[23] It is important to contrast this with health *equality*, which means that everyone gets the exact same care. For example, the clinic that is open to everyone from 9 a.m. to 5 p.m.

provides health equality, whereas the clinic that schedules appointments after hours so patients who work during the day can have access provides health equity. Looking at these examples, it is clear that health equity and patient centricity are closely linked. Moving toward health equity will require addressing SDOH in order to improve health outcomes.

Letitia[24] is a patient advocate and a member of ZS's VoiceZS research panel. For many years, she ran her own personal training business, until fatigue overcame her. As a self-employed African American woman, she prided herself on exemplifying a healthful lifestyle and knew something was wrong. However, her doctor did not agree. He discounted her concerns and, moreover, repeatedly blamed her for gaining weight, suggesting she cut the midnight snacking. Unable to shake her doctor's conviction that her weight gain was merely the result of personal failings, she finally worked up the courage to seek a second opinion. Her new doctor ultimately unearthed the cause of her fatigue and weight gain: a rare, chronic kidney disease.[25] The definitive diagnosis empowered her to get through the next day and the day after that and meant she could finally receive therapy to help control the symptoms of her unfortunately incurable condition. She accepted that she couldn't beat it, but knowing what she was up against allowed her to regain control of her own life. It also prompted her to become an advocate supporting other patients like her.

Figure 1-2: Health Equity Framework[22]

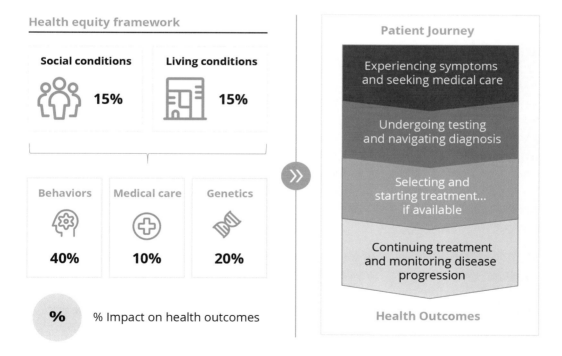

In Letitia's journey, her unwillingness to accept the first opinion and ascribe her symptoms to personal failings was a significant reason she was able to move the needle on her care. She insisted on finding a doctor who would listen and dig deeper to uncover the underlying condition causing her symptoms.

For many minority groups and other underserved populations, mistrust of the medical establishment is a real factor.[26] Doctors may hold unconscious biases that influence how they communicate with patients and affect their decisions about whether to order additional tests.[27] Meanwhile, patients from historically underserved communities may be reluctant to follow through and complete the tests.[28] Even with a confirmed diagnosis, patients of color are less likely to receive appropriate treatment in many cases.[29] In truly addressing the ideals of patient centricity, we must listen to and partner with patients from a highly diverse set of communities so as to ensure our solutions meet their needs and advance the cause of equity in healthcare.

Whether driven by the lack of understanding of the patient's healthcare journey, the complex challenges of the disease state itself or the inequality that many patients and families experience, it is clear that much more is required across the healthcare continuum in order to identify how pharma can deliver on the promise of patient-centered solutions and care. All the while, patients will continue to face a mix of fear, anxiety and hope surrounding the ever-present challenges of managing their disease states.

Paula's Story

So, now that we've zoomed out to discuss some of the larger forces at play in the healthcare ecosystem, let's zoom in again and bring the focus back to the individual patient experience. Paula was a scrub nurse, working long hours in surgery to help others address their own medical conditions and needs. In the midst of one memorable 13-hour shift, while supporting a complex surgical procedure, Paula heard a huge pop, felt a sharp pain and realized that she had dislocated her shoulder. With no one on staff to relieve her, she continued with her duties to support the surgery. Talk about putting the patient first! She took a couple of days off to rest. Unfortunately, a few nights later, she woke up screaming in pain. Something was very wrong with her arm.

Paula patiently underwent various tests; meanwhile, she was regularly dislocating her shoulder. She went for MRIs, scopes and physical therapy, but nothing provided relief from the intense pain. She felt fortunate that her doctors believed her experience of the pain and continued to partner with her to help her find the root cause: "None of the doctors ever doubted me that something was wrong, even when the results came back negative." So, they continued to conduct tests, ultimately diagnosing Paula with complex regional pain syndrome (CRPS).[30] Although CRPS was a diagnosis Paula could walk away with, she quickly realized it wasn't something that doctors understood very well. As she learned more about the condition, she realized most people with CRPS that go to their doctor aren't taken very seriously. Doctors inadvertently question or challenge CRPS patients' experiences by, for example, expressing skepticism about the level of pain they say they live with, or suggesting that they just haven't followed up properly with their physical therapy. Paula felt grateful to be a nurse who could talk to her healthcare team as both a patient and healthcare professional. Her doctors took her seriously as a result.

Paula recalled her first surgery, this time not as a confident nurse but rather as a scared patient:

> I remember my very first surgery. I worked in the operating room, and my surgery was at my hospital. I had the privilege of picking my team, from anesthesia to assistants. I knew everyone in that room! But when that gurney clinked up next to the OR bed, I felt so alone and isolated. I started panicking inside. I remember thinking, "Is this what it is like for our patients?" I vowed that, when I returned to work, I would change how I did my job. I just never returned. Nobody did anything wrong that day, but nobody did it right by me as the patient either. I knew each and every one of the people in my room. I knew the surgery in and out because I had assisted on it. I knew the sights and sounds, and yet I still was lost in fear. A simple hand-hold would have fixed the problem.

First-line treatment for CRPS can take several forms, including physical therapy, psychotherapy, a variety of different types of medications (none of which are currently approved by the U.S. FDA specifically for CRPS) or other types of surgical or drug intervention.[31] Paula found relief from nerve blocking agents,[32] despite mixed scientific opinion as to the utility of these agents in long-term care of CRPS. Unfortunately, her private insurance was "blocking the blocks" (her pun here, albeit not much of a laughing matter). Paying out of pocket was impossible for her. Her insurance company ruled that her pain could be managed through opioids. The opioids didn't do much to help her pain, but, with the barriers she was facing, she felt they were better than nothing, so she continued with the treatment. This was a life-altering decision for Paula, as she could not work while taking opioids. She had to give up her life's work that she was so passionate about in exchange for mediocre relief from her crippling pain.

After several years of fighting for coverage and fighting her pain, her journey took an even darker turn, driven by the emotional toll that such an intense, life-altering ordeal can have on patients and their families and friends. Paula became depressed and angry: "I shouldn't have been in the position I was in." She felt like no one was listening.

Despite her depression, Paula was not ready to give up. She found new connections through social media: other sufferers of CRPS to whom she could relate. A newfound sense of connectedness helped reduce her loneliness and the guilt she carried due to the burden she felt she was putting on those in her immediate circle. Through her social media interactions, Paula became an advocate, focusing on bringing attention to CRPS and on driving home one of the key insights she gleaned from her experience as a patient: There is a person behind everything we do in healthcare.

While Paula's diagnosis was straightforward, her journey highlights many of the different challenges a patient may face. Like many other patients, she experienced acute barriers to accessing life-changing therapies due to the complex insurance ecosystem. Her story also highlights how much the patient experience matters and how isolating and scary it is contending with a disease. Whether simple or complex, mild or severe, acute or chronic, a disease can turn the lives of patients and their loved ones upside down. While Paula's story isn't intended to provide answers to challenging issues with insurance claims, it is intended to reflect the extent and complexity of the issues patients face in their journey. And, for pharma to be truly patient centric, these are the voices we need to amplify.

Key Takeaways

- The patient journey, from getting an accurate diagnosis to living with the condition (with or without available therapeutics), can often be long, arduous, confusing and stressful. It is in these situations that we need to better understand each step of the journey and the toll it takes on the patient and family. This can include the physical toll of the condition as it worsens while seeking care, the emotional toll of dealing with the unknown (or the ramifications of what is known), the logistical challenges of obtaining care and the financial burden of out-of-pocket costs for therapies.

- It is important to understand this journey and each of the steps so that the various stakeholders at each step can envision opportunities to put patients' needs first and develop programs and policies that help patients and their families carry the weight of any associated burdens, ultimately creating the best possible experience out of a potentially life-altering situation.

- It is critical to recognize and understand the differences in the opportunities available across our society and our globe. Health equity should be at the forefront in conversations on patient centricity, as those who are most in need are not always the most likely to have access (financial or otherwise) to available care and support. Understanding social determinants of health and their impact on the patient experience is crucial to developing wide-reaching care and support programs.

Acknowledgments

The authors would like to thank the many ZSers that contributed to the shaping and writing of this chapter. They would also, perhaps more importantly, like to recognize the many stories from patients, families and caregivers that provide us with the real understanding of the healthcare odyssey. Many patients and families struggle day-to-day emotionally, physically and financially, and we are hopeful that the ideas that come from this book, and bringing true patient centricity to the forefront in healthcare, will lead to significant advances and hope for those who are struggling.

The Cure SMA Industry Collaboration (SMA-IC) was established in 2016 to leverage the experience, expertise and resources of pharmaceutical and biotechnology companies, as well as other nonprofit organizations involved in the development of spinal muscular atrophy (SMA) therapeutics to more effectively address a range of scientific, clinical, and regulatory challenges. It is currently comprised of our partners at Novartis Gene Therapies, Biogen, Genentech/Roche Pharmaceuticals, Scholar Rock, and SMA Europe. Funding for the Voice of the Patient Report was provided by members of the 2018 SMA-IC, which included Astellas Pharmaceuticals, AveXis, Inc., Biogen, Genentech/Roche Pharmaceuticals, Cytokinetics Inc., Novartis Pharmaceuticals and Ionis Pharmaceuticals, Inc.

Endnotes

1. Name changed for the purposes of this book.

2. James A. Dickerson, "Lesser-Spotted Zebras: Their Care and Feeding," in Canadian Family Physician 62, no. 8 (August 2016): 620-621, https://www.ncbi.nlm.nih.gov/pmc/articles/pmc4982713/.

3. Shire, "Rare Disease Impact Report: Insights from Patients and the Medical Community," Global Genes, April 2013, https://globalgenes.org/wp-content/uploads/2013/04/shirereport-1.pdf.

4. Name changed for the purposes of this book.

5. ZS Patient Journey Research, 2020.

6. Name changed for the purposes of this book.

7. ZS Patient Journey Research, 2020.

8. CureSMA, "About Spinal Muscular Atrophy," accessed June 20, 2021, https://www.curesma.org/about-sma/.

9. Rosangel Cruz et al., "Voice of the Patient Report: A Summary Report from an Externally-Led Patient Focused Drug Development Meeting Reflecting the U.S. Food and Drug Administration (FDA) Patient-Focused Drug Development Initiative," Cure SMA, January 10, 2018, https://www.curesma.org/wp-content/uploads/2018/01/sma-vop-for-publication-1-22-2018.pdf.

10. Queensland Government, "About the Patient Travel Subsidy Scheme," last modified February 19, 2018, https://www.qld.gov.au/health/services/travel/subsidies/about.

11. "The Story Behind the VIP Sibling Project," VIP Sibling, https://vipsibling.com/about/.

12. "VIP Sibling Project."

13. "VIP Sibling Project."

14. Name changed for the purposes of this book.

15. ZS Patient Journey Research, 2020.

16. Bram Sable-Smith, "Insulin's High Cost Leads to Lethal Rationing," NPR, September 1, 2018, https://www.npr.org/sections/health-shots/2018/09/01/641615877/insulins-high-cost-leads-to-lethal-rationing.

17. Paul Howard, "New Prescription Charges Coalition Report: 'Still Paying the Price': Cost of Prescriptions Prevent People from Getting Necessary Medication," Lupus UK, June 29, 2017, https://www.lupusuk.org.uk/prescription-costs-report/.

18. Nambi Ndugga and Samantha Artiga, "Disparities in Health and Health Care: 5 Key Questions and Answers," Kaiser Family Foundation, May 11, 2021, https://www.kff.org/racial-equity-and-health-policy/issue-brief/disparities-in-health-and-health-care-5-key-question-and-answers/.

19. Kate Raphael et al., "Social and Health-System Factors That Affect Health: A Review of Literature," Drivers of Health, accessed September 4, 2021, https://driversofhealth.org/wp-content/uploads/sdh.whitepaper_v8.pdf.

20. National Center for Health Statistics, "Health, United States, 2015: With Special Feature on Racial and Ethnic Health Disparities," CDC, 2016, https://www.cdc.gov/nchs/data/hus/hus15.pdf; Nicole Scholz, "Addressing Health Inequalities in the European Union: Concepts, Action, State of Play," European Parliament, February 2020, https://www.europarl.europa.eu/regdata/etudes/idan/2020/646182/eprs_ida(2020)646182_en.pdf.

21. Agency for Healthcare Research and Quality, "2019 National Healthcare Qualities and Disparities Report," accessed September 4, 2021, https://www.ahrq.gov/sites/default/files/wysiwyg/research/findings/nhqrdr/2019qdr-core-measures-disparities.pdf; World Health Organization (WHO), "Healthy, Prosperous Lives for All: The European Health Equity Status Report (2019)," 2019, https://www.euro.who.int/en/publications/abstracts/health-equity-status-report-2019.

22. ZS Meta Analysis, "Understanding and Addressing Social Determinants of Health," 2019.

23. P. Braveman et al., "What Is Health Equity?" Robert Wood Johnson Foundation, May 1, 2007, https://www.rwjf.org/en/library/research/2017/05/what-is-health-equity-.html.

24. Name changed for the purposes of this book.

25. ZS Patient Advocacy Research, 2021.

26. Katrina Armstrong et al., "Racial/Ethnic Differences in Physician Distrust in the United States," in American Journal of Public Health 97, no. 7 (July 2007): 1283-1289.

27. Megan Johnson Shen et al., "The Effects of Race and Racial Concordance on Patient-Physician Communication: A Systematic Review of the Literature," in Journal of Racial and Ethnic Health Disparities 5, no. 1 (February 2018): 117-140.

28.   William J. Hall, "Implicit Racial/Ethnic Bias Among Health Care Professionals and Its Influence on Health Care Outcomes: A Systematic Review," in American Journal of Public Health 105, no. 12 (December 2015): e60-e76.

29.   Lauren A. Eberly et al., "Identification of Racial Inequities in Access to Specialized Inpatient Heart Failure Care at an Academic Medical Center," in Circulation: Heart Failure 12, no. 11 (November 2019): e006214, https://doi.org/10.1161/circheart-failure.119.006214; Salimah H. Meghani, Eeseung Byun and Rollin M. Gallagher, "Time to Take Stock: A Meta-Analysis and Systematic Review of Analgesic Treatment Disparities for Pain in the United States," in Pain Medicine 13, no. 2 (February 2012): 150-174, https://doi.org/10.1111/j.1526-4637.2011.01310.x.

30.   According to the NIH, "People with CRPS have changing combinations of spontaneous pain or excess pain that is much greater than normal following something as mild as a touch. Other symptoms include changes in skin color, temperature, and/or swelling on the arm or leg below the site of injury. Although CRPS improves over time, eventually going away in most people, the rare severe or prolonged cases are profoundly disabling." National Institute of Neurological Disorders and Stroke, "Complex Regional Pain Syndrome Fact Sheet," last modified October 14, 2020, https://www.ninds.nih.gov/disorders/patient-caregiver-education/fact-sheets/complex-regional-pain-syndrome-fact-sheet#what%20is%20complex%20regional%20pain%20syndrome?.

31.   National Institute of Neurological Disorders and Stroke, "Complex Regional Pain Syndrome."

32.   One intervention involves "sympathetic blocks—in which an anesthetic is injected next to the spine to directly block the activity of sympathetic nerves and improve blood flow." National Institute of Neurological Disorders and Stroke, "Complex Regional Pain Syndrome."

Chapter 2:
The Forces Propelling Patient Centricity

Sharon Suchotliff

Ro's Story

A carved Buddha wall-hanging peeps coyly down at the laminate floor, meditation music hangs over the lobby like a snug cloud of incense and a pod coffee machine is on hand to serve me my choice of hot beverage. I choose tea.

I've filled out some easy paperwork, and, although the front-desk person and I are both behind masks, this experience feels as familiar as stepping into a spa for a massage appointment back in the BC (Before COVID-19) days—except, instead of looking forward to a relaxing spa treatment, I'm checking in at a well-appointed infusion center in Fremont to receive therapy for my inflammatory bowel disease (IBD).

In no time at all, I'm whisked into a private room with a recliner chair and flat-screen TV. After the friendly nurse measures me in various ways, I'm reclined at a dozy angle, with a warm blanket over my feet, a Sprite in hand and a bickering couple entertaining me on HGTV. Oh, and a very expensive drug drip-dropping into my veins.

How did I get here?

In 2015, on a trip to India, I got sick. Very sick. What I thought was food poisoning turned out to be ulcerative colitis (UC). Like its cousin Crohn's disease, UC is an auto-immune disease that affects the digestive tract. I'll spare you the details. Let's just say UC is painful, bloody shit.

Back in the U.S., my doctor recommended I get on an infusion treatment for UC. The first infusion center I went to was a hospital-like facility with a familiar and standard-issue medical setting: multiple beds, beeping machines, privacy curtains if I needed them and competent, friendly nurses.

But a month later, I moved to Burlingame, California, and had to find a local GI. This new GI, who I thought I'd identify with because she was a younger woman like me, spent a total of maybe 20 minutes with me over two-and-a-half years of treatment. Her infusion set-up was in a back room in her office; the choice of seating was between two office chairs and another chair that looked like it had lived a full life in a dentist's office in the 80s. If my infusions were during the lunch hour on Thursdays, as they often were, I'd invariably smell the Chinese takeout that a sales rep would bring the clinic staff.

These were difficult years. My disease, and therefore my life, felt out of my control. My doctor would casually say things like, "Well, we'll just have to take it out," in regard to the ultimate outcome of my disease—the "it" in this context being my colon and "out" meaning surgical removal. I'd be sitting there thinking, "Look lady, I'm not opposed to the idea, but can we maybe slow down a little, get to know my colon a bit better, maybe understand its love language more?" At the time, I didn't know how to verbalize these feelings of frustration over the fact that too many major decisions about my body and health were being weighed without my input. It was like my doctor forgot that there was a whole person attached to my colon!

Finally, I switched doctors and facilities. My new doctor's clinic was attached to the local hospital. The infusions would happen at a specialized cancer infusion center. Hopefully, I'd have more of a rapport with the doctor this time. I'd certainly try to be more proactive.

At first, the approach worked. I fell in love with the nurses at my infusion center. For the last two-and-a-half years, I've looked forward to my bimonthly infusions to chat with a trio of the most generous and hilarious women I've met in their profession. They made my experience feel human—like I was connected to a group of people who cared about me, and I cared about them in return.

Meanwhile, my relationship with my doctor was now at least more formalized. He was plugged into a messaging service that flowed through the hospital system's app, which I'd downloaded. Appointments were easier to book. But, again, I felt like I was having to navigate this disease with little guidance. When I was about to start a new job, I was the one who suggested I get a colonoscopy, because I hadn't had one in three years, and I wanted to level-set on where my disease was.

If you're still with me, we're nearing the spa. Hang in there.

About a year ago, I started periodically sending messages to my doctor saying I was in acute pain, and he'd suggest short-term treatments—steroids, enemas and double-whammy steroid enemas—in addition to the regular infusions I was receiving. I think it should have been clear to him that I wasn't really progressing with the treatment regimen I was on—it was certainly clear to me. But it wasn't until two months ago that he ordered a full blood panel, and we found that my body was producing antibodies in response to the infusion treatment, meaning I was rejecting it completely. The magic test number should have been under 10; mine was 100. Off the charts! And so he recommended we try a different treatment. I said: "Sure, why not?"

Cue some insurance paperwork and blood tests and then, finally, my insurance company told me I had been approved for the new infusions. But the catch was I couldn't get the treatments at my old infusion center—I needed to go to this new clinic, a private clinic not associated with the hospital system. I cried thinking about how I wouldn't see my nurses again. And then I went to the new infusion center, settled into the spa-like chair and chilled out while watching HGTV.

So why am I whining?

Because, if anyone in the medical profession had asked me what I wanted, I would never have talked about comfy chairs or flat-screen TVs.

I would have said I'd like to stay at my old infusion center, where I felt connected and cared for.

I would have said that, at a time when the coronavirus is sapping this country's healthcare system, I'm actually really uncomfortable receiving treatment in a luxury setting. I would have said that I don't really care about the fancy atmosphere, or even the drug, as long as I can tangibly see that I am improving—however gradual that improvement is. I would have said that it makes me sad and sick to see fellow UC sufferers in my Facebook group talk about life with UC without health insurance. What made me more worthy than them to get this care? I would have said I'd like to talk to someone, person to person, who can walk me through the different medications and available surgical options and help me anticipate what the next 10, 15, 25 years of this journey will look like.

Look, I'm glad for the shy Buddha on the wall, but I could live without him. I'd like this to actually feel like a journey—a guided journey, not a series of random events in which I have sometimes had agency but more often than not felt completely sidelined.

Midway through the HGTV show that's on the TV during this most recent visit, a pharmaceutical ad comes on. You know the kind: an older woman with stunning cheekbones and a beautiful frown is deeply saddened that she can't play with her grandchild like she used to. A soothing voice asks if you suffer from this condition too. Name of the medicine. Side effects quickly enumerated, but you are focused on the woman's silver-fox husband who is smiling at her over a glass of wine at sunset. "Talk to your doctor."

Well, I have. I have talked to my doctor. And it's brought me to a luxurious, spa-like treatment center. But that's not what I wanted. No one asked me. To me, this place seems to have been designed by people who've never talked to a patient. So, to the healthcare industry at large, I'd like to say that we may not all have enviable bone structure and laughing spouses at sunset, but here's an idea: "Talk to your patient."

The Movement Toward Patient Centricity

While the broader healthcare ecosystem has been engaging in a patient-centered trans-formation for decades, it's only in recent history that pharma has embraced the idea of bringing patients into key decisions relating to their health. The UCB 2010 annual report, titled "Aspiring to Be the Patient-Centric Biopharma Leader," was a significant milestone. It was one of the first public statements from a pharma company about the importance of adopting a patient-first approach.

Since 2010, there has been broader recognition within the pharmaceutical industry that, in order to facilitate treatment success, it is vital to fully consider the values, preferences and expressed needs of the individual patient. But has the industry taken meaningful action? As Jane Griffiths, former company group chairman of Janssen in Europe, the Middle East and Africa, put it: "If we reflect a little, we see that, while we have the patient in mind, we might not always understand exactly what they want. Do oncology patients always want to live longer or do they want a better quality of therapy?"[1] According to Bharat Tewarie, former CMO of UCB: "It's been over a decade since pharma has put a stake in the ground. But have we really made progress on the real-world impact in the eyes of our patients?"

Today there is an increased drive for pharma to become patient centric. Why the change? In recent years, a perfect storm has started to come together. Far-reaching external shifts that were already nudging the industry toward patient centricity, including changes in consumer behavior and expectations, growing competition, advancements in technology and new data and analytic capabilities, have combined to exert a strong force on pharma. New developments in the healthcare space, such as patient-focused regulatory guidelines and new interpretations of value by payers and providers, have added to the pressure. And the final elements—the business realities of the profitability of drug development and shifting product pipelines—have contributed to the turmoil, making patient centricity no longer an optional component of the business but a necessity for survival.

A Perfect Storm: The External Environment

Changes in Consumer Expectations and Behaviors

There is no denying the growing influence of patients and caregivers in healthcare decisions. With close to half of Americans enrolled in a high-deductible health insurance plan,[2] the cost of care continues to shift to patients, who are becoming more informed and vocal about their treatment. With the proliferation of health-related information across the web and the emergence of "Dr. Google," patients are increasingly coming into their doctor's office with a medication or treatment preference in mind. This trend is not only present in the U.S.; ZS research has shown that those outside the U.S. are often just as likely, or even more so, to go to a doctor's appointment with a treatment in mind (see Figure 2-1). Knowing that physicians will grant a patient request for a medication more than half the time, depending on the medication,[3] patients are becoming more and more important to pharma as stakeholders; as such, pharma's focus on their experience has grown.

In the words of physician and futurist Dr. Eric Topol of Scripps Research Translational Institute, the new mantra for the patient experience is: "I want what I want when I want it" (IWWIWWIWI).[4] Over time, many of the activities we all used to have to do in person or through a phone call—depositing checks at a bank, making travel reservations, ordering takeout—have migrated to websites and apps on our computers or phones. As the world outside of healthcare—think Amazon, Starbucks and Netflix, among others—continues to shift to on-demand experiences, people are expecting that same level of personalized, instant service from healthcare and from pharma. With that, the COVID-19 pandemic and the associated lockdowns and isolation have intensified the need to self-manage many aspects of our physical and mental health, resulting in a substantial increase in the use of health-related mobile apps, including trackers, online fitness classes, weight management programs, telemedicine platforms, and online therapy and mental health services. As the ways in which people interact with the world change, so must the ways in which pharma engages with patients.

According to Laurie Meyers, executive director of engagement and experience design at Genentech, all of this means that "we need to meet people where they are and on their own terms." To deliver on this idea, Meyers pulled together a cross-functional team, including patients, caregivers and other stakeholders, to help inform and design a two-way secure messaging platform that allows patients and caregivers to call, text, instant message and engage with Genentech via email. Meyers shared in a recent interview with ZS: "What we hear loud and clear from [patients] is, 'I want you to listen to me. I want you to make this easier. It's too complicated. You're a small piece of my overall life, and a small piece of my overall healthcare.' "[5] Developing a platform that provides on-demand, instant information and engagement with pharma was one step, among many, that Genentech took to recognize how consumer behavior has changed and to address evolving patient expectations.

Figure 2-1: Across the Globe, Patients Are Going into Their Doctor's Office with a Treatment Preference and a Specific Treatment in Mind[6]

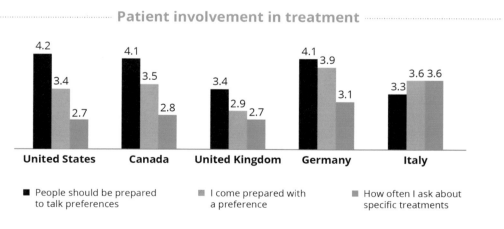

Numbers indicate "Level of agreement with the statement from 1-5"

Competition

Patients now have more choices for treatment than ever before. Consider the proliferation of diabetes medications, for instance: Between 1982 and 2015, 74 different medications to treat type 2 diabetes, including generics, were approved in the U.S.,[7] and many others have been approved since, with even more in the pipeline. As competition in many therapeutic categories has increased, the patient experience has become a key area where pharma companies can demonstrate their value and differentiate themselves from competitors. Take the example of immunology: As a variety of biologic treatments came to market starting in the early to mid-2000s, pharma companies began investing heavily in patient support programs to drive differentiation through the patient experience, since efficacy between products is similar. These trends are sure to continue. Pharma must compete on value beyond just efficacy and clinical results.

Similarly, as the number of clinical trials increased exponentially over the last 20 years, from 1,255 registered clinical trials in the year 2000 to 362,524 trials registered in 2020,[8] there has been growing competition both for patients to participate in clinical trials and for investigators to run the trials. This shift has triggered pharma companies to try and become a "sponsor of choice" for investigators considering taking on new trials. A big part of becoming a sponsor of choice means improving the experience for patients in the trial, which, in turn, typically betters the experience of clinical trial sites and investigators. Improving the experience of sites improves the perception of the sponsor and often leads to an openness to collaborate again on future trials.

In recognition that the patient experience is crucial for both the development and commercial sides of their operations, pharma companies have started to dedicate specific resources to focus on better meeting patient needs. As Anne Nijs, transformation lead for rare conditions at Roche, remarked in a recent interview: "Operating in a fully patient-centric manner demands new ways of working and a fresh understanding of what it takes to create value."[9] To that end, Roche created a mix of new positions aimed at collaborating on the ground with patients as they engage with the healthcare ecosystem. One of the new roles is even titled "patient journey partner"![10] The patient journey partner's mandate is to engage with all stakeholders who directly influence the patient journey for a given condition, to gain a deep understanding of the patient experience and to work together to co-create meaningful solutions that address patients' needs. The people in these senior level roles are embedded within markets, are empowered to pull in Roche resources to improve outcomes for their patients, and have received the marching order to "do it faster."

The New Definition of Value

Increasingly, payers and health technology assessment (HTA) bodies are demanding that pharma demonstrate tangible value to patients and their health, especially for conditions that involve expensive treatments, a multitude of treatment options, high symptom burden or a need for palliative care. Whereas clinical outcomes were once the core focus of value, today there is a recognition that what's important to patients and their preferences also has an intrinsic value. As a result, validated Patient Reported Outcomes (PROs) have become more significant. For example, after receiving an initial negative HTA rating in Germany, which restricted access and reimbursement for Xalkori, a treatment for metastatic non-small-cell lung cancer (NSCLC) with a specific mutation, the brand was able to gain more favorable status once they included a PRO on health-related quality of life.[11] While there is a lot of variability in the ways U.S. payers and global HTAs consider PROs in decision-making, there is general agreement that PROs will become increasingly more important in the next five to 10 years.

Additionally, as the healthcare ecosystem in the U.S. continues to shift from a fee-for-service model to value-based care, pharmaceutical manufacturers will be expected to play a more significant role in improving the patient experience and outcomes. Pharma is just starting to experiment with different value-based approaches. For example, in an agreement between insurance company Harvard Pilgrim and Eli Lilly, the insurer pays a lower price for Eli Lilly's type 2 diabetes drug, Trulicity, if patients do better on competing diabetes drugs.[12] These types of value-based arrangements tie payer rebates to the product's real-world performance, creating accountability to ensure that actual outcomes match clinical trial results. As David Ricks, chairman and CEO at Eli Lilly, explained: "We're putting our money where our mouth is—not just making claims about superiority but measuring outcomes."[13]

For provider organizations, the changing definition of value can be tied to healthcare's "Triple Aim": improving patient experiences, outcomes and the economics of healthcare. As provider organizations are increasingly incentivized to improve on these measures, they are looking more broadly at managing care at the population level, which often requires navigating the needs of heterogeneous populations. For pharma, this means that generating value for its customers (the HCPs) requires a focus on health equity by seeking to understand and support diverse populations.

This phenomenon became even more pronounced during the COVID-19 pandemic, when a great divide emerged in terms of health outcomes between those with access to care and those without. In response, many pharma organizations mobilized quickly to provide free medications, transportation to care, telemedicine services and at-home treatment options; some have even instituted new functions dedicated to a focus on health equity. For example, companies like Merck,[14] Genentech,[15] Takeda[16] and BMS[17] are taking a vocal stance on the importance of health equity and its significance to the future of their businesses. All four major companies now have dedicated resources, programs and funding to increasing the representation of diverse populations in their clinical research, improving the health literacy of their patients and caregiver materials, and customizing their patient support services to meet the needs of marginalized communities.

Advancements in Technology

Other major forces of change have been the accelerating advancements in technology, which enabled a wide spectrum of new tools and capabilities in the healthcare space, like electronic health records, remote monitoring, telemedicine and many more. One of the biggest developments in technology is the shift in the underlying infrastructure that is currently under way: the move from 4G to 5G. Faster data speeds on the 4G network enabled our consumption of more than 13 hours of media each day in 2020; 5G will deliver not only faster data but, perhaps more importantly, much lower latency. For those of us who aren't up on the tech jargon, low latency essentially means that devices can talk to each other with almost no delay. This development is what will enable, for example, safe driverless cars that can communicate with each other nearly instantaneously about a car suddenly braking half a mile ahead, and will spur the continued development of connected devices.

We certainly have seen an explosion of connected devices over the last few years (see Figure 2-2). Everything from your watch to your thermostat, lights, scale and even kitchen gadgets are now connected through Wi-Fi. All of these connected devices collect data and can provide key signals about our health status and needs. For example, many retirement communities now utilize a small sensor on residents' refrigerators to help passively monitor their health, with the idea that, if a resident has not opened his or her fridge in 24 hours, there's a need to intervene.

For pharma, these advancements in technology mean that there are now better ways to reach and support patients. Through technology, it is now possible to overcome some of the most challenging aspects of participating in a clinical trial, such as physically getting to the trial site for routine tests or making sure patients can adhere to medication schedules. Janssen sought to alleviate some of the logistical burdens for patients participating in clinical trials by piloting a suite of digital technologies called iSTEP (Integrated Smart Trial and Engagement Platform). iSTEP integrates medication tracking and adherence with a patient-facing mobile app that includes learning modules, videos and tutorials designed to keep patients motivated to take the drug as scheduled. The pilot showed a 92% medication compliance rate and 84% patient satisfaction rate.[19] Considering that as many as 40% of patients enrolled in a trial become non-adherent to the product after 150 days, this technology has the potential to significantly impact retention in clinical trials.[20]

The creative use of technology to facilitate trials has especially picked up speed during the COVID-19 pandemic; the sudden imposition of social distancing forced pharma's hand in the development of more extensive digital and virtual experiences (decentralized clinical trials) in order to continue with clinical research (more on this in Chapter 6). The pandemic also led to a growing culture of collaboration in healthcare; we're increasingly seeing partnerships not only between companies in life sciences but also with other sectors, such as technology. Big pharma and big tech are increasingly realizing they have more to gain from working together than from competing.

Figure 2-2: The Number of Internet-Connected Wearable Devices Globally Is Expected to Reach 1.1 Billion by 2022 (*2020-2022 numbers projected)[18]

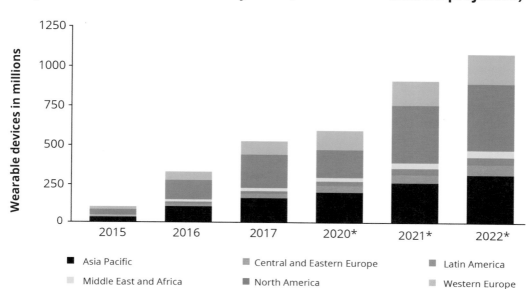

This is just the tip of the iceberg. As technology continues to become faster, smarter and more immersive, we have the opportunity to not only improve patients' current experiences but to also simulate and anticipate future needs. For the drive toward true patient centricity, technology is critical to streamlining and improving access to care. It can empower patients, caregivers and providers to get the right information at the right time and improve decision-making, which leads to better outcomes. There's no turning back now; and, as we note in Chapter 6, virtual and augmented reality solutions for digital health and clinical trials are fast evolving from experimental practices to the norm.

Availability of Data and Advanced Analytics Capabilities

Artificial intelligence (AI) and machine learning are becoming critical tools, given the exponential growth of data from our mobile and connected devices and all of our interactions with connected media. For pharma, the degree to which AI applies not only to "high science" and drug discovery but also to consumer analytics will dramatically change the ways in which the industry can engage meaningfully with patients. While many consumer-packaged goods (CPG) companies are using some form of predictive analytics to offer suggestions to customers,[21] pharma is slowly but surely adopting this approach to create "next-best-action" suggestion engines that can help people manage their health more effectively. AbbVie is one of the companies at the forefront of initial applications. Through a fully integrated, multi-channel program that tracks data in real time, AbbVie has been able to leverage AI and machine learning to anticipate and respond to potential disruptions in a patient's care journey.[22] For patients, this has meant more support in getting, taking and staying on course with their treatments, ultimately leading to better health outcomes (more on this in Chapter 9).

Mainstream and emerging real-world data (RWD) sources offer pharmaceutical companies an opportunity to understand patients with greater depth and breadth than has been possible until now. Looking at patient insurance claims data can give pharmaceutical companies a view into healthcare utilization (number of visits to the doctor or emergency room) and into clinical information, such as diagnoses and procedures. Emerging data sources, like electronic health records, genomics, labs and biomarker testing data, can provide a much more detailed clinical view of patients, helping to draw out connections between such factors as demographics and responses to treatments. The emerging data that comes from these varied sources is essential for pharmaceutical companies that need to identify areas of the greatest unmet need and can illuminate the impact of factors like biomarkers or even marketing activities (more on this in Chapter 11).

Partnerships with companies in and outside of the pharmaceutical industry can yield tremendous value by giving pharma access to new technologies that capture patient data. For example, through its partnership with the healthcare technology company 23andMe, GlaxoSmithKline (GSK) can access millions of people's genomic data for drug development and also learn from patients' responses to questionnaires about their overall health and experiences living with particular ailments.[23] As a direct result of the partnership, GSK and 23andMe have launched their first joint clinical development program to test a new drug that targets specific types of tumors.[24] Meanwhile, companies like Alphabet's Verily Life Science, which has staked their entire business model on the ability to develop tools and devices to collect, organize and activate health data, have announced partnerships with Novartis, Otsuka, Pfizer and Sanofi.[25]

Patient-Focused Drug Development

Regulatory bodies in the U.S.[26] and EU are increasingly requiring the inclusion of the patient voice and patient experience in drug development. In the U.S., the Patient-Focused Drug Development (PFDD) program aims to ensure that the pharmaceutical industry meaningfully includes a diverse and representative sample of patients and their perspectives, priorities and needs in drug development and in the evaluation of new treatments.[27] Under PFDD guidance, the FDA has started to roll out its perspective on where, when and how pharmaceutical companies should incorporate patient input into clinical development; the FDA is increasingly looking for pharma companies to demonstrate that they are collecting data on the impact of treatments on patients' functioning, quality of life and experience and also which outcomes patients deem important and why.[28] Outside of the U.S., the European Medicines Agency (EMA) regularly brings in patient organizations and patient experts to provide guidance and input, beginning even before a company submits a product for approval, and has emphasized the growing importance of working with patients throughout the drug development process.[29]

Beyond the formal guidance issued by regulatory agencies, several industry groups are becoming increasingly vocal and influencing the ways in which pharma companies incorporate the patient voice into drug development. This is especially significant in the EU, where private-public partnerships, such as the European Patients' Academy on Therapeutic Innovation (EUPATI) and Patients Active in Research and Dialogues for an Improved Generation of Medicines (PARADIGM), are at the forefront, developing tools and resources for patients and pharmaceutical companies to enable and motivate meaningful engagement. Another such organization, Patient Focused Medicines Development (PFMD), brings together a diverse group of health stakeholders from pharma, patient advocacy, provider organizations and others to share experiences and case studies openly and in a non-competitive environment, with the goal of advancing best practices for patient engagement in research and drug development.

Pharmaceutical companies have taken notice of the evolving guidance of regulatory bodies and the public statements of industry groups, and many are developing formal processes and mechanisms to bring patients into the drug development process and capture data (more on this in Chapters 5 and 6). These include patient experience dossiers, which provide an overview of the condition from the patient perspective. Such reports bring together findings from a variety of sources, such as input from patient panels, patient advocacy groups and co-creation sessions with patients, to inform protocol development and marketing materials. These dossiers are intended to provide the initial view of the patient experience and provide a baseline understanding of the potential burden for participating in a given trial.

At Boehringer Ingelheim (BI), a patient experience assessment is drafted in preparation for the start of any clinical development program. The assessment is a living document that describes patients' perspectives about currently available treatment options, unmet needs, treatment goals and expectations for clinical trials, using publicly available information as well as BI internal patient experience data. This document is then continually updated throughout the clinical development process to ensure the patients' (and sometimes caregivers') perspectives are understood and considered in key decisions. According to Dr. Hilary Wilson, BI's director of patient engagement,

> Companies now understand just how critical patient input is throughout the development life cycle; but until patient insights are systematically integrated into the way in which we work, we will fall short on consistently delivering products and services that address unmet patient needs. The patient experience assessment program was designed to do exactly this: Create an evidence-based foundation for development teams to understand what matters most to patients, outline gaps in the organization's understanding of the patient experience and provide a framework to define a strategy to close evidence gaps. When this type of scientific data is made available to teams before clinical development is initiated,

decisions about product and program design are naturally made with the patient voice represented from the very beginning.

These powerful shifts in the external environment—changing consumer behaviors and expectations, regulatory guidance, payer demands and advancements in technology and analytics capabilities—make it clear that, if pharma doesn't change today, the industry could risk going the way of companies like Kodak or Blackberry. Kodak famously failed to take seriously the disruptive potential of digital photography for its business. Despite market research that clearly demonstrated that the adoption of digital technology would likely overtake film photography, a series of CEOs pointed to their predecessors' failure to make the transition to digital, stated their own intention to do so and then failed to effect change. Blackberry, another famous riches-to-rags story, failed to anticipate that the future of smartphones would be driven not by business customers but by consumers. Despite a clearly demonstrated end-user preference for touchscreens, Blackberry continued to produce devices with keyboards, because the company could not conceive of its devices as anything other than high-powered mobile phones. By contrast, Apple and Android conceptualized their phones as palm-sized computers and were able to meet users' demands. There are obvious lessons in both of these cases for pharma to heed. Patient centricity is no longer a choice; it's an imperative for existence.

Business Realities: The Internal Drivers of Change

Just as the external world has been increasingly demanding that pharma focus on the patient, there are also very real drivers for patient centricity that have arisen out of pharma's business model itself. The types of returns on investments the industry once commanded are no longer a guarantee, especially as pharma moves into increasingly more rare, targeted and complex therapeutic categories. Add that to the enduring challenges around medication adherence, compliance and persistence, and it's clear why pharma's business practices must change and must do so now.

The ROI of Clinical Trials

A notable change for pharma is the fact that R&D is no longer as attractive as it once was. In 2018, the return on investment in R&D dropped to 1.9% from just over 10% in 2010.[30] Considering that only about 13% of drugs and vaccines and just over 3% of cancer treatments make it to market,[31] there is a clear motivation for pharma to get R&D processes right. And yet, close to 80% of phase III clinical trials fail to meet their enrollment timelines, which can cost pharma companies upwards of $500,000 per day in lost revenue.[32]

In response to these trends, some pharma companies have adopted a strategy of acquiring assets to commercialize, as opposed to investing in their own development pipelines. This strategy leaves companies little opportunity to influence clinical development programs and shape the outcomes. As an R&D approach, this strategy is really just a stopgap. The only way to change the downward trajectory of R&D profitability is to turn the process on its head: start with the patient, not the idea. Just as software companies completely changed their approach to software development in the early 2000s through Agile, focusing first and foremost on the needs of people over process, so must pharmaceutical companies.

Pharma's Portfolio and Pipeline

Part of the need for change arises from the fact that, over the last 20 years, highly effective and reasonably tolerable treatments for the world's most prevalent chronic conditions have already been discovered and brought to market. Products such as Pfizer's Lipitor for high cholesterol, GSK's Advair for chronic obstructive pulmonary disease (COPD) and asthma, and AbbVie's Humira for a whole host of inflammatory autoimmune diseases have changed the game for hundreds of millions of people who now have treatments for the first time and can live longer, healthier lives. These blockbuster brands once accounted for 60% of sales for the top 10 leading pharma companies.[33] But the future of the pharma business is no longer in treating widespread chronic conditions, such as heart disease or high blood pressure. We've already successfully addressed the biggest unmet needs in those disease areas.

The unmet medical needs that remain today are increasingly in cancer, neurology and rare disease, where treatments are highly targeted, potentially curative and require complex administration and typically the use of a specialty pharmacy. For example, emerging blockbuster drugs that treat a variety of cancers, such as Keytruda and OPDIVO, are highly targeted immunotherapy treatments and require a lengthy in-office infusion and biomarker testing before a patient may even qualify.

Similarly, cell and gene therapies are a huge potential market for pharma companies. By 2025, the FDA expects to approve 10 to 20 cell and gene therapy products each year to treat or cure a whole host of conditions.[34] There are extreme complexities that cell and gene therapies will introduce for patients, including navigating incomplete reimbursements, keeping up with long-term disease monitoring and engaging with a complicated manufacturing process. Pharma now needs to help patients address these novel challenges, ranging from steering patients and their families through the sometimes lengthy and complicated treatment process to managing multifaceted logistics, like travel and the potentially permanent side effects that might come with preparing the body to accept the treatment (which could, for example, cause sterility for some people).

One pharmaceutical company, a leader in the treatment of the rare, life-shortening degenerative neuromuscular disease Friedreich's ataxia (FA), has always made it a priority to work with patients as it develops treatments. While conceptualizing its next innovation in treatment, the company shared its idea with FA patient, advocate and successful podcast host (among many other things) Kyle Bryant. According to Kyle: "They [the pharma company] were so excited to talk to me about their plans, I almost felt bad bursting their bubble." The company was considering options for pill size in a new investigational treatment. A smaller pill seemed appropriate as the company assumed it would be more manageable for patients to swallow—a reasonable expectation. But in discussions with Kyle, he was able to share with them the challenges FA patients face as they lose mobility and dexterity. In fact, Kyle shared that "[A larger pill] would be more easily manipulated by my fingers and I would be able to pick it up. I would also be able to better feel it in my mouth and throat to ensure that I am swallowing it."

Understanding these highly specific needs of people managing complex diseases is key to improving outcomes for patients and for the future success of pharma's business. And what is best suited for the patient is not always the most obvious solution. For many people fighting cancer or living with a rare disease, treatment success is not necessarily defined by a positive clinical outcome but by which treatment is tolerable and what helps them live more manageable lives.

The $500 Billion Problem

Even before the COVID-19 global pandemic, the impact of medication non-adherence and compliance had an outsized impact on the U.S. healthcare system, estimated at $528.4 billion in 2016.[35] This number might not be all that surprising, considering that 30% of prescribed medications are not filled and 50% of medications are not taken as prescribed (more on this in Chapter 9).[36] This is too high a price to pay and has enormous negative consequences for patients, the healthcare ecosystem and the pharma industry.

These staggering statistics should be a call to arms for the pharma industry. No longer can we accept sub-par patient experience and clinical outcomes. To thrive in the evolving and increasingly competitive pharmaceutical industry, companies must take a serious look inward and acknowledge what needs to change. This is not only because it's the right thing to do for patients—increasingly, it's also a business imperative. In the succinct words of Ro: "Talk to your patient."

Key Takeaways

- Patient centricity is a top priority for the pharmaceutical industry and a strategic imperative for senior leaders.

- External forces, such as changing consumer behavior and expectations, advances in technology and data availability, increasing competition, regulatory guidance and the new definition of value, are pushing pharma to make changes to meet the demands of the evolving environment.

- Within the industry, emerging business realities make a focus on the patient mission critical; these include the declining ROIs of R&D, the changing pipeline and the ongoing challenges around patient adherence, persistence and compliance.

- Pharma companies face the risk of being outpaced by their competition or displaced by players external to healthcare if they fail to embrace these changes and evolve.

- Companies have demonstrated that they can overcome key business challenges (e.g., AbbVie improving adherence, Janssen improving clinical trial compliance, Takeda improving employee motivation, etc.) through patient-centric approaches, leading to positive impacts for both the patient and the business.

Acknowledgments

The author would like to thank the following people for their contributions and input in writing this chapter: Andrew Benzie, Kyle Bryant, Nan Gu, Pratap Khedkar, Stefan Kloss, Rohini Kumar, Laurie Meyers, Aaron Mitchell, Ed Schoonveld, Tanya Shepley, Pranav Srivastava, Bharat Tewarie, Michael Thomas, Vijesh Unnikrishnan, Albert Whangbo and Dr. Hilary Wilson.

Endnotes

1. Hugh Gosling, "Patient-Centricity: Ghost in the Machine," Pharma Times Magazine, May 2016, http://www.pharmatimes.com/magazine/2016/may_2016/patient-centricity_ghost_in_the_machine.

2. Robin A. Cohen, Michael E. Martinez and Emily P. Zammitti, "Health Insurance Coverage: Early Release of Estimates from the National Health Interview Survey, January–March 2018," National Center for Health Statistics, August 2018, https://www.cdc.gov/nchs/data/nhis/earlyrelease/Insur201808.pdf.

3. John B. McKinlay et al., "Effects of Patient Medication Requests on Physician Prescribing Behavior: Results of a Factorial Experiment," in Medical Care 52, no. 4 (April 2014): 294-299, https://doi.org/10.1097/MLR.0000000000000096.

4. Eric J. Topol, "Topol on Medicine in 2015: Letting Go," Medscape, September 24, 2021, https://www.medscape.com/viewarticle/836971.

5. Laurie Meyers, "Q&A with Genentech: How Patient Centricity Is Evolving with COVID-19," interview with Hensley Evans, ZS, November 10, 2020, https://www.zs.com/insights/qa-genentech-how-patient-centricity-evolving-covid-19.

6. ZS Research, 2020.

7. Evgenia Gougari et al., "A Comprehensive Review of the FDA-Approved Labels of Diabetes Drugs: Indications, Safety, and Emerging Cardiovascular Safety Data," in Journal of Diabetes and Its Complications 31, no. 12 (December 2017): 1719-1727, https://doi.org/ 10.1016/j.jdiacomp.2017.08.005. https://www.sciencedirect.com/science/article/pii/S1056872717302003

8. National Library of Medicine, "Trends, Charts, and Maps," last modified September 23, 2021, https://clinicaltrials.gov/ct2/resources/trends.

9. Anne Nijs, "Roche's Infinity Model: Helping to Transform the Lives of Patients with Rare Diseases," interview by Jan Asher and Anton Chtcherbakov, McKinsey & Company, July 15, 2021, https://www.mckinsey.com/industries/pharmaceuticals-and-medical-products/our-insights/roches-infinity-model-helping-to-transform-the-lives-of-patients-with-rare-diseases.

10. Roche, "Patient Journey Partner (PJP)," accessed September 24, 2021, https://www.roche.com/careers/jobs/jobsearch/job.htm?id=E-202104-109616&locale=en&title=patient+journey+partner+%28PJP%29#jobfacts.

11. Andrew P. Brogan et al., "Payer Perspectives on Patient-Reported Outcomes in Health Care Decision Making: Oncology Examples," in Journal of Managed Care & Specialty Pharmacy 23, no. 2 (February 2017): 125-134.

12. Moe Alsumidae, "Non-Adherence: A Direct Influence on Clinical Trial Duration and Cost," Applied Clinical Trials, April 24, 2017, https://www.appliedclinicaltrialsonline.com/view/non-adherence-direct-influence-clinical-trial-duration-and-cost.

13. Shelby Livingston, "Value-Based Contracts Key to Solving U.S. Drug Pricing 'Crisis,' " Modern Healthcare, June 9, 2017, https://www.modernhealthcare.com/article/20170609/NEWS/170609875/value-based-contracts-key-to-solving-u-s-drug-pricing-crisis.

14. Merck, "Merck Announces Fifth Round of Global Grants to Tackle Maternal Mortality and Promote Health Equity Worldwide," March 2, 2021, https://www.merck.com/news/merck-announces-fifth-round-of-global-grants-to-tackle-maternal-mortality-and-promote-health-equity-worldwide/.

15. Genentech, "Advancing Inclusive Research," accessed September 25, 2021, https://www.gene.com/patients/advancing-inclusive-research.

16. TEConomy Partners, LLC, "The Biopharmaceutical Industry: Improving Diversity & Inclusion in the Workforce," PhRMA, December 2020, https://www.phrma.org/-/media/project/phrma/phrna-org/phrma-org/pdf/s-u/teconomyphrma-dI-report-final.pdf.

17. Ann Powell, "Reflecting on the First Anniversary of Our BMS Commitments in Diversity, Inclusion and Health Equity," Bristol Meyers Squib, August 12, 2021, https://www.bms.com/about-us/global-diversity-and-inclusion/our-commitments.html.

18. Lionel Sujay Vailshery, "Number of Connected Wearable Devices Worldwide by Region 2015-2022," Statista, January 22, 2021, https://www.statista.com/statistics/490231/wearable-devices-worldwide-by-region/#statisticContainer; Statista, "Number of Connected Wearable Devices Worldwide by Region from 2015 to 2022," graph, February 2019, https://www.statista.com/statistics/490231/wearable-devices-worldwide-by-region/#statisticContainer.

19. Marco Ricci, "Janssen Makes iSTEP clinical Trials Digital Platform Open to All," Pharmaphorum, October 16, 2017, https://pharmaphorum.com/news/janssen-istep-clinical-trial-adherence/.

20. Moe Alsumidaie, "Non-Adherence: A Direct Influence on Clinical Trial Duration and Cost," Applied Clinical Trials, April 24, 2017, http://www.appliedclinicaltrial-sonline.com/non-adherence-direct-influence-clinical-trial-duration-and-cost.

21. Guillaume Charlin et al., "Unlocking Growth in CPG with AI and Advanced Analytics," Boston Consulting Group, October 15, 2018, https://www.bcg.com/en-ca/publications/2018/unlocking-growth-cpg-ai-advanced-analytics.

22. ZS, "Redefining Patient Centricity in Pharma," presentation, 2019.

23. Denise Roland, "How Drug Companies Are Using Your DNA to Make New Medicine," The Wall Street Journal, July 22, 2019, https://www.wsj.com/articles/23andme-glaxo-mine-dna-data-in-hunt-for-new-drugs-11563879881?mod=article_inline&adobe_

24. U.S. National Library of Medicine, "Study of the Safety and Effectiveness of GSK6097608 in Participants with Advanced Solid Tumors," published June 25, 2020, last modified July 27, 2021, https://clinicaltrials.gov/ct2/show/nct04446351.

25. Amirah al-Idrus, "Novartis, Otsuka, Pfizer, Sanofi Join Verily's Project Baseline," Fierce Biotech, May 21, 2019, https://www.fiercebiotech.com/biotech/novartis-otsuka-pfizer-sanofi-join-verily-s-project-baseline.

26. U.S. Food & Drug Administration (FDA), "FDA-Led Patient-Focused Drug Development (PFDD) Public Meetings," last modified December 22, 2021, https://www.fda.gov/industry/prescription-drug-user-fee-amendments/fda-led-patient-focused-drug-development-pfdd-public-meetings.

27. FDA, "CDER Patient-Focused Drug Development," July 27, 2021, https://www.fda.gov/drugs/development-approval-process-drugs/cder-patient-focused-drug-development; FDA, "FDA-Led Patient-Focused Drug Development"; Center for Drug Evaluation and Research (CDER), "Patient-Focused Drug Development: Collecting Comprehensive and Representative Input," FDA, last updated June 16, 2020, https://www.fda.gov/regulatory-information/search-fda-guidance-documents/patient-focused-drug-development-collecting-comprehensive-and-representative-input.

28. CDER, "Patient-Focused Drug Development."

29. EMA, "From Lab to Patient: The Journey of a Medicine Assessed by EMA," accessed January 17, 2022, https://www.ema.europa.eu/en/from-lab-to-patient-timeline; EMA, "Overview of Patient Involvement Along the Medicines Lifecycle at EMA," accessed January 17, 2022, https://www.ema.europa.eu/en/documents/other/overview-patient-involvement-along-medicines-lifecycle-european-medicines-agency_en.pdf.

30. Deloitte Centre for Health Solutions, "Ten Years On: Measuring the Return from Pharmaceutical Innovation 2019," Deloitte, 2020, https://www2.deloitte.com/content/dam/Deloitte/uk/Documents/life-sciences-health-care/deloitte-uk-ten-years-on-measuring-return-on-pharma-innovation-report-2019.pdf.

31. Alex Berezow, "Clinical Trial Success Rates by Phase and Therapeutic Area," American Council on Science and Health, June 11, 2020, https://www.acsh.org/news/2020/06/11/clinical-trial-success-rates-phase-and-therapeutic-area-14845.

32. Priya Temkar, "Accelerating Study Start-Up: The Key to Avoiding Trial Delays," Association of Clinical Research Professionals, February 1, 2017, https://acrpnet.org/2017/02/01/accelerating-study-start-up-the-key-to-avoiding-trial-delays/.

33. Nefees Malik, "Has the Era of Blockbuster Drugs Come to an End?" in BioPharm International 20, no. 2 (December 1, 2007): para. 1, https://www.biopharminternational.com/view/has-era-blockbuster-drugs-come-end.

34. Alex Chatel, "Gene Therapy Manufacturing Trends: Accelerating the Path to Industrialized Gene Therapy Manufacturing with High Capacity, Scalable, Fixed-Bed Bioreactors," Contract Pharma, May 5, 2021, https://www.contractpharma.com/issues/2021-05-01/view_features/gene-therapy-manufacturing-trends/.

35. Jonathan H. Watanabe, Terry McInnis and Jan D. Hirsch, "Cost of Prescription Drug-Related Morbidity and Mortality," in Annals of Pharmacotherapy 52, no. 9 (2018): 829-837, https://doi.org/10.1177/1060028018765159.

36. Katy Anderson, "Why You Should Take Medication as Prescribed," SingleCare, last modified on April 16, 2021, https://www.singlecare.com/blog/news/1-3-patients-dont-take-medications-as-prescribed/.

Chapter 3:
Defining Patient Centricity

Sharon Suchotliff and Hensley Evans

Tony's Story

Tony had been living with high cholesterol for years, but it wasn't until his total cholesterol jumped from 189 to 261 in a two-year span that he started taking medication—despite the fact that he worked in healthcare and knew about the association of high cholesterol with increased risk of a heart attack. The medication was moderately effective, but, three years later, a new physician, worried about his LDL cholesterol specifically, did a tomography scan and saw calcium deposits in his coronary arteries. Tony found a cardiologist who conducted an angiogram, saw a massive blockage and recommended surgery immediately. The next day, Tony underwent double bypass surgery at the age of 49. Determined not to let it slow him down, he recovered quickly and was back to traveling for work six weeks later. Over the next 13 years Tony took medication in an attempt to get and keep his LDL down, trying several different statins, but they were only ever moderately successful.

When Repatha, a new monoclonal antibody treatment designed to be taken with statins, launched in 2015, Tony believed he'd be a great candidate for the medication. Although his physician had not specifically recommended Repatha, Tony asked for a prescription, even though he knew that the process of getting insurance coverage might be more complicated and that the drug was administered via injection. Tony shared: "I knew I was a great candidate for this product. I have kids, hobbies, and a flourishing career—I wanted to stick around for that."

Since starting Repatha, Tony was able to significantly lower his LDL to 24 mg/dl—well below the 100 mg/dl guideline for a healthy heart. But now there were other challenges. Tony's prescription was originally approved by his insurer, but, after his employer changed insurance companies, Tony had to go through the entire authorization process again. He hit speedbump after speedbump in dealing with the insurers, the specialty pharmacies and even his physician. As Tony recalled,

> *I needed to remind my cardiologist why I need to be on this medication, and one time my doctor suggested that I stop taking my statin because he thought my LDL was too low! What's even more frustrating is the process of getting an extra prescription delivered to me when I am going on vacation and will be out of town for a few weeks. But I know how to navigate the system and could do something about it.*

Tony's exasperating experience getting and staying on Repatha is unfortunately a common one—it could as easily apply to a person who isn't fluent in English and doesn't know who to call or what to ask for, or to the busy mom of three who juggles work and home and doesn't have the time or bandwidth to deal with navigating all the roadblocks Tony encountered. "I think that if I wasn't who I am, I would have long ago given up on taking Repatha," said Tony.

Luckily for Tony, he just so happens to be Anthony Hooper, former executive vice president of global commercial operations for Amgen, the maker of Repatha. Tony's vast experience in healthcare means that he can understand the rationale insurance companies have for removing drugs from formularies or requiring prior authorizations, but, as he says, "Repatha is not a lifestyle drug—it's a life-saving drug."

Tony's experience moved him to take a closer look at what patients taking Amgen drugs go through. During his tenure at the company, Amgen invested significantly in improving the patient experience. Some of the patient research conducted by Tony's team at Amgen also taught him that patients often have many other priorities—affording rent, getting to work, caring for children—that can supersede healthcare issues: "Very few people want to be patients. We have to make the experience better, easier—start to treat them like customers. I can order anything I want on Amazon, and it's delivered to my home. Getting a prescription should be similar. Everything else is on autosupply. Why not my medications?"

The majority of the resources the pharmaceutical industry produces for the patient today are not actually designed for the patient. We provide information that, although factual and "accessible," may not serve the fundamental purpose of helping a patient achieve uninterrupted benefit from a medication.

As a life sciences industry, we spend a lot of time and money developing tools and services to address the needs of people taking our medications without really thinking about patients' convenience accessing and using these resources or how any hindrances to care might disrupt other parts of patients' lives. It's not until we put ourselves in patients' shoes that we understand the real impact. Patient centricity is our call to action as an industry to deliver real value to patients in support of their health journeys.

What Is Patient Centricity?

Even though the phrase "patient centricity" has been part of the healthcare industry's vernacular for more than a decade, translating what it means within a pharma company's culture and business objectives is challenging. As Laurie Myers, executive director of engagement and experience design at Genentech, noted: "If you ask 10 people what it means to be patient centric, you'll probably get 10 different answers, and that can lead to 10 very different experiences for patients who interact with us." According to Dr. Dara Richardson-Heron, chief patient officer for Pfizer at the time of writing, patient centricity is about working together to "develop and implement creative and innovative ideas and solutions designed to maximize patient safety, ensure that patients' voices are heard, increase diversity in clinical trials and overcome barriers to accessing quality and affordable healthcare."[1] At Merck, Dr. Julie Gerberding, executive vice president and chief patient officer, talks about patient centricity as "moving from thinking 'product, product, product' to 'patient, patient, patient.' "[2]

Having varying definitions of patient centricity within the pharma industry isn't a bad thing—but the diversity of definitions has led to a similarly wide range of approaches organizations are taking on the path to becoming more patient centric. What is critical is for a company to define a clear patient centricity "North Star" that guides their company's culture and business decisions.

Defining Patient Centricity

At ZS, we define patient centricity as having an organizational culture, business practices and capabilities that put patients at the heart of decisions, meet patient needs as articulated by patients themselves and drive business outcomes. However, the specific wordsmithing of the definition isn't as important as the four key elements of patient centricity, or what we call the Four I's: Insight, Integrate, Improve and Impact. These Four I's address the role of the patient perspective (Insight), company culture and business practices (Integrate), delivering a better experience through key capabilities (Improve) and ensuring sustainability by focusing on areas of mutual benefit for the patient and business (Impact). While many companies have patient centricity as a goal, the key to actually achieving a sustained focus on the patient is following through all the way from insights to impact. We'll outline each of the Four I's in more detail below.

First, though, it's important to note that, while patient centricity is related to and includes patient advocacy, patient engagement and patient experience, these aren't the same things. A few working definitions:

- **Patient advocacy:** Collaborating with and supporting patient organizations to amplify the patient voice and deliver on patient needs.

- **Patient engagement:** Two-way interactions between an organization and patients or advocacy groups to gain insights into the patient perspective, invite their input during decision-making and ultimately co-create products and services.

- **Patient experience:** The patient's subjective experience of interacting with the product, the company and the company's support and solutions.

Similarly, patient centricity is intricately related to health equity and reducing disparities in care. By putting individual patients and their needs at the heart of our decisions, we can take a big step toward understanding and potentially eliminating health inequities. To reach either goal of patient centricity or health equity, pharma must cross the same bridge guided by a common compass: the Four I's.

The Four I's of Patient Centricity

Insight

Any truly patient-centric endeavor starts with understanding people (who are sometimes also patients) and their experiences. And this means all different types of people that are part of the patient population of interest. This fundamental human understanding is what we mean by "insight." In pharma, we often believe we know what people want—but, when we ask them directly, we discover that their real needs are completely different. For example, a top pharma company working on a rare disease, for which tracking the occurrence of symptoms is key to successful disease management, decided to develop a mobile app to make that process easier for people living with the condition. When the company brought in patients to advise on the development of the app, they discovered that patients had already been using effective means to track their symptoms themselves—they'd been doing it their entire lives and were quite content using their own methods. That was a key insight. The company was dedicating precious time and resources to develop a solution to a problem that didn't actually need solving. What patients felt they really needed was an alert system to let their loved ones know when they were having a bad day and might need medical care. Through this interaction, the company learned a valuable lesson about how important it is to hear from patients themselves and not make assumptions about their experiences.

In another example, a pharma company struggled to enroll patients in a trial for a potentially life-changing treatment. The company believed that the reluctance of patients to enroll was because they felt uncomfortable with the protocol requiring them to provide semen samples at regular intervals throughout the trial. However, through ethnographic research and a series of interviews and surveys, the company discovered that patients were actually fine with the protocol, were very open to the trial and eager to learn more about the requirements. As it turned out, it was the principal investigators (PIs) and clinical research coordinators (CRCs) who were uncomfortable—they lacked the education, training and confidence to talk with patients in accurate and relatable ways. The company responded to these insights by co-creating a three-pronged plan with patients, CRCs and PIs. The approach included drafting new brochures and pamphlets to support gaps in the discussion between PIs and patients, consulting with key opinion leaders (KOLs) in sexual health to make informational videos for investigators modeling how to have effective conversations about semen samples and using role play during training to help investigators get comfortable with the subject. In acting on these insights, the company transformed the patients' experiences of enrollment and accelerated the trial recruitment rate by a factor of 20 (see Figure 3-1).

Figure 3-1: Accelerated Enrollment Through Patient Understanding[3]

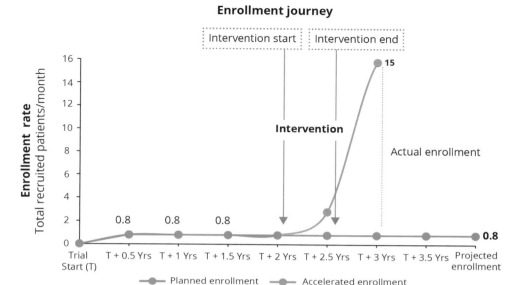

Integrate

Of course, the deepest and most unique insights in the world won't help if there are no mechanisms in place to integrate these perspectives into an organization's culture and decision-making. A simple litmus test is to ask: "Did we make any different decisions as a result of the insights we gleaned from patients?" If the answer is no, there's a problem either with the insight ("Did we ask the right questions?") or with the way the organization disseminated or acted upon the insight. Companies can integrate patient-centric approaches into their overall ways of working by:

- Developing a common patient-centered lexicon adopted at all levels within the organization

- Incorporating patient-centric approaches into learning and development programs

- Building patient-focused measures into KPIs or performance metrics for each employee's function or role

- Creating business processes that orient the company's culture around the patient

Although shifting a company's culture takes time and concerted effort, through our work at ZS we've seen several pharma organizations take meaningful steps to enable and support a change in employee mindsets and behaviors. In 2015, UCB reorganized all business units and renamed them "patient value units." The company also changed all job titles to orient every function around the value each role brings to patients. UCB has continued to add new patient-focused roles. For example, in 2019 the company added a new role called Head of Insights to Impact, which is responsible for leading a team across finance, strategy and operations to leverage insights and align company resources to have the greatest impact for patients. This bold move clearly demonstrates the importance UCB places on considering what matters to patients when driving business outcomes.[4]

At Ipsen, a global biopharmaceutical company, all medical teams receive training on what patient centricity means at the company through workshops and simulations; the company is also rolling out an Ipsen Patient Centricity Training Curriculum through their e-learning platform for all employees who already work, or may work, with patients and patient organizations. Ipsen also made patient centricity a core component of the certification program that is required before anyone in the company engages with patients.

Investing in tools and infrastructure that make it feasible for employees to obtain patient input as part of their workflows is critical. Several pharma organizations have created "patient expert" panels that employees can consult as a way to help bridge a direct connection with patients. These panels help employees working across the product life cycle get guidance from and collaborate with patients on activities like the development of clinical trial protocols, patient support programs, marketing and other initiatives.

At Genentech, collaboration with a patient council has helped the company gather insights from a diverse group of patients early and often and shift the company mindset from thinking of patient input as "nice to have" to a "must have." In the second half of 2020, Genentech employees engaged with members of the patient council over 270 times on topics ranging from how to design a clinical trial for a multicultural population, to patient perceptions of digital technologies, to what "self-service" options patients want pharma to provide. The company frequently holds "ask-me-anything"-style open forums with the patient council. These forums help employees get comfortable collaborating with patients and also illuminate the many ways in which pharma has failed to deliver a good experience for patients, helping the company identify where and how to intervene. According to Laurie Myers, who is responsible for the patient council as executive director of engagement and experience design at Genentech, this work has enabled a shift in the organization's mindset from a culture of, "you *should* get patient input [on projects] to *why wouldn't* you get the patient perspective."

Improve

Once a company successfully embeds insights into key business processes, it's still crucial to ensure that the capabilities and resources necessary to deliver an improved patient experience are in place. Early experience with a novel therapy for the treatment of a rare pediatric disease showed a drug maker just how confusing the process of undergoing treatment could be for patients and their parents. This early insight signaled to the company that relying on a traditional pharma script for their call center might create confusion and additional stress and frustration for parents of potential patients As you can imagine, parents had a whole host of complex questions about what the treatment entails, the process and what happens to their children's bodies after a treatment. Rather than relying on staff typically utilized for patient support centers, the company invested in hiring highly educated PhDs who had a deep understanding of the science but who also knew how to explain it in plain terms, and with empathy, to parents and patients (especially as the FDA later approved further applications of the treatment in other disease areas).

Another way to deliver on a better patient experience is using automated tools and digital resources to ensure that patients can understand materials intended to support them. For example, companies like Bristol-Meyers Squib[5] and AstraZeneca developed internal tools to make sure their materials contain accessible language that patients and caregivers can easily understand. The use of these tools is part of the approval process for all patient-facing materials and is embedded as part of the workflow, ensuring that patients won't have to struggle to decipher important information about their condition and the available treatments.

Impact

The final key to sustainable focus on patient centricity is to find the sweet spot where patient and business interests overlap in a win-win opportunity. The past decade is littered with examples of programs that companies developed by drawing on patient insights and that succeeded in delivering a better experience for patients—but didn't deliver any impact for the organization. That's simply unsustainable for pharma. We need to look for opportunities for mutual benefit for both patients and the business and then focus our efforts there. Imagine if we could condense Tony's lengthy experience trying to get his medication into 48 hours. This would mean that he would have little or no disruption in treatment, which in turn would result in less risk of Tony dropping off—a benefit to Tony and to Amgen.

In a study published in 2019, AbbVie showed that Humira patients who engaged in the Humira patient support program had 29% higher adherence, 22% lower discontinuation rates and 35% lower disease-specific annual medical costs than patients who didn't participate.[6] Having help in managing complex treatment regimens clearly benefited the participants' health and also reduced their healthcare costs. Although it wasn't directly measured in the study, imagine how these types of patient support programs could improve a patient's quality of life! And, given the improved adherence and lower discontinuation rates, there's also an obvious business benefit for AbbVie.

In another example from Eli Lilly, the company demonstrated that patient-centric approaches can lead to clinical trial success. Working across clinical trial programs, Lilly took a multi-pronged approach to tackle challenges around clinical trial awareness, recruitment and retention. For example, the company designed simulations that brought together researchers, study coordinators, doctors and patients to walk through a trial protocol. In one simulation for a migraine treatment trial, the company learned that the time frame for patients to complete diary entries wasn't feasible. In another trial, Lilly discovered that a proposed protocol requiring central electrocardiograms wouldn't be possible for sites in Europe. According to Anne White, former vice president of Lilly Research Laboratories: "These situations could have resulted in protocol violations and patient dropouts. Instead, the issues were fixed before the trial even started." Patient-centric approaches like these have helped Lilly reduce drug development time by nearly two years, resulting in both huge savings for the company and an opportunity to bring drug treatments to patients faster.[7]

Making Patient Centricity a Reality

As we've established, making patient centricity a reality requires four things, which we call the Four I's:

- Collecting deep and meaningful **Insights** from diverse and representative patients

- Nurturing a culture and set of business practices that **Integrate** the diverse patient perspective into decision-making

- Building capabilities that allow the organization to deliver an **Improved** patient experience

- Measuring and demonstrating the win-win **Impact** for the patient and business

We've given some examples of specific initiatives that illustrate these Four I's. But how do companies build these capabilities at the enterprise level? To understand how pharma companies across the industry are igniting and supporting patient-centric change, ZS conducted research with more than two dozen mid- to large-sized global pharma companies. We explored the types of capabilities companies invest in, the organizational models and functions they put in place, the activities they conduct to drive a change in mindset and the standard operating procedures (SOPs) that help to advance patient centricity, among other elements.

Our findings point to four capability dimensions that enable patient centricity within a pharma organization: leadership and culture; structures and practices; data, analytics and technology; and cross-industry collaboration (see Figure 3-2). Within each of these four dimensions, we assessed the progress an organization has made toward becoming more patient centric. We rank this progress on a 1-to-5 scale, with a score of 1 representing emerging, basic capabilities and 5 representing a transformational organization. To date, no pharma company has reached a score of 5.

Figure 3-2: The Capability Dimensions of Patient Centricity

Leadership and culture

Where patients fit in the organization's overarching strategic development plan

Strategic vision

Cultural mindset

Portfolio and pipeline strategy

Resourcing

Structure and practices

How company structure affects patient centricity

Business practices

Governance and decision making

Key performance indicators

Education and development plan

Data, analytics and technology

The company's approach to capturing, acquiring and working with patient data

Knowledge management and insight sharing

Data and analytics strategy

Technology

Cross-industry collaboration

Identifying partners to ideate, foster, pilot and implement patient-centric initiatives

Healthcare ecosystem partnerships

Regulatory roadmap and engagement plan

We define the four dimensions of patient centricity capabilities as follows:

Leadership and culture: This dimension refers to where patients fit in the organization's overarching strategic plan. We look at whether there's a clear, communicated vision for patient centricity; the extent to which a focus on the patient has permeated the cultural mindset; and how the company uses the patient perspective to make business decisions. A company with a score of 1 to 2 might have a vision for patient centricity, but the vision hasn't yet been formalized. In these organizations, patients are important as end users but are not yet viewed as a focal point for the business. A company that is advanced (i.e., has a score of 3 to 4) will have a unified strategy for patient centricity, from early research through clinical development and commercialization.

Structures and practices: This dimension is where the rubber meets the road. Beyond merely stating a commitment to the patient, what are the business processes and mechanisms the organization has put in place to enable patient centricity in practice? These include KPIs that signal the significance of the patient's role in the pharma company's business decisions and activities, training and development programs to ensure employees understand and internalize what patient centricity means in their day-to-day roles and SOPs that exist to support a true focus on patients and connect their needs to those of the business. Early in their patient centricity journey, companies might start with informal structures, relying on particularly motivated individuals to take the initiative and carry out patient-centric activities without a directive or specific mandate. As companies advance, we start to see dedicated staff and budgets allocated to patient centricity as well as formalized goals, incentives and processes to encourage and support patient-centric behaviors.

Data, analytics and technology: This dimension encompasses an organization's approach to capturing, acquiring and working with patient data and insights, as well as the technology infrastructure in place to facilitate the patient experience. For example, we assess the types and variety of data collected, the various methodologies for gathering patient insights and how insights are distributed throughout the organization. Companies with a score between 1 and 2 will have some technology and systems in place to collect and analyze patient data, but they're generally ad hoc and discrete. In these organizations, patient data and insights are siloed and used for one-off purposes. Companies on the higher end of the spectrum will tap into and combine many different types of data sets, including marketing insights, real-world data and behavioral insights, in a systematic and streamlined fashion. These companies maintain connectivity of data from discovery through to drug delivery and use these data and insights to deliver tailored support and improved experiences for patients.

Cross-industry collaboration: This final dimension involves the extent to which an organization has a strategy and partnerships in place to support patients in the broader healthcare ecosystem. We look at the breadth and depth of partnerships with regulatory bodies, patient advocacy groups, digital and connected health companies and others in the healthcare ecosystem—as well as companies outside of healthcare. Companies on the lower end of the patient centricity index will have one-off partnerships with patient advocacy groups, professional provider organizations, digital health solutions companies and other such healthcare organizations aimed at addressing a specific, distinct need. As companies progress to the higher end of the index, they start to develop long-standing, deep, mutually beneficial relationships and explore partnerships with regulatory bodies that help to advance patient engagement activities.

Pharma's Progress in Patient Centricity

To measure these four dimensions, ZS developed the Patient Centricity Maturity Index to show how pharma companies have progressed in advancing patient centricity. We first documented our findings in 2018 (see Figure 3-3). We repeated the study in 2021, and, although 85% of the companies we studied have made progress, the ZS Patient Centricity Maturity Index highlights that no one pharma company is transformational on any dimension of patient centricity. And many in the industry agree. A 2019 ZS survey of patient centricity professionals revealed that 93% of participants felt that a focus on patient centricity is critical, yet less than 20% believed their organizations had made significant progress in becoming more patient centric.[8] Companies are largely still experimenting and piloting efforts to embed patient centricity. We also note that no one company leads across all four dimensions of patient centricity maturity, and that's typically purposeful. The decisions as to which dimensions a pharma company focuses on tend to be related to the company's therapeutic areas, pipelines and strategies best suited to advance in those areas.

For example, leaders at the company represented by the red diamond in Figure 3-3 decided that understanding and anticipating patient needs and behaviors would be a key competitive advantage to help defend against encroaching generic competition. For almost a decade and up to this day, the company has invested in building advanced data and analytics capabilities to map patient behaviors and needs across the healthcare journey. This information provides the backbone of all commercial planning, enables the delivery of strong patient services and drives the company's activities around its portfolio of products. In both the 2018 and 2021 studies, the red company clearly led in the dimension of data, analytics and technology. Only now is the company leadership starting to work on embedding a patient centric culture and mindset that permeates across the organization.

Many companies that have started on the journey to becoming more patient centric tend to focus on patient centricity in one part of the organization, such as R&D or commercial, or in a specific business unit, such as oncology or rare disease, but not across the entire organization or throughout the product life cycle. The company represented by the lavender diamond in Figure 3-3 led in the dimension of structures and practices in 2018

Figure 3-3: 85% of Companies Have Improved Across the Four Dimensions of the ZS Patient Centricity Maturity Index Since 2018

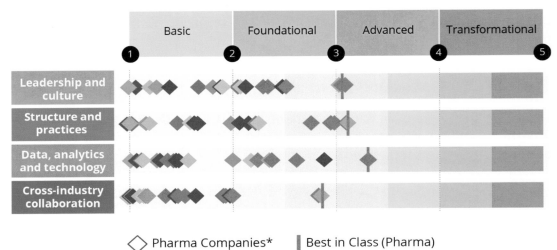

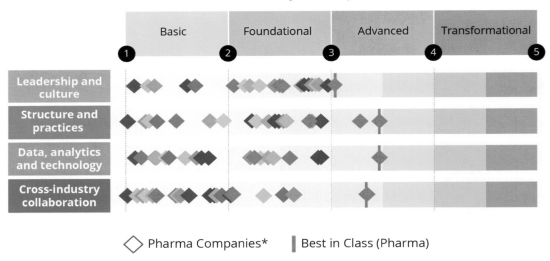

due to its world-class center of excellence (CoE) for patient centricity. The CoE focused on enabling the various units within the company to include the patient perspective in drug development across priority therapeutic areas in the pipeline. By appointing a team of subject matter experts (SMEs) to partner with teams across different functions and therapeutic areas, the CoE identified best practices and SOPs and provided trainings and guidance at critical milestones in early research and clinical development. Leaders in functions across the organization were deputized by the U.S. president of the organization to advance patient centricity within their functions and ensure their teams adhered to new processes. This approach aimed to create momentum and accountability for patient centricity in the drug development process as the company prepared to enter new therapeutic categories, with less of a focus on commercial activities.

We often hear from clients that there's an assumption that companies working in rare disease are more patient centric than those working in more prevalent conditions because of the requirements of working with the rare disease community. However, ZS research has found that this isn't the case—none of the companies at the higher end of the Patient Centricity Maturity Index focus exclusively on rare disease. For example, the company represented by the gray diamond in Figure 3-3 leads in the dimension of leadership and culture in the 2021 study. This company operates in a disease that affects more than 38 million people around the globe, and listening to the patient voice has been critical to the company's ability to advance treatment and prevention options. For this organization, ensuring that all employees recognize the imperative of understanding the perspectives of those living with or at risk of the disease has been a key differentiator in an increasingly competitive market. As of 2018, the organization had effective mechanisms in place to collaborate with patients and caregivers and gather their insights, but it was still experimenting with various types of data and slowly starting to consider an overarching patient-centric strategy and technology platform to provide patient support.

Since our first benchmarking work in 2018, much of the progress we've seen organizations make has been in the dimensions of leadership and culture and structures and practices, with many companies moving from basic to foundational capabilities. This shift demonstrates some of the first steps companies typically take in their journey to become patient centric: building a vision for patient centricity and then investing in the business processes to make that vision a reality. Because of the level of effort, time and financial investment required, we've seen slower progress in the dimension of data, analytics and technology, but this is an area that many companies are prioritizing as the next area of focus.

Our 2021 study also reveals that much of the progress over the last few years has focused on the commercial side of pharma organizations. This is partly because some of the earliest patient-focused efforts within pharma came out of marketing. Pharma has more experience and a foundation to build on when it comes to branded medications. Over the next few years, we expect the focus to expand and emphasize the R&D parts of pharma organizations as companies move from experiments and pilots in patient-focused drug developed to established capabilities and SOPs.

The emphasis on the commercial side of pharma organizations is also part of the reason we saw slower movement between 2018 and 2021 in the dimension of cross-industry collaboration. Much of the work to date in this dimension has been around partnerships with patient advocacy groups along with a smattering of partnerships in health tech and a few with payers and provider organizations. During the COVID-19 pandemic, we saw many pharma companies experimenting more broadly and with more far-reaching partnerships with other pharma companies as well as with regulators, providers, infusion centers and payers. As patient-focused drug development (PFDD) continues to gain momentum, we expect to see much more movement in this dimension as pharma seeks to partner more broadly with patients, regulators and others in the ecosystem to include the patient perspective, expand the diversity of patients represented and improve patients' experiences as participants in clinical trials and as end-users of treatments.

The ZS Patient Centricity Maturity Index provides a valuable resource for understanding where progress has been made and how pharma organizations can continue to advance patient-centric efforts. Despite many people asking, however, it doesn't provide us with a specific formula for success. True patient-centric transformation requires persistence, consistent investment and time. It requires a clear vision and leadership that articulates a specific internal definition of patient centricity and that demands accountability for progress and impact. The rest of this book lays out both the challenges that remain and the various ways in which pharma can not only advance but transform. Our hope and ambition is that over the next few years, we'll see companies on the PCI not only advance but show us the way for pharma to become transformational. Are you ready to walk hand-in-hand with patients?

Key Takeaways

- At ZS, we define patient centricity as having an organizational culture, business practices and capabilities that put patients at the heart of decisions, meet patient needs as articulated by patients themselves and drive business outcomes.

- Making patient centricity a reality requires four things, which we call the Four I's:

  - Collecting deep and meaningful **Insights** from patients

  - Nurturing a culture and set of business practices that help to **Integrate** the patient perspective into decision-making

- Building capabilities that allow the organization to deliver an **Improved** patient experience

- Measuring and demonstrating the win-win **Impact** for the patient and the business

- Being patient centric does not need to come at the expense of company profits. Companies like AbbVie, Eli Lilly and others have demonstrated that patient centricity can lead to benefits for both the patient and organization.

- It's not necessary to lead across all dimensions of patient centricity. It's critical to focus on the dimensions that are most relevant to the company's business and strategic priorities. Emphasis on a specific dimension will shift over time as the company expands its capabilities.

- The ZS Patient Centricity Maturity Index shows that no pharma company is transformational yet, but many are actively exploring how to incorporate more patient-centric approaches.

Acknowledgments

The author wishes to thank Pascale Cavillon, Emily Goldsher-Diamond, Oleks Gorbenko, Anthony Hooper, Barbara McCullough, Laurie Meyers, Alyson Nelson, Mark Saunders, Pranav Srivastava, Victoria Summers, Bharat Tewarie, Maria Whitman and the ZS Patient Centricity Advisory Board members for their contributions to this chapter.

Endnotes

1. Pfizer, "Working with Patient Organisations," accessed January 17, 2022, https://www.pfizer.co.uk/getting-to-know-our-chief-patient-officer.

2. Gareth Phillips and John Elliott, "The Path to Patient Centricity: Closing the 'How' Gap," Ipsos, August 2018, https://www.ipsos.com/sites/default/files/ct/publication/documents/2018-09/ipsos-healthcare-the-path-to-patient-centricity-august-2018.pdf.

3. ZS Research, 2019.

4. UCB, "Kim Moran: Head of U.S. Insights to Impact," accessed January 17, 2022, https://www.ucb-usa.com/ucb-in-the-u-s/u-s-leadership-team/kim-moran#:~:-text=kim%20moran-,head%20of%20u.s.%20insights%20to%20impact,the%20greatest%20impact%20for%20patients.

5. "The Universal Patient Language," UPL, accessed January 17, 2022, https://www.upl.org/.

6. Diana Brixner et al., "Patient Support Program Increased Medication Adherence with Lower Total Health Care Costs Despite Increased Drug Spending," in Journal of Managed Care & Specialty Pharmacy 25, no. 7 (July 2019): 770-779, https://doi.org/10.18553/jmcp.2019.18443.

7. Ed Miseta, "Lilly Uses Patient Awareness & Access to Cut Clinical Trial Timelines," Life Science Leader, May 2, 2018, https://www.lifescienceleader.com/doc/lilly-uses-patient-awareness-access-to-cut-clinical-trial-timelines-0001.

8. Hensley Evans and Sharon Suchotliff, "Why Do We Struggle to Deliver on Patient Centricity Despite Knowing It's Critical?" ZS, October 30, 2020, https://www.zs.com/insights/why-do-we-struggle-to-deliver-on-patient-centricity-despite-know.

Chapter 4:
Why Has Pharma Struggled to Change?

Hensley Evans

The Enormous Gap Between Intention and Reality

The past two years have seen huge shifts in how the pharmaceutical industry thinks about the patient experience, as healthcare systems worldwide struggle to simultaneously manage periodic surges in COVID-19 infection rates while still providing ongoing care to patients with other acute and chronic diseases. If ZS clients are any indication, interest in patient centricity has accelerated tremendously as a result. But, as Chapter 3 illustrated, even two years ago in 2019, a ZS survey of pharmaceutical executives in the U.S. and Europe showed overwhelming agreement that increasing the focus on patient centricity was critical.[1] And yet, less than one in five executives believed they had made meaningful progress.

It's interesting to note that senior executives saw less of a gap than middle management. When asked whether they agreed that their organization had made progress in developing a mindset that placed patients, caregivers and communities at the forefront of organizational decision-making, almost half of senior executives agreed (47%), compared with only 18% of middle managers. At ZS, we have also observed this "optimism gap" anecdotally in our benchmarking work with specific clients: senior leadership tends to believe (or at least claim) that the company is making rapid progress, while people in roles that directly work to implement patient-centric approaches are far more skeptical about the speed of change. One hypothesis for this disparity is that, as patient centricity gains traction as an important business objective, middle managers are more likely to talk to senior executives about success stories and to downplay the challenges. Another hypothesis is that senior leadership often either doesn't grasp many of the hurdles that exist or may be defining patient centricity progress in different terms than middle managers. Perhaps CEOs and senior leaders are focused on more narrow definitions (better medicines and patient access) than middle managers, who are trying to solve for broader challenges in the patient journey. Whatever the case, all agree there is a gap between vision and reality.

Key Barriers to Change

What *is* holding the pharmaceutical industry back from making real progress? In our survey, we asked about the key barriers organizations face in implementing patient-centric solutions. We had hypothesized that many respondents to the survey would point to regulations and compliance (an oft-cited concern). Particularly outside of the U.S., we often hear that companies struggle to figure out how to deliver value to patients—especially when it comes in the form of direct communications—while staying within the boundaries of market regulations. Somewhat surprisingly, though, this didn't show up in the top survey responses. Instead, we heard about four underlying challenges: a siloed organizational structure, the lack of a consistent focus on the patient, poorly aligned incentives and KPIs, and a struggle to make a compelling business case for change.

Figure 4-1: Perceived vs. Actual Barriers to Patient Centricity[2]

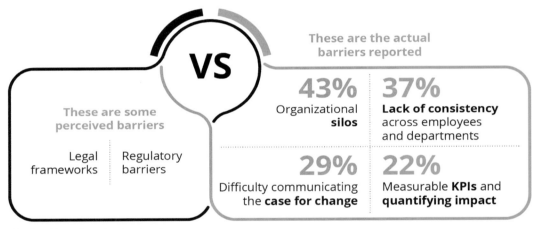

These are the actual
barriers reported

These are some
perceived barriers

Legal
frameworks

Regulatory
barriers

43%
Organizational
silos

37%
Lack of consistency
across employees
and departments

29%
Difficulty communicating
the **case for change**

22%
Measurable **KPIs** and
quantifying impact

Barrier - % are based on top two boxes

Organizational Structure: Product Life Cycle Versus Patient Lifestyle

One of the biggest challenges is that the majority of pharma product manufacturers are functionally organized around the product development life cycle. Pharma's model is thus quite different than that of organizations with customer-based structures designed to tailor services to specific customer needs (for example, healthcare providers organized into urgent, outpatient and emergency care) or that of organizations with market-based divisional structures that allow the companies to implement strategies based on similar characteristics within each market (McDonald's is a notable example, with divisions for international lead markets, high growth markets and foundational markets). One noted disadvantage of a functional organizational structure is the difficulty of coordinating across functional areas. In pharma's case, the challenge of coordination can slow the adoption of patient-centric initiatives. Several members of the ZS Patient Centricity Advisory Board—made up of leaders from mid- to large-cap pharma organizations who focus on patient centricity within their organizations—noted that silos and lack of coordination across functional groups were major barriers to implementing more patient-centric approaches in their companies.[3]

Although there are obviously differences in organizational structures across pharmaceutical manufacturers, the majority use some form of matrix structure that includes both functional groups and product or disease area structures (a.k.a. business structures). At the most fundamental level, the business functions of a pharmaceutical company are to discover and develop new medicines, to produce and distribute those medicines and to market those medicines—and these functions typically drive the organizational structures. Although the details vary widely, typical functional units include R&D, production and commercial operations (marketing and sales), while the business units are organized around the specific products or therapy areas contained within the organization's portfolio. Most organizations try to create business processes that allow for the sharing of information across functional areas and business units, but, in practice, many wind up with "siloed" structures that don't communicate efficiently, which makes it challenging to disseminate patient perspectives or insights throughout the organization. Each part of

Figure 4-2: Matrix Structure in Pharmaceutical Organizations

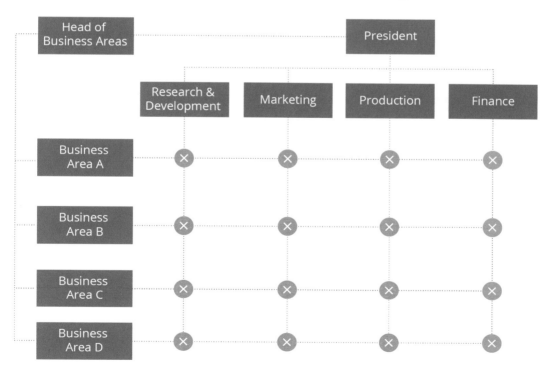

the organization collects specific data and patient insights based on that unit's specific needs and then effectively files this information away after it's used. Because each team typically has only enough team members to serve its own specific needs, most don't have the additional time or financial resources that would be needed to structure the data or information in such a way as to make it accessible to others in the organization. With valuable new insights from patients falling through the cracks between the various disconnected internal structures, organizations miss the opportunity to develop a coordinated strategy that responds efficiently and effectively to patients' needs.

These disjointed functional structures also create friction when it comes to implementing enterprise-level initiatives around patient centricity. Multiple organizations have created patient-focused roles up to and including c-suite roles, such as chief patient officers or chief patient affairs officers, but in most organizations these positions are not quite so senior. ZS internal research in 2020 found that two-thirds of the patient centricity leaders were VPs, directors, or department heads. However, where these roles sit in terms of functional area is often based on where the current patient centricity efforts of the organization are focused and how far along the organization is in its patient centricity evolution. This generally dictates (and often limits) the scope of influence of these teams or individuals. Often, these roles are placed outside of both R&D and commercial organizations, reporting instead into corporate affairs, medical affairs, strategy or business operations; at the time of writing, Pfizer's chief patient officer reported into corporate affairs, and Ipsen's chief patient affairs officer sat within global medical affairs.[4]

Positioning these roles outside R&D or commercial has some obvious theoretical advantages in terms of being able to work across functional areas and business units, but it also has some practical disadvantages. These other teams tend to have limited budget authority; as such, they are required to "pass the cup" to fund initiatives, face challenges generating buy-in across the organization and lack authority to enforce the adoption of specific initiatives. Some organizations (including Sanofi, Takeda and GSK) are now looking to address some of these disadvantages by embedding patient centricity teams within R&D—with the rationale that this will not only create better accountability but that embedding the patient voice into early discovery and development will solve some of the common challenges later in the development life cycle. While this thinking does have merit, it of course creates some additional challenges in pulling patient-focused initiatives through to the commercial side of the organization.

Medical affairs teams are now in an interesting position within pharma organizational structures because they straddle R&D and commercial functions. In about half of organizations, medical rolls up to R&D, while in about 30% it stands alone; in the remaining 20%, medical reports into the commercial part of the organization. As specialty medicines are coming to dominate the pipelines of many organizations, medical functions are growing in both size and influence. More teams are starting to think about what patient centricity really means in the context of medical functions, as medical affairs teams are increasingly seen as the most appropriate conduit between pharma and patients, and for a number of reasons. First, they typically have established relationships with patient advocacy organizations and thus have access to insights into the patient perspective from these groups. Medical affairs teams also possess all the clinical data and can package this into relevant narratives for each audience, including patients. While medical teams are looking to bridge the internal organizational silos and convey patient insights across the functions, a lack of clear accountability for patient insights or authority to drive patient decisions in the R&D and commercial spaces continues to make this challenging.

Lack of Consistent Focus

Several of our advisory board members cited an inconsistent emphasis on patient centricity within organizations as a key challenge that manifests in several ways. First, senior leadership perspective has a huge impact on the degree of strategic focus placed on the patient, and, when executive-level leadership changes, this can cause huge swings in the overall approach to patient initiatives. Second, within specific asset or brand teams, one or two passionate individuals often drive patient-focused innovation. Without a clear mechanism for these team members to measure impact or share best practices, successful approaches fail to scale. The fact that many patient-focused roles are part-time or an "extracurricular" activity only exacerbates this problem, as these individuals have limited incentives to invest much time and energy into these activities. While some organizations with more sophisticated patient centricity or engagement centers of excellence or team structures do include roles focused on patient innovation across functions or brands, the majority of pharma companies are still early in their development and have less formal patient-centricity structures. Finally, even when business processes are put in place with the intention to standardize the inclusion of the patient perspective, they fall flat if they aren't aligned with corporate objectives and culture.

Senior Leadership Changes

When an organization brings in new senior leadership, it's often because the board or CEO is looking to initiate change—so it shouldn't come as a surprise when fairly radical organizational change follows. Because patient-focused initiatives have often struggled to demonstrate a clear link to business impact, they are frequently a target of reorganizations. One company that spent years creating a center of excellence devoted to the patient perspective saw this group dissolved when leadership changes occurred. The new business unit general manager decided that, contrary to what his predecessor believed, "the patient isn't a key decision-maker." Several organizations have created centralized patient engagement functions only to disband them a year or two later to embed patient functions into business units directly, citing the need to move these functions closer to decision-making or the importance of incorporating these skills and capabilities directly into brand teams. While in theory this could help distribute accountability for patient engagement, in practice we have seen that this results in individuals having only a small fraction of their time dedicated to patient-centric initiatives, and these often wind up being deprioritized. While there may be cases where there is a solid rationale for these changes, the constant flux can create "patient centricity whiplash" and lead middle management to conclude that too much focus on the patient may be a risky career move. This creates incentive for managers to pay lip service about patient centricity to corporate PR without instituting tangible initiatives or adding line items to their budgets.

Additionally, while many senior leaders now acknowledge the need for more patient focus, not all do—and, regardless of point of view, very few have had direct patient experience themselves. None of the current CEOs of the top 20 pharma organizations have spent time in specifically patient-focused roles.[5] Small wonder that many leadership teams are less comfortable with patient initiatives than with those focused on HCPs or other, more traditional, stakeholders: We know what we know.

Variability in Patient Focus Within Organizations

Even within an organization with visible and vocal leadership support for patient value, the degree to which leaders in different functional areas agree that patients should be a key focus varies widely, and interpretation of how to actualize patient centricity is frequently left to individuals within various teams. Within the same organization, some business units may have a clear and dedicated focus on the patient, while others may remain unconvinced of the value of patient centricity. Passionate and inspired individuals often do create initiatives that are founded in patient insights, integrate those insights into decision-making and implement approaches that improve the patient experience—at least, for one particular trial or for one brand in one country. But, since most organizations lack the infrastructure to collect, evaluate and disseminate findings from these organically generated "pilots," the impact fails to scale, and the organization doesn't integrate the knowledge. When those particularly passionate individuals working to spur the shift toward patient centricity eventually move on, the lessons learned go with them.

In organizations that structure patient engagement or patient centricity roles as a part-time or "extracurricular" activity on top of someone's primary responsibilities, this problem is even more pronounced. Patient ambassadors, patient-centricity champions and other such roles in many organizations attract individuals who are passionate about centering patients and willing to put in extra time to help support ventures designed to benefit patients. These individuals, while enthusiastic supporters, sometimes lack the skills or experience needed to be as effective as possible, and organizations don't always prioritize training and skill-building initiatives for these "extra" activities. More to the point, with only part of their focus on patient initiatives, people in such roles also lack the time and individual incentives to make significant and sustained impact within the organization.

These grassroots and diffuse efforts can help inspire cultural adoption but generally don't lead to consistent or widespread implementation.

Organizational Mindset and Culture

Several organizations have attempted to use process to solve this problem. As an example, one business unit with a mandate to integrate patient insights into drug development implemented an updated asset planning process with specific patient insights milestones. Unfortunately, the organization didn't make additional resources available to the team to accommodate more robust patient input gathering, so these milestones became mere "box-checking" exercises. Since there wasn't a connection to key organizational objectives, senior leadership didn't push the team to provide more depth behind their patient insights or use the insights to drive changes in critical decisions, and the process became a documentation exercise that failed to deliver real value for the patient.

One "symptom" of this lack of a consistent focus on the patient is the tendency for R&D to hand off assets to the commercial team that have significant patient experience challenges. Many of the most important functional characteristics of a medicine (dosing, mode of administration, etc.) are determined during drug development, when clinical outcomes and side effects are also identified. If the R&D team has not carefully considered the patient experience, and specifically the experiences of a representative set of patients, the commercial team is then left to construct patient support programs that are, in the words of one patient engagement leader, "bug fixes" to address patient or HCP barriers that result from under-conceived functional characteristics. Although most patient support programs are designed with the help of patient input, many of the barriers they address (inconvenient or intimidating administration, difficult access, confusing dosing, harsh side effects) just stem from a lack of patient centricity in the product design. Even worse, these services and support programs are often designed at the eleventh hour, so most teams don't actually know for certain whether the "bug fixes" will address the barrier. Integrating early "proofs of concept" for services and support into the clinical trial process would go a long way towards avoiding these late-stage issues.

One example of the types of challenges that could be addressed earlier in the life cycle is Novartis' Gilenya launch. In 2010, Novartis won the race to launch the first oral disease modifying therapy for MS, beating Biogen's Tecfidera to the punch. But then Novartis ran into some problems: Gilenya's label included a first dose observation (FDO) requirement, and, at launch, not every prescriber was qualified as an FDO center for patients. In order to start therapy, patients sometimes had to travel long distances to an unfamiliar physician's office, and this presented a significant barrier to many patients who didn't have easy access to transportation or who were confused about the process of scheduling their FDO and ensuring their first dose was delivered to the right place. Subsequent to launch, Novartis redesigned the process, eventually launching Gilenya@home. In this new, more patient-friendly version of the initiation process, the baseline assessments and FDO process could be conducted by contracted healthcare professionals who would come to the patient's home (pre-COVID-19). The more convenient process made physicians more comfortable prescribing to a broader set of patients—and made the patient experience significantly better.

KPIs and Incentives Aligned to Shareholders Versus Patients

Despite lots of talk from many leaders about the urgency of focusing on patient value, most pharma organizations have struggled to establish clear links between patient centricity initiatives and business value or to develop metrics that can measure the impact that patient initiatives are having on the organization. As a result, KPIs and incentives within the functional teams in pharma remain primarily product-related and are much more closely aligned to perceived shareholder value than to the value for other stakeholders (such as patients). But, in truth, patient and business value are often aligned well (as the Novartis example above illustrates).

Research and Development

In the R&D space, the lack of alignment between patient centricity and established KPIs is especially pronounced. Choosing patient-focused assets early on in discovery doesn't necessarily align with team success metrics or incentives. During early drug discovery and translational research, teams comprised mainly of scientists (PhDs and MDs) work to identify molecules that show promise in addressing disease. They can do this in one of two ways: target-based discovery (TBD) or phenotypic screening. To use layman's terms, TBD allows scientists to look for molecules that act against specific "targets" known to play a role in certain diseases; TBD might, for example, identify molecules that interact with immunoglobulin E (IgE), an antibody that plays a role in the immune system. Phenotypic screening, on the other hand, essentially takes molecules that are already known to have a biological impact (in cell or animal models) without necessarily understanding how exactly the molecules work in the body. So target-based discovery looks at molecules where we know "how" they work but don't know if they will have any biological effect, whereas with phenotypic screening we know that they have an impact (at least in models) but don't know how they work.

In theory, this means that TBD would enable a more patient-centric approach—allowing researchers to focus on diseases with a high unmet need, to identify targets associated with that disease and then to seek compounds that act against those targets. Unfortunately, TBD approaches tend to have a much higher attrition rate than phenotypic screening, because not all of the compounds wind up having a biological impact; in other words, they don't have any clinical or subjective impact on the disease or on other bodily functions.

Since one of the primary KPIs in early discovery is success rate (i.e., how many compounds make it through to clinical trials), many organizations choose molecules based on the likelihood of success, rather than based specifically on the therapy area or degree of unmet patient need. As R&D returns for pharma companies continue to decline, there is substantial pressure to choose assets that are more likely to make it through clinical trials, rather than focusing first on patient need.

While positive trial outcomes are obviously a requirement for an asset's progression, they are not sufficient by themselves; despite positive early outcomes, many drugs do not move forward because of insufficient market opportunity. For those that do move forward, analysts eagerly await trial result announcements, and share price responds—sometimes dramatically—to the news. In fact, the market response to trial results is quite asymmetrical, with a bigger penalty for negative news (1.7% share price loss on average) than the reward for positive results (0.4% share price increase on average).[6] Despite all the data showing that it is incredibly difficult to get an asset successfully through the clinical trial process, it seems that the market "expects" good news.

Delays are often viewed as a signal of potential bad news, so sticking to trial milestones is an important metric—not to mention that trial delays cost money, both due to the additional time and investment in a particular asset and the postponement of potential revenue from the drug if eventually approved. "First Patient First Dose (FPFD)" is a key milestone, as is trial completion. A Google search using the phrase "first patient dosed" returns a list of recent press releases from companies large and small announcing the initiation of clinical trials—and also lots of articles on Yahoo! Finance, Market Watch and similar sites with recommendations for potential investors on when and whether to buy stock. There is also anecdotal evidence that share price declines after trial delay announcements, particularly recently with COVID-19 treatments and vaccines, but also in several other notable cases prior to the pandemic. In a bid to avoid taking a hit in the stock market, Eli Lilly and Incyte went so far as to deliberately wait to announce baricitinib resubmission on Good Friday in 2017 when the market was closed for the bank holiday. But the strategy didn't seem to help much—Eli Lilly's shares dropped 5.6% the following Monday, while Incyte's fell 13%.

Meanwhile, during the earliest stages of clinical research, a lot of decisions are made about dosing schedules, the best way to administer the medicine (e.g., orally, via injection, via infusion) and how to engineer the molecule to avoid impacting other pathways beyond the specific target. If the asset is successful in clinical trials, these decisions obviously affect the ultimate patient experience. So, while many organizations talk about the importance of having patient input early on in the discovery and design process, as well as during clinical trial design and the selection of key endpoints for inclusion, these initiatives require extra time to incorporate the step of seeking and then addressing patient feedback—and, as we saw above, time is at a premium. Choosing to take the time to integrate the patient perspective may result in a product that more closely aligns with patient need in the long run but doesn't necessarily align with the short-term metrics and market incentives. However, it may turn out that taking the time to get input from a diverse and representative set of patients early actually reduces time later, since one of the biggest time hurdles during development is trial enrollment. If the value proposition of the therapy resonates with patients, recruiting may be accelerated. (For a detailed discussion of this topic and some concrete examples that illustrate the benefits of soliciting patient input during R&D, see Chapter 6.)

Medical

Of all the functions in current pharma organizations, medical probably has the best chance for clear alignment between their KPIs and patient needs. Medical is responsible for engaging with key opinion leaders, physicians and investigators in a non-promotional context. Within this capacity, medical oversees market development pre-launch, thus helping to set the context for patients' unmet needs and treatment goals, so it's becoming more important for medical teams to be more connected to patient insights and input. Medical is also responsible for post-marketing (phase IV) and investigator-initiated clinical trials. As such, medical teams often need to address evidence gaps: patient populations that weren't included in original trials but are a significant proportion of people impacted, important patient-reported outcomes or other alternative endpoints, or changing standards of care that the product will need to satisfy. Medical needs to be able to bring together disparate data sets—ranging from clinical studies to commercial data and real-world evidence (RWE)—and use this data to inform interactions with a wide range of stakeholders, all in the ultimate pursuit of improving patient outcomes.

For most medical teams, KPIs are thus linked to two factors: key opinion leader (KOL) engagement (with varying approaches to measuring both quantity and quality) and post-marketing evidence generation. Although there is no direct conflict between better quality engagement of KOLs and patient needs, it would be ideal if medical teams could build in metrics that measure the impact of KOL engagement on addressing patient needs—for example, by engaging KOLs along with patient advocacy groups in the co-creation of patient solutions and tools. In some cases, post-marketing evidence generation may already address specific patient populations with unmet needs, so there is hope that in medical affairs there is more alignment between business incentives and patient needs. Many medical teams are starting to think along these lines.

Commercial

Commercial units might seem like they'd be the parts of an organization most naturally and obviously oriented toward patients. Commercial functions include sales and marketing, the latter incorporating patient support programs, DTC promotion (in the U.S.) and disease awareness campaigns (both in the U.S. and elsewhere) designed to help consumers and patients become better informed about the health challenges they may be experiencing. However, while these patient-facing promotional tactics certainly have the potential to deliver benefits to patients, most of the metrics and measures in place for these programs are deeply pharma-centric.

By watching any broadcast television program, it might be hard to believe that DTC advertising really only took off in the late 1990s and early 2000s. (We should note here that, while DTC is sometimes taken as synonymous with TV advertising, DTC includes many other channels and doesn't have to include TV at all.) Until 2013, most spending on DTC focused on primary care brands and blockbusters. Prior to this date, the old adage that "half of my advertising spend is wasted—I just don't know which half" left marketers convinced that, unless they had a very large potential patient audience, DTC wasn't a smart marketing investment. But, starting in 2014, specialty brands began to invest and then dominate DTC spending, despite the fact that these potential audiences were much smaller than, say, those for Lipitor or Ambien. Oncology brands entered the DTC market with Opdivo's approval in 2015, followed shortly by Keytruda. Even companies producing treatments for HIV—which marketers had long held was inappropriate for DTC—began disseminating ads in late 2017. Had pharma finally realized how important patients were to decision-making?

Well, yes. And also no. Even when manufacturers consider patients, the focus from a DTC perspective is much more on how pharma can influence patients' decision-making instead of on how patients can inform pharma's decision-making. And, in the case of specialty and oncology brands, with lifetime patient value (LPV) starting at $10,000 and ranging upwards from there into six figures, even if pharma is successful in influencing the decision-making of a small number of patients, the ROI of these DTC investments is substantial. Pharma might not be great at patient centricity, but the industry is certainly good at math, and this has continued to drive the expansion of DTC for specialty brands to this day—including during the COVID-19 pandemic. While increased consumer response to DTC advertising isn't necessarily a bad thing for patients, companies base optimization of these campaigns primarily on a business metric (new starts) instead of a patient metric (better outcomes).

Companies also generally measure patient support programs (PSPs) in commercial terms rather than patient terms. While programs stay away from measuring ROI directly, they do use "stay times" (increases in patient adherence or decreases in patient discontinuation) as common measures. Humira is well known for having robust patient support programs, and AbbVie was the first to publish data (in JMCP in 2017) demonstrating an increase in time on therapy for patients enrolled in the company's programs.[8] Several other companies, including UCB[9] and Otsuka,[10] have followed suit since then. While the original study didn't address the revenue impact for AbbVie, it would certainly be easy enough to do some back-of-the-envelope math to calculate the impact of that increase in stay time. Brands often develop PSPs specifically to address commercial challenges, such as motivating patients to begin and maintain treatment.

Figure 4-3: Specialty and Oncology Brand DTC Investment[7]

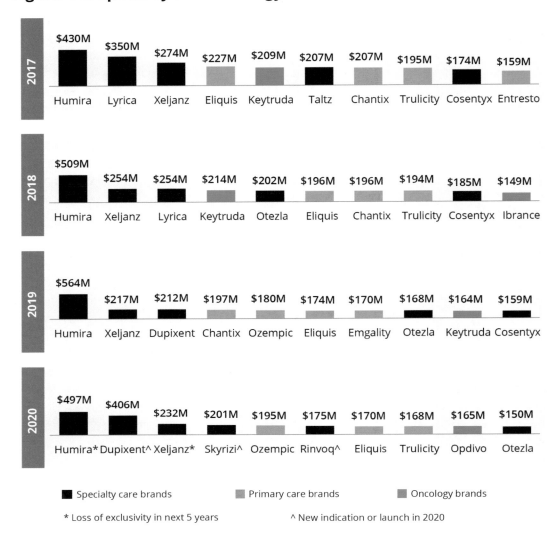

2017
| Humira | Lyrica | Xeljanz | Eliquis | Keytruda | Taltz | Chantix | Trulicity | Cosentyx | Entresto |
| $430M | $350M | $274M | $227M | $209M | $207M | $207M | $195M | $174M | $159M |

2018
| Humira | Xeljanz | Lyrica | Keytruda | Otezla | Eliquis | Chantix | Trulicity | Cosentyx | Ibrance |
| $509M | $254M | $254M | $214M | $202M | $196M | $196M | $194M | $185M | $149M |

2019
| Humira | Xeljanz | Dupixent | Chantix | Ozempic | Eliquis | Emgality | Otezla | Keytruda | Cosentyx |
| $564M | $217M | $212M | $197M | $180M | $174M | $170M | $168M | $164M | $159M |

2020
| Humira* | Dupixent^ | Xeljanz* | Skyrizi^ | Ozempic | Rinvoq^ | Eliquis | Trulicity | Opdivo | Otezla |
| $497M | $406M | $232M | $201M | $195M | $175M | $170M | $168M | $165M | $150M |

■ Specialty care brands　　■ Primary care brands　　■ Oncology brands

* Loss of exclusivity in next 5 years　　^ New indication or launch in 2020

Meanwhile, PSPs in categories where patients have significant needs are often lacking if there isn't a commercial rationale for providing support. In 2017, ZS conducted a meta-analysis of patient insights research and patient support program benchmarking across four key therapeutic categories: immunology, endocrinology, cardiovascular disease and oncology.[11] We found that, in general, immunology brands offered a wider range of support services to meet patient needs, including in-person device training, peer-to-peer support and nurse call centers, while oncology brands lagged significantly behind the other three specialties.[12] In the past, oncology brand leaders typically believed that—given the severity of the disease—patients would defer to physician recommendations, so there was less need to provide patient education and support than in other categories where patients had more options or could delay or avoid treatment. However, we are starting to see oncology leaders recognize the important decision-making roles patients and caregivers are playing in oncology, especially as more options enter what is already a crowded market. Even in late-stage cancer where patients have limited treatment options, a non-trivial percentage of patients refuse treatment even against the direct recommendations of their physicians—so, clearly, they do have agency in their choices throughout the disease journey.[13]

The Platform Isn't Burning (But Is That Smoke I Smell?)

One of the biggest barriers to change is perhaps the simplest: to date, there has been no "burning platform." In a 2020 study published in JAMA, the authors found that, between 2000 and 2018, pharma companies outperformed companies in other sectors by nearly 80%, with net income as a percentage of revenue at 13.8% versus 7.7%.[14] While there are certainly numerous factors driving pharma toward patient centricity (as we outlined in Chapter 2), the status quo is, at least for the time being, still working pretty well. Despite the declining R&D ROI, pipelines are more robust than ever, and new drug approval counts are rising. Even in 2020, despite COVID-19, the FDA approved 53 novel medicines, and approval time for these medicines actually decreased.[15]

But pharma has long suffered from a terrible reputation in public opinion polls. A 2017 Harris poll showed that only 9% of Americans believed that pharma puts profits over patients. In 2019, pharma "slipped" from its long-held position at next-to-last to take over the bottom spot in Gallup's industry reputation rankings. In 2021, the federal government re-took last place, and pharma moved up, likely due to some positive glow as a result of COVID-19 vaccine development.[16] Still, this "good news" means that 51% of consumers view the industry negatively while only 31% view it positively, for a "net" rating of -20%. The feds take last place at a net -28%. While this improvement represents a small step in the right direction, pharma still has a long way to go to catch up with even the legal industry (currently beating pharma by 16% points)—so no one should be congratulating themselves just yet.

Nonetheless, we are optimistic. Chapter 2 outlined several external and internal drivers that have slowly been shifting the pharma industry perspective on patient centricity. Meanwhile, in the past 18 months, COVID-19 dramatically changed the landscape of how patients access healthcare, and, as a result, pharma organizations have been forced to change how they incorporate the patient perspective. We are hopeful that perhaps the silver lining of COVID-19 will be that it serves as the final push the industry needs to create ongoing momentum for patient centricity going forward.

Key Takeaways

- While 93% of pharma executives overwhelmingly agree that patient centricity is critical to their organizations' future success, few (19%) believe they have made meaningful progress to date.

- Our research identified four underlying challenges:
  - A siloed organizational structure
  - The lack of a consistent focus on the patient across business units and over time
  - Poorly aligned incentives and KPIs
  - The lack of a burning platform

- There are signs that the industry is making more substantial changes in response to COVID-19, which may provide the push pharma needs toward sustained patient centricity.

Acknowledgments

The author wishes to thank Lisa Bance, Sarah Jarvis, Aaron Mitchell, Bharat Tewarie, Tanvi Vedhera and the ZS Patient Centricity Advisory Board members.

Endnotes

1. Hensley Evans and Sharon Suchotliff, "Why Do We Struggle to Deliver on Patient Centricity Despite Knowing It's Critical?" ZS, October 30, 2020, https://www.zs.com/insights/why-do-we-struggle-to-deliver-on-patient-centricity-despite-know.

2. Patient Centricity Survey, 2019.

3. ZS Patient Centricity Advisory Board, June 2019.

4. ZS Benchmarking Study of Patient Centricity Organizational Structures, December 2020.

5. ZS Desk Research of Top 20 pharma CEOs using LinkedIn and other publicly available sources.

6. Kantar Strategy, 2020.

7. Thomas J. Hwang, "Stock Market Returns and Clinical Trial Results of Investigational Compounds: An Event Study Analysis of Large Biopharmaceutical Companies," in PLoS ONE 8, no. 8 (August 2013): e71966, https://doi.org/10.1371/journal.pone.0071966.

8. Diana Brixner et al., "Patient Support Program Increased Medication Adherence with Lower Total Health Care Costs Despite Increased Drug Spending," in Journal of Managed Care & Specialty Pharmacy 25, no. 7 (July 2019): 770-779, https://doi.org/10.18553/jmcp.2019.18443.

9. Douglas C. Wolf et al., "Adherence Rates and Health Care Costs in Crohn's Disease Patients Receiving Certolizumab Pegol With and Without Home Health Nurse Assistance: Results from a Retrospective Analysis of Patient Claims and Home Health Nurse Data," in Patient Preference and Adherence 12 (2018): 869-878, https://doi.org/10.2147/ppa.s148777.

10. Malik Greene et al., "Evaluation of Patient Support Program and Adherence to Long-Acting Injectable Aripiprazole for Patients Utilizing Injection Local Care Centers," in Current Medical Research and Opinion 35, no. 1 (January 2019): 97-103, https://doi.org/10.1080/03007995.2018.1536651.

11. ZS Meta-Analysis of PSP Programs vs. Patient Needs Across CV, Endocrinology, Immunology and Oncology, January 2017.

12. ZS Powering Up Your Oncology Patient Support Program, November 20, 2019.

13. Moshe Frenkel, "Refusing Treatment," in Oncologist 18, no. 5 (May 2013): 643-636, https://doi.org/10.1634/theoncologist.2012-0436.

14. Fred D. Ledley et al., "Profitability of Large Pharmaceutical Companies Compared with Other Large Public Companies," in Journal of the American Medical Association 323, no. 9 (2020): 834-843, https://doi.org/10.1001/jama.2020.0442.

15. FDA, "Novel Drug Approvals for 2020," accessed January 17, 2022, https://www.fda.gov/drugs/new-drugs-fda-cders-new-molecular-entities-and-new-therapeutic-biological-products/novel-drug-approvals-2020.

16. Gallup, "Business and Industry Sector Ratings," accessed January 17, 2022, https://news.gallup.com/poll/12748/business-industry-sector-ratings.aspx; The Harris Poll, "Harris Poll: Only Nine Percent of U.S. Consumers Believe Pharma and Biotechnology Put Patients Over Profits; Only 16 Percent Believe Health Insurers Do," accessed January 17, 2022, https://theharrispoll.com/only-nine-percent-of-u-s-consumers-believe-pharmaceutical-and-biotechnology-companies-put-patients-over-profits-while-only-16-percent-believe-health-insurance-companies-do-according-to-a-harris-pol/

SECTION TWO INTRODUCTION:
What Does It Take?

Are you energized and excited to think about how you and your organization can do more to become patient centric? One of the challenges a number of teams have found over the years is that the phrase "patient centricity" is often misinterpreted to mean altruistic efforts that only serve the patient. We believe that true patient centricity is finding opportunities to align the incentives of various stakeholders so that we create win-win solutions: initiatives that deliver benefits to the patients as well as benefits to pharma, payers or the healthcare system as a whole and, in some cases, all of the above.

Although the opportunities are (almost) limitless, we've identified five key places where we believe the incentives of patients can align strongly with the business objectives of pharma organizations. For example, patients benefit greatly when pharma understands them as whole people and designs assets and solutions that help address their holistic needs and not just a small subset. At the same time, if pharma does deliver product/solution combinations that are informed by and responsive to a broader set of patient needs, and thereby delivers more value to patients, these assets are then more likely to be clearly differentiated in the market from those of competitors and more likely to succeed commercially. In Chapter 5, we explore how moving from a narrow understanding of a particular disease or treatment to understanding the daily experience of the whole person—for whom that disease or treatment is only one aspect of a full life—can have substantial benefits for pharma. One notable example highlights how listening to the patient perspective led one company to recognize that some patients might be missing treatments not only because of potential side effects, but because of travel challenges; that company is now pursuing at-home administration in specific geographies.

On the R&D side, patients want and need pharma to develop new lifesaving or life-improving medicines and bring them to market faster. But pharma struggles to complete trials on time, on budget and with the right, diverse patient populations participating. By integrating the patient voice throughout the discovery and development process, pharma can both deliver better medicines faster and more efficiently find and recruit the right patients for trials. Trials are thus another area where delivering a better experience for patients serves the interests of both patients and pharma. In Chapter 6, we look at several examples of successes and failures here, including the initial trials for Levitra, where wording on the trial questionnaire excluded certain patients from trial participation: the language included questions about vaginal penetration, which of course excluded any men who have sex with men (MSM) participants.

As more and more organizations launch assets into new markets and portfolios become dominated by rare or specialty therapies, it becomes even more important that consumers and patients have a baseline awareness of the conditions or diseases these assets can address. Back in Chapter 1, we saw how long it can take for patients with a rare disease to receive a diagnosis—and this isn't only true in cases of rare disease. In Chapter 7, we look at how pharma can help accelerate complex diagnoses, legitimize treatment of health issues that have been ignored or overlooked and increase people's understanding of the risks and benefits of novel treatments. AbbVie's unbranded disease awareness campaign for endometriosis is an excellent example of how driving more effective conversations between patients and healthcare providers (HCPs) can help patients get to diagnosis earlier.

Chapter 8 explores an age-old question: Does direct-to-consumer (DTC) promotion help or hurt patients? Does it enable them to find the care and treatment they need more quickly, or would they find their way to treatment regardless? The COVID-19 pandemic has really shifted the patterns of consumer media consumption (we think for good) and changed the way consumers interact with and respond to branded DTC and disease awareness campaigns. As the Nurtec example highlighted in Chapter 8 shows, digital and social have become powerful tools to connect directly with consumers. Telemedicine and digital and connected health also continue to grow to serve both patients and others in the ecosystem. DTC can play a key role in getting patients to an accurate diagnosis more quickly and to the most appropriate treatment to get them to the best possible outcome.

We know that even when patients do receive a prescription for medication, up to 30% of these patients never fill their first script. Cost, confusion, inconvenience and many other factors play into this disturbing data point. What's more, over half of patients who take medication for a chronic condition drop off therapy within one year. This contributes to an estimated $528 billion cost to the healthcare ecosystem annually. The last chapter in this section, Chapter 9, looks at what organizations are doing to help patients get their medications, start therapy and stay adherent. One example shows how Gilead is using regional partnerships to help support the holistic health needs of people living with HIV/AIDS in the U.S. If we can transform the treatment experience and eliminate some of the addressable causes of drop-off, we can help deliver better clinical outcomes and lower healthcare costs overall, as well as increased business impact for manufacturers.

Our hope is that at least one of these chapters will be directly relevant to anyone reading this book, and will help you generate some new ideas for how you can not only bring more patient centricity into your organization but build a bulletproof business case for doing so.

Chapter 5:
Understanding People,
Not Patients

Fiona Taylor and Albert Whangbo

Even if you aren't a car person, you've probably heard of the Ford Edsel.[1] It holds a special place in the hearts of marketers for being such a spectacular failure. Launched in 1957, the Edsel was supposed to be the new car of choice for middle-class Americans; instead, Ford lost $350 million on it.[2] So what went wrong? Ford made critical product decisions based on competitor offerings and assumptions about what its target customers wanted rather than actual customer input. The company built up hype that it was creating the car of the future; meanwhile, the Edsel's design was based on what customers had wanted in the early 1950s. The designers put in bells and whistles (like a floating speedometer that would glow if the driver exceeded a pre-set speed limit!) that customers didn't see the value in. The Edsel's design was too ostentatious and priced out of reach for much of the company's target market. Ford thus failed to regularly listen and learn from its customers—and paid the price. Even minimal market research would have revealed how customer preferences were evolving toward more compact and fuel-efficient vehicles, and perhaps the Edsel would have been spared its notoriety as an infamous design and marketing failure. Ford's mega-flop from over 50 years ago still offers an important lesson for pharma today: the value of deeply understanding customers during product development and commercialization.

The Patient Insight Gap

As the Edsel example demonstrates, proceeding on assumptions and failing to put customers at the center of critical decisions can be very costly. The $350 million Ford lost in 1950s dollars would equal about $3.8 billion dollars today![3] For life sciences companies, the investments made to develop and commercialize new products are regularly at a similar scope and scale, which means the risks are just as great. What can pharma do to avoid similarly devastating mistakes?

Patient centricity is the answer. As described in Chapter 3, achieving patient centricity requires the Four I's:

- Collecting deep and meaningful **Insights** from patients

- Nurturing a culture and set of business practices that help **Integrate** the patient perspective into decision-making

- Building capabilities that allow the organization to deliver an **Improved** patient experience

- Measuring and demonstrating the win-win **Impact** for the patient and business

This chapter will focus on why it is important to collect deep and meaningful insights from patients and how to do it well. Without patient insights, companies can only guess at how to integrate the patient perspective, change the patient experience and improve patient outcomes. Particularly in today's increasingly crowded marketplaces, pharma development and commercialization decisions must start from a place of empathy with the people who are experiencing a disease. We must seek to understand their lived experiences, needs and priorities and carefully consider how a new product might fit into their world.

Yet, when development teams go to design a new drug, they typically don't begin by talking to and listening to patients in order to understand their lived experience. Instead, the traditional approach to drug development starts with the creation of a target patient profile (TPP), which contains hypothetical clinical data to support the product's efficacy, safety and tolerability claims. Many of the key insights that go into decision-making at this stage of development—including demand estimates and forecasts to inform trial design and go/no-go investment decisions—are based on physician responses to the TPP.

What are the possible negative consequences of starting from the product rather than the patient? It creates a critical insight gap. Putting a disproportionate focus on clinical product attributes ignores critical patient considerations and reinforces inaccurate assumptions about the drivers of product choice and adoption. Compared to patients, physicians often have quite different perceptions about a disease and the drivers (or burdens) of treatment. Physicians' treatment objectives are often based on managing specific clinical indicators, such as blood pressure, blood glucose, progression-free survival, etc. These are not always aligned with patients' treatment objectives. Patients tend to place a higher emphasis on immediate symptom relief, improved quality of life and convenience.[4] Also, physicians often have limited visibility into important aspects of the patient or caregiver experience, such as the challenges of dealing with side effects, the logistical challenges of receiving treatment, the cost burden, the social stigma and the emotional strain of living with a chronic, incurable or potentially fatal disease. As a result, a research and insights plan that relies too heavily on physician inputs creates blind spots for pharma.

Incorporating patient insight early in the process allows companies to create a patient-centric TPP that clearly articulates important elements of the patient experience and highlights any emotional burden that may be associated with taking the product. Some companies are already starting to integrate the patient voice into their TPPs, even constructing target patient value propositions (TPVPs) as an add-on to traditional TPPs. Figure 5-1 shows a hypothetical before-and-after, with a traditional TPP approach and one that more explicitly assimilates the patient experience and needs into the product description.

Figure 5-1: Shifting from a Traditional Target Product Profile to Integrate Patient-Centric Components

Standard target product profile

Indication/target population	T2D patients with renal impairment
Dosage and administration	Twice daily, Oral, 5mg
Efficacy	**Efficacy** 1% of reduction in HbA1c with oral Product X **Weight loss** Body weight reduction by 5 lbs
Safety	**Mortality** Statistically significant 25% relative reduction in all-cause mortality **Diabetic retinopathy** Limited occurrence of diabetic retinopathy (3%)
Pricing	**Pricing** 15% discount to parity vs. SoC

Figure 5-1 (continued)

Patient-centric target product profile		Difference from standard TPP
Indication	T2D patients with renal impairment	Target population and indication can be separated to capture patient unmet needs
Target population	For patients over 60 with any level of renal impairment, are more anxious about complications and are especially interested in options that delay insulin	
Dosage and administration	Twice daily, Oral, 5 mg Non-invasive administration via an easy-to-swallow pill, allowing for better patient experience and disease management.	Patient experience with the product
Patient-reported outcomes	**Patient lifestyle** 10% improvement vs. SoC of QoL score which assesses disease impact on patient well-being and lifestyle including social and physical activities	Patient reported outcomes related to patient lifestyle
Efficacy	**Efficacy** 1% of reduction in HbA1c with oral Product X **Weight loss** Body weight reduction by 5 lbs	
Safety	**Mortality** Statistically significant 25% relative reduction in all-cause mortality **Diabetic retinopathy** Limited occurrence of diabetic retinopathy (3%)	
Pricing	**Pricing** 15% discount to parity vs. SoC	
Patient Access	**Patient access** Expected delay to insulin up to 2 years, translating into annual economical saving for patients and higher access to patients	

While patient insights are vitally important in early development, they must also be integrated throughout the commercialization process. Foundational elements of patient research typically include an in-depth analysis of the patient journey that explores both the functional and emotional aspects of a patient's experience. The scope of commercial activities is wide, spanning patient segmentation research, patient support program design and communication testing, which includes developing patient brochures, websites and TV ads. In many cases now, launching a new product also entails creating digital health solutions. (Pitfall alert: The app store is littered with thousands of apps, developed with great intentions and promising ideas but often without input from patients. Many sit idle because they provide insufficient value to patients; as with any patient solution, customer insight is critical).

Consulting with patients can yield unexpected results. Consider this case of a client with which ZS recently worked. The client, a company working in immunology, launched a long-acting intramuscular injection into a well-established oral market. Prior to launch, research with physicians suggested low preference for the new injection; physicians cited concerns about the invasiveness of the injection procedure and the inconvenience of having to schedule regular office visits for administration. However, when the company surveyed potential patients, the brand team was surprised to learn that the patients expressed strong enthusiasm for the new treatment option. The patients highlighted how, despite the potential inconvenience of monthly appointments or injection site pain, the long-acting product would alleviate the heavy burden of having a daily reminder of their disease. As a result of this finding, the client began exploring ways to make the injection more convenient for patients, such as setting up alternative injection sites, like retail pharmacies or even patients' homes with help from a nurse service. Had the company only considered physician feedback, it would have taken a narrow launch strategy. But, given the unexpected enthusiasm patients voiced for the injection treatment, the company was able to confidently launch the product while taking meaningful action to enhance accessibility, thus fostering a better patient experience.

In a similar example, a company launched a daily controlled-release pill that would compete with a treatment taken twice per day. The response from physicians in pre-launch market research was tepid. In their view, the new treatment reduced the flexibility to adjust dosing; they didn't recognize the single dose as a meaningful improvement. However, research with patients and their caregivers showed that the simpler dosing schedule provided a clear benefit. Had the company listened only to physician feedback, its commercial teams would not have realized the importance of investing in patient marketing and support campaigns. Equipped with insights from patients, however, the company was able to make sure patients were aware of the new treatment option through direct-to-patient marketing and educational materials that resonated strongly with the patient audience.

Putting insufficient weight on patient perspectives in clinical development and commercialization ultimately leads to inaccurate assumptions that distort pharma companies' views of their products' market potential and likely rate of adoption. This has implications for many downstream decisions:

- **Product design**: Companies may emphasize the wrong features or fail to address major shortcomings early, when the cost to do so is much lower and there is opportunity to maneuver (e.g., by measuring additional endpoints in a clinical trial or including a particular patient subgroup).

- **Forecasting**: Inaccurate predictions about product adoption often lead to sub-optimal pricing and under- or over-investment in commercialization. They also have negative consequences for stock prices when the product's performance does not meet expectations.

- **Manufacturing**: Failure to understand the factors driving patient demand frequently results in under- or over-supply.

- **Promotional strategy**: Blind spots with respect to patient and caregiver roles in making treatment decisions can lead to a sub-optimal marketing mix and poor media planning and cause companies to overlook critical promotional channels.

- **Patient service design**: A lack of understanding about the patient and caregiver experience can result in underinvestment in patient support overall, overinvestment in low-impact solutions and failure to meet critical patient needs.

The cost of establishing a foundational understanding of patient perspectives represents only a tiny fraction of the total development and commercialization expenses involved in bringing a new product to market. However, proceeding without understanding the patient can lead to costly missteps in each of these areas and ultimately compromise the ability to advance patient outcomes through patient centricity.

After making it through the development and approval hurdles, the need to listen to patients continues! What are the experiences of the first patients starting therapy? How well is a patient support program addressing patient needs? There are many aspects of the patient experience that pharma companies can and should track: new patient starts, duration on therapy, reasons for initiating and discontinuing therapy, patient support program use and impact, and the success of DTC communications.

How to Achieve Deep and Robust Patient Insights

The best way for pharma to overcome its blind spots when it comes to understanding patients is to expand the approach for gathering insights. It is critical to regularly and iteratively include the patient perspective. Each product's value proposition, potential benefits, tradeoffs and features must be tested early and often with patients. In recent years, research and insight teams have taken steps to become more "customer-centric."

For many pharma companies, this has meant soliciting input from stakeholders beyond just physicians, including patients, caregivers, nurses and other medical staff. This offers an immediate benefit of giving planners better insights into the forces that drive brand choice and patient retention. Furthermore, taking a broader view of treatment with the patient at the center will help pharma companies prepare for industry-wide changes: more and more companies are shifting their commercial go-to-market models beyond physician-focused sales representatives to a wider variety of field roles, including field reimbursement representatives, nurse educators, patient case managers and representatives focused on accounts.

All of this raises one fundamental question: What are the best ways to gather patient insights? Let's first consider the still underutilized but more standard qualitative research approaches, then we'll dive deeper into emerging solutions, such as real-world data (RWD), behavioral science and co-creation.

Qualitative Research

No patient insight plan is complete without listening directly to patients. The way to listen can take many different forms and cannot be a one-time-only undertaking. Every opportunity to engage with a patient is an opportunity to hear a new story, empathize with a different experience and potentially arrive at a new ah-ha! moment.

Deeply immersive ethnographic research can be a rich place to start. Historically, this has entailed having a researcher visit a patient's home, often with a videographer to record the experience. Typically, the scale of ethnographic research is small, as the objective is depth rather than breadth; for instance, the researcher might spend a day with each of two to 10 patients, documenting their lived realities in thorough detail. Ethnographic approaches furthermore enable powerful immersive experiences, helping each member of the research team develop profound empathy for patients.

Nowadays, driven primarily by the advancements in smartphones (and the dire need to get the most out of smaller research budgets, of course), a lot of ethnography has shifted into patients' own hands. Rather than a researcher physically walking into patients' homes, patients welcome the research team into their lived experience through multi-media immersion, sharing videos, photos and voice recordings using fit-for-purpose research apps. Consider, for example, Debbie,[5] a mother suffering from chronic migraines who shared her experience with ZS.[6] With the click of a button, she uploaded a photo that showed us the mountain of clean laundry that she had managed to wash and dry but couldn't fold and put away because she had been overcome by a migraine. Through a video she uploaded, we witnessed her agony as she lay on the floor, blinds drawn, and talked us through the moment of onset of yet another crippling headache.

Although not the same as crossing the threshold into patients' homes and passing time with them in person, these mobile ethnographies or e-journals are more cost effective than home visits, lowering the barrier to conducting such research and offering researchers the ability to engage a larger patient sample. Such methods also enable researchers to reach patients across a broader geographic spread (whether within a single country or around the world) and even provide access to intensely private moments, like the onset of Debbie's migraine, that are typically inaccessible to an in-person ethnographer. With studies spanning multiple days or weeks, patients can share with us the moment that a symptom manifests or tell us how they feel when they walk out of the pharmacy without their new prescription because the co-pay was too high. In fact, because they are talking to their phone, their most trusted confidant, rather than a strange researcher, patients often divulge more than they might otherwise share. Participants have described the experience of creating an e-journal as cathartic, like writing in a diary, while the research team gains valuable knowledge from having unprecedentedly intimate access to the participants' lived realities.

A key ingredient of robust qualitative patient research is to provide participants the space to tell their stories. Whether engaging with patients in a focus group discussion or talking to them one-on-one in person, on the phone or over a Zoom video call, truly listening to patients requires time, patience and a few well-formulated questions. Those of us working on research teams need to ensure that the ways in which we seek patient insights to inform patient centricity are also patient centric. We must meet patients where they are and reflect empathy in the language we use, inviting their trust that we will fully understand and value their stories. We must always remember that patients are more than their medical histories; they are human beings with a host of unique experiences and perspectives to share. In-depth patient interviews should center around the individual person and reflect how each person's condition fits into the larger narrative of his or her life. Failure to incorporate that broader perspective will result in a myopic view of the patient's lived experience and lead to missed opportunities to improve the patient experience or patient outcomes.

Hearing a patient's full story can prompt meaningfully different strategic decisions, because each opportunity to capture patient input can provide actionable insight into the patient experience and how to improve it. For instance, a study to test the layout of patient informational brochures for a new oncology product can allow for critical improvements to the corresponding patient support program if patient voices are heard and amplified. Patient stories can also be the catalyst sparking big ideas for change. Listening as cancer patients share their struggles with long commutes, exhausting and emotionally draining days at the hospital and the burden of relying on a loved one to be able to make it to each treatment infusion (IV) just might be the thing that turns an IV into a sub-cutaneous injection that can be administered in their local doctor's office or, taking it a step further, the spark for the development of at-home modes of administration.

Many pharma companies are making shifts toward gathering patient insights but still lack mechanisms for systematically capturing patient experiences or for integrating patient-centric solutions early in development and carrying them through into organizational processes. A company may conduct research to understand the patient journey and come away with recommendations for an additional clinical endpoint that better reflects the symptoms that matter most to those patients. The ability to act on such recommendations enables patient insights to be effectively integrated into the relevant organizational functions, so that critical findings such as these, which often go beyond the scope of the original research objectives, can be disseminated and leveraged in brand- or organizational-level decision-making.

Traditional qualitative and quantitative primary market research—the tried-and-true methods like in-depth interviews, focus groups, surveys and ethnographies—are essential inputs to any patient insight plan. However, organizations that wish to dive deep into patient-centric insights are increasingly embracing data analytics and new qualitative methodologies that can super-charge insights into both the whats and whys of patient preferences and behavior. Below, we explore three of these new approaches: real-world data (RWD), behavioral science and co-creation. These approaches solve three different problems that cannot be addressed by traditional research alone. RWD provides longitudinal insights at a scale that is unattainable through traditional quantitative research and allows pharma to extrapolate what we learn about sample patient groups to the broad patient population. Meanwhile, behavioral science and co-creation are typically called upon to help crack sticky problems, such as how to motivate patients to use prophylactic treatment to prevent long-term complications of a disease or how to improve patient outcomes through better compliance. These approaches augment the power of traditional research methodologies.

Real-World Data

RWD is an indispensable asset for quantifying patient preferences and behavior. Such data might include, for example, pharmacy and medical claims derived from insurers and/or pharmacies and electronic medical records from provider systems. Pharma companies have long used longitudinal RWD sources to describe patient journeys and measure patient outcomes, such as healthcare resource utilization and cost burden across patient demographics and clinical characteristics. However, even though most companies leverage RWD at some point in their products' life cycles, most also underutilize this valuable resource. Table 5-1 captures just a few ways that organizations can make better use of RWD.

Digging a little deeper into RWD can reveal startling insights about the patient experience. For example, a ZS study of claims data from patients with non-alcoholic steatohepatitis (NASH)—a largely asymptomatic, underdiagnosed condition affecting patients who often live with multiple chronic illnesses—reinforced our understanding of the tremendous comorbidity and concomitant therapy burden many patients face.[7] One patient had interacted with nearly 40 different HCPs over a six-year period. During the same period, the patient filled an average of 40 prescriptions annually to treat seven different comorbidities, including diabetes, hypertension, neuropathic pain and gastroesophageal reflux disease (GERD). However, we also observed that the patient's mix of prescriptions changed over time, particularly following critical events such as a heart attack and diabetic foot ulcer. It was clear that the patient's treatment priorities were highly dynamic and being driven by a kind of triage process in response to both chronic and acute disease states.

Table 5-1: Illustrative RWD Analyses and Last-Mile Applications

Basic RWD application	Advanced RWD analytics	Last-mile use: The "so what"
Map the overall patient journey at the global level	Map journeys at a local level, highlighting regional differences and opportunities to improve patient outcomes along the pre- to post-Rx spectrum	Combine RWD with a variety of other data inputs (physician behaviors, patient demographics, social determinants) to identify the drivers of local differences, and use the insights to develop targeted interventions
Identify key decision points along the patient journey	Use artificial intelligence (AI) models to predict when patients will need to make key decisions and the most likely outcomes	Use event prediction to trigger appropriate interventions (e.g., informing HCPs or providing patient support) that can lead to better patient outcomes
Use clinical characteristics as an input to patient segmentation	Build patient segments based on archetypal journey pathways (event sequences) derived from longitudinal RWD	Use patient segment constructs combined with opt-in data to optimize the matching of channels and content to support patients
Invest in aggregated third-party insights derived from RWD	Conduct in-depth custom studies that provide much greater flexibility for using RWD to explore emerging issues and business questions	Invest in building an RWD analytics capability that can be deployed across data sources, captures institutional knowledge and is plugged into an intelligent engine for patient and/or HCP engagement

Figure 5-2: RWD Illustrates That a Patient's Treatment Needs and Priorities Can Shift Over Time[8]

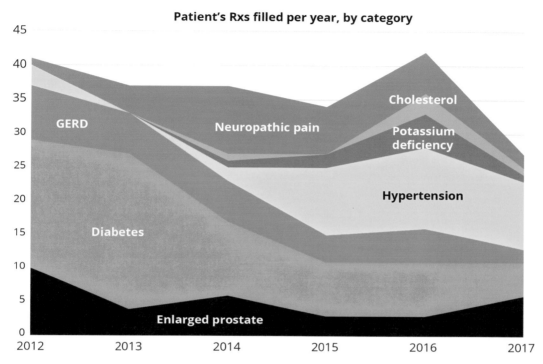

Given the challenges with which NASH patients frequently contend in determining how to balance and prioritize care for multiple conditions, it's critical that a pharma company working to create treatments for NASH think not just of a "NASH patient" but a "person with NASH." The former view is premised on the assumption that patients' treatment decisions are driven solely by the need to alleviate their NASH symptoms. But NASH is often a very small piece of the puzzle, as patients tend to focus on whatever conditions and symptoms are causing them the most pain, discomfort or inconvenience at any given moment. If, for example, a pharma company were trying to change the treatment paradigm in NASH by requiring patients to start a new treatment that can preserve liver function, the company would need to shape its call to action in a way that acknowledges that patients are likely heavily burdened with multiple comorbidities and treatment regimens, along with the associated financial and quality of life implications. RWD does not specify the solutions that pharma needs to create for patients, but it does give pharma visibility into the complexity of patients' care and their unmet needs.

The view that RWD provides of patients' health and the drivers of health outcomes is becoming both richer and more expansive with the adoption of new data sources. While administrative claims and electronic medical records are well-established for capturing patients' healthcare resource utilization and clinical outcomes, new sources are emerging that carry a lot of promise for enriching quantified patient-centric insights beyond the

85

clinical setting. One of the most promising emerging sources for life sciences is a broad category of data called social determinants of health (SDOH). SDOH include socioeconomic markers (e.g., education, occupation, access to healthcare services and access to food), demographics (e.g., age, gender, race and living environment) and social connectedness. SDOH dimensions have a huge impact on health risks and outcomes.[9]

Incorporating SDOH data—much of which federal, state and local governments gather and make publicly available—into models of patient behavior can have a strong impact on the descriptive power of those models, as well as on their predictive accuracy. For example, ZS recently worked with a client to identify untreated patients in an infectious disease market. A predictive disease model based solely on healthcare resource utilization data from insurance claims achieved 88% accuracy. However, adding SDOH such as employment status, poverty levels and housing access—even at a local geographical level—into the model improved accuracy to 98%, demonstrating the explanatory power of social determinants. The implications for this client are powerful: the company is now equipped with knowledge about not only the clinical experience of their patients but also the context in which their patients live. This enables the client to better identify opportunities to serve its patients, including partnerships with organization and funding initiatives targeted at underserved and vulnerable populations.

As the scope of RWD continues to expand, so too will its power to drive patient-centric insights. We already see RWD helping to explain the role of medical decisions and socio-economic factors on patient outcomes—insights that are helping pharma companies uncover blind spots when it comes to reaching and serving specific sub-populations. The next frontier for patient-centric data will be to enable even greater individualization of healthcare delivery and support. It is likely in the next few years that we will see an accelerating adoption of genomics and biomarker data to enable personalized medicine. We should also expect to see increasing sophistication in our ability to capture individual patient attitudes, so that we can understand not only what is happening in the patient journey but also the whys behind patient choices and behaviors.

Behavioral Science

Understanding—and later motivating—patient behavior requires deep knowledge of patients' needs and attitudes. Acquiring this knowledge requires a comprehensive understanding of patients' conscious decision-making and emotional experiences, as well as cognitive factors. Given the weight of medical decisions, patients often approach them with a high level of conscious deliberation and diligence. Yet a patient's decision may be inextricable from emotions they feel and unconscious factors that are difficult for them to articulate. Cognitive factors have their roots within an unconscious system of shortcuts that governs an estimated 60% of human cognition. These shortcuts, known as heuristics, are what allow us to, for example, drive to work while engaging in a conversation with a friend. Understanding this unconscious system is where behavioral science, the study of the mind and its processes, comes in. Behavioral scientists have named and defined these factors and designed experiments to test for their presence. Perhaps most importantly, from the perspective of pharma, integrating behavioral science helps us determine ways to impact these decision-making processes. In its ability to provide new windows into the subconscious mechanisms by which patients make decisions, and to open up new solutions to tap into those mechanisms, behavioral science is becoming a critical tool in the patient insight toolkit.

Figure 5-3: Our Brain Uses Hundreds of Mental Shortcuts to Make Decisions

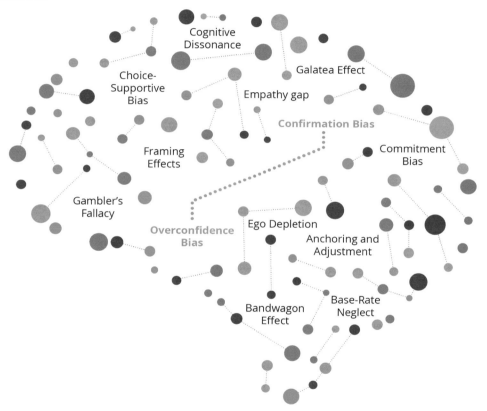

Pharma companies often struggle to achieve their key behavioral objectives because patients' decision-making rules—their cognitive biases—are not generally revealed through direct question-and-answer approaches and are therefore challenging to uncover through traditional research. Behavioral scientists instead use carefully designed experiments to test for specific biases within the patient population of interest. Equipped with this knowledge, brand teams can then shape their positioning, messaging and creative tactics to resonate more with patients. Such insights also better enable companies to inform patients' decisions about starting or staying on therapy and help companies ensure their patient support programs and services meet the mark, thus improving patient outcomes.

In 2021, ZS designed and fielded 20 behavioral science experiments across more than 620 adults in the U.S.[10] Each experiment was designed to test a separate cognitive factor to learn which tactics would prompt people to change their stance from being hesitant to get a vaccine to being willing to receive one. Our study had two aims: 1) investigating COVID-19 vaccine hesitancy, and 2) looking at adult vaccine hesitancy for previous vaccines. Out of 20 different interventions tested, we found six that were effective in overcoming COVID-19 vaccine hesitancy (see Figure 5-4). However, only two of them also impacted decision-making about established adult vaccines: social facilitation (reminding people that others are watching and that their decisions affect their interaction with others) and confirmation bias (in this context, priming someone's attitude towards vaccination by having them think about why someone would want to get vaccinated). This finding that the relevant factors differ across different adult vaccine decision-making highlights the risk of extrapolating insights from even closely related therapeutic areas. Many public health efforts to overcome vaccine hesitancy are based on common practice rather than scientific evidence. Insights fueled by behavioral science can ensure resources are directed toward the most impactful ways to overcome vaccine hesitancy rather than toward solutions that are commonly used but tend to have a lesser impact.

As another example of the benefits pharma can derive from applying behavioral science, one ZS client used behavioral insights techniques to uncover hidden biases that were preventing patients from starting prophylactic treatment for a chronic disease. The insights ultimately helped improve patient outcomes, which was one of the client's biggest business objectives. Patients using the standard treatment for acute events face an increased risk of developing severe joint damage. Physicians strongly advocate that patients treat the condition prophylactically rather than waiting until they experience an acute event, but this advice has failed to persuade many patients, who continue to prefer to treat only when it is essential, at the time they are experiencing an acute event. The client had conducted multiple rounds of research to try to crack the problem, but standard marketing interventions failed to drive behavioral change. So the company decided to take a different tack and look at the problem through the lens of behavioral science.

Analysis of research conducted with both patients and physicians uncovered a bias called hyperbolic discounting: the idea that people will be more willing to agree to expend effort in exchange for a specific benefit if they can put in the effort at a future time (rather than immediately). And the inverse is also true: people are less willing to expend effort in the short term for a benefit that will happen in the future. The people living with this chronic disease were under the belief that the benefit—preventing long-term joint damage—was in the distant future. Thus, they were unwilling to undertake the effort required for prophylactic treatment in the short term.

Equipped with this knowledge, the brand team was able to adjust its patient-oriented content to focus on immediate benefits for patients: namely, experiencing less anxiety about acute events and contending with fewer emergency room visits as a result.

Figure 5-4: Cognitive Factors Identified in ZS Vaccine Hesitancy Study[11]

Prospect theory
Individuals place more emphasis on gains rather than losses and as a result, will try to make decisions that contribute to gains.

Effort justification
Increasing the effort involved with achieving a goal will change the value we place on the goal itself.

Confirmation bias
Our preconceived expectations or preferences influence our decision making in new or ambiguous situations.

Halo effect
People consistently make irrational associations and assumptions between things that feel like they should be related but are not.

Social facilitation
The presence of others can promote accountability and improve judgment in given situations compared to their performance when alone.

Anchoring effect
Exposure to arbitrary numbers can influence peoples' number-based estimates or behaviors.

By highlighting what mattered to patients in the short term, the company could motivate patients to make the switch and help them derive the long-term benefits that the treatment change would accomplish (i.e., less joint damage). The team also helped physicians shift their call-to-action language by putting the effort of changing treatment regimens in the future; for example, physicians asked patients if they would be willing to switch to prophylactic treatment in a month—to which many more said yes.

A robust, experiment-driven behavioral science solution is not required in all patient insight work, but it can provide a turboboost to the insights engine when companies are looking to solve challenges that haven't responded to more typical approaches. Understanding which biases are present and what impact they are having can mean the difference between patients accepting a life-changing new treatment or not, complying with their care plan to maximize the health benefit they are able to achieve or finally completing that potentially life-saving cancer screening before it is too late.

Co-Creation

If behavioral science lends itself to robust experimentation, co-creation sits at the opposite end of the spectrum in that it involves a highly exploratory design-thinking approach. It provides a way for pharma companies to work alongside patients in order to move from identifying a problem toward innovating impactful solutions. Using human-centered design processes, co-creation brings patients to the proverbial drawing board to create solutions that are not just for patients but also by patients. From the companies' perspective, co-creation ensures that the time, effort and resources invested into new solutions produce usable, feasible and desirable results. Although co-creation is neither a new patient insight solution nor a pure insights generation method, we would be remiss not to mention it in a discussion about enhancing patient centricity through the better understanding of patients. It bridges insights and actions as a powerful tool to drive patient centricity.

Figure 5-5: Three Ways in Which Collaborating with Patients Unlocks Value

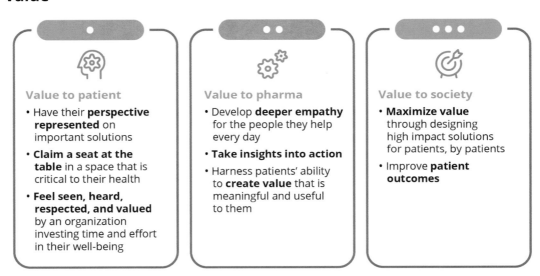

Value to patient
- Have their **perspective represented** on important solutions
- **Claim a seat at the table** in a space that is critical to their health
- **Feel seen, heard, respected, and valued** by an organization investing time and effort in their well-being

Value to pharma
- Develop **deeper empathy** for the people they help every day
- **Take insights into action**
- Harness patients' ability to **create value** that is meaningful and useful to them

Value to society
- **Maximize value** through designing high impact solutions for patients, by patients
- Improve **patient outcomes**

Co-creation itself can take many different forms, such as simulations with healthcare professionals or in online forums to allow patients time to react to different ideas and contribute to their refinement. For instance, in one ZS study, a client was able to use virtual-reality simulations to understand and optimize the enrollment process for clinical trial participants (more on this in Chapter 6). Another ZS co-creation study brought together numerous stakeholders, including GPs, endocrinologists and patients, to conduct simulations of HCP-patient interactions about healthcare decision-making for type 2 diabetes (T2D).[12] In particular, this research focused on developing patient-centered solutions to overcome T2D patients' hesitancy about using non-insulin injectables. The solutions developed were very different than what we would otherwise have identified based on the preceding phases of traditional qualitative and quantitative research alone. For example, patients suggested that instead of their doctors taking more time to talk to them theoretically about switching to an injection (a solution that assumes what's missing is more effort to convince the patient), the doctor should give the injection pen to the patient to touch and feel (an experiential solution that acts to alleviate patients' fear of "scary needles").

In another example of applying co-creation to achieve big impact, Eli Lilly's oncology team launched its CoLab and CoDesign programs to take patients through day-long dress rehearsals of a trial in order to spot any weaknesses or opportunities for improvement. These co-creation programs were key contributors to Eli Lilly's reduction of average trial enrollment time from four years down to three; and also enabled the company to tighten the gap between first patient dose and product launch from 10 years to eight and a half.[13] Genentech meanwhile has formalized the adoption of co-creation by instituting a Patient Co-Creation Council (PCC). The PCC engages patients and caregivers to work in partnership to develop products, services and solutions that improve the patient and caregiver experience.[14]

Like behavioral science, co-creation is a high-impact solutioning strategy with specific applications, such as designing a patient support program, learning how to better address sensitive topics with patients or seeking ways to connect with disengaged patients. Since it involves the development of solutions for and by patients, it is an invaluable tool as pharma endeavors to make the shift toward patient centricity.

Integrating Patient Insights

Many pharma companies today seek relevant patient insights to address specific business problems. But to achieve patient centricity, the bar is much higher. An important evolution is to integrate patient insights throughout product development and commercialization in a coherent, cohesive and integrated way. This will allow pharma to create products that better meet patient needs, which will in turn inspire greater demand for those products. Diverse and representative patient insights can thus fuel the virtuous circle ("win-win-win") by which we can simultaneously deliver better patient experiences, boost business outcomes and improve the economics of healthcare.

Figure 5-6: Win-Win Outcomes for Patients and Pharma through Patient-Centric Approaches[15]

Value to patients

Therapies that better meet patients' needs are developed faster

Clinical trials include populations that **better reflect the diversity of patients**

| Pre-clinical | Clinical |

Value to pharma

Rapid identification of new target molecules and indications

Identify and enroll patients for trials faster, **better retention**

Differentiated value proposition

Value to patients

Positive experience on therapy; including service experiences that meet **individual needs**

Better outcomes; support **around and beyond** the pill

| Launch | Inline |

Value to pharma

PROs can be utilized in **market access and pricing negotiations;** enable innovative value-based pricing models

Getting the right patients on therapy faster

Demonstrate **improved outcomes and strengthen positioning and label**

The Edsel provides a lesson to pharma of what not to do: a large company wrongly assuming it knows what its customers want and suffering a major financial setback as a result. We'll never know how the Edsel story would have played out if Ford had solicited ongoing customer feedback rather than extrapolating from what it had learned in the past about customers. However, we can contrast the Ford Edsel debacle against the success of another well-known consumer brand that has taken a highly customer-centric approach and actively listened to customers from its very beginning: Starbucks. The ubiquitous global chain has met spectacular success by creating the personalized experience that its customers want and by opening a channel of communication to allow customers to directly share their suggestions.[16] In 2008, Starbucks launched its My Starbucks Idea platform, which allows customers (and employees) to share ideas they have for new products, make suggestions about changes to existing products and even request for discontinued products to be brought back. By regularly tapping into this channel for customer insight, Starbucks has been able to fuel its growth; for example, customer feedback is what prompted the company's successful expansion into a variety of dairy-free milk alternatives.

Pharmaceutical drug development is inarguably more complex than determining whether to offer oat, soy or almond milk (or all of the above). But we can nonetheless take from the Starbucks example these two fundamental lessons: 1) listen to customers, and 2) establish mechanisms to integrate customer input. These lessons are essential to achieving both patient centricity and business success in the modern era.

Key Takeaways

The pharma industry has a "patient insights gap"; there is a tendency to make assumptions about what patients want and need, when the reality may be quite different.

- The insights gap has a negative impact on all stages of drug development and commercialization, from R&D through to marketing.

- Robust research methodologies, both qualitative and quantitative, are available to provide an in-depth understanding of the patient experience, but they remain underutilized.

- Moving the needle toward patient-centric insights will require pharma to ask new questions and adopt new methods, including RWD analytics, behavioral science and co-creation.

- Making continued progress toward true patient centricity will require organizations to regularly gather patient insights and integrate them throughout all product development and commercialization processes.

- Having a clearer picture of the full patient context will translate into benefits for patients as well as business impact for pharma.

Acknowledgments

The authors would like to thank the following people for their contributions and input in writing this chapter: Jacob Braude and Nan Gu.

Endnotes

1. Richard Feloni, "4 Lessons from the Failure of the Ford Edsel, One of Bill Gates' Favorite Case Studies," Business Insider, September 5, 2015, https://www.businessinsider.com/lessons-from-the-failure-of-the-ford-edsel-2015-9.

2. Shah Mohammed, "'Ford Edsel' Brand Failure Case Study and Business Lessons," Medium, April 5, 2017, https://shahmm.medium.com/ford-edsel-brand-failure-a-design-thinking-perspective-eea92d2e90ec.

3. Feloni, "4 Lessons from the Failure."

4. ZS Patient Experience Index (PXi) Study, 2020.

5. Name changed for the purposes of this book.

6. ZS Migraine Patient Journey, 2017.

7. Optum's de-identified Clinformatics®Data Mart Database (2007-2019).

8. Optum's de-identified Clinformatics®Data Mart Database (2007-2019).

9. Edwin Choi and Juhan Sonin, "Determinants of Health," Goinvo, last modified April 14, 2020, https://www.goinvo.com/vision/determinants-of-health/.

10. Jacob Braude, "How Behavior Science Can Solve Healthcare Hurdles As Large As Vaccine Hesitancy," ZS, June 22, 2021, https://www.zs.com/insights/how-behavioral-science-can-solve-vaccine-hesitancy.

11. ZS Vaccine Hesitancy Study, 2021.

12. Amy Marta, Hensley Evans and Fiona Taylor, "Behavioral Insights for a Hungry Healthcare Market," ZS, accessed January 18, 2022, https://www.zs.com/insights/behavioral-insights-for-a-hungry-healthcare-market.

13. Joseph Kim, "What the Patient Voice Taught Lilly About Clinical Trial Design & Recruitment," Clinical Leader, June 4, 2019, https://www.clinicalleader.com/doc/what-the-patient-voice-taught-lilly-about-clinical-trial-design-recruitment-0001; Emily Wasik, "State of Patient Centricity 2020: Advancing from Patient-First Intentions to True-Co-Creation," Economist Impact, May 29, 2020, https://eiuperspectives.economist.com/healthcare/state-patient-centricity-2020-advancing-patient-first-intentions-true-co-creation.

14. Genentech, "Create with Us," accessed October 22, 2021, https://www.gene.com/patients/create-with-us.

15. ZS Patient Centricity executive-level presentation, 2021.

16. Gigi Devault, "How Starbucks Uses Market Research to Propel the Brand," The Balance Small Business, last modified June 25, 2019, https://www.thebalanc-esmb.com/starbucks-use-of-market-research-propels-the-brand-2297155.

Chapter 6:
Removing Barriers to
Participation in Clinical Trials

Nikita Reznik and Lisa Bance

I used to be a person. Following my diagnosis, I stopped being a person and became a patient. However, after choosing to enroll in a clinical trial, I suddenly realized I was not even considered a patient anymore. I simply became a study subject.

– Clinical Trial Participant, DIA 2016[1]

The Need for a Patient Focus in Clinical Development

The decision to enroll in a clinical trial is one of the most important, personal decisions in the lives of patients and their families and often comes with a sense of hope for better health and empowerment to advance the science for others. But the experience of participating in a trial can become another source of disappointment and frustration for patients. Ideally, patients would have consistent support throughout the process, from the decision to enroll all the way through to the trial's final phase. In practice, however, sponsors and sites often have limited resources to cover a large volume of trials, and patient interactions can feel impersonal and lack the desired support. As a result, clinical trial participants may start feeling dehumanized, as though they're merely "study subjects" and "N-numbers."

A clinical trial should be a partnership between trial investigators and patients, who incur personal risk to help advance science and develop new medicines. Engagement with patients as partners is vital for success. To state the obvious, clinical trials can't happen without trial participants; investigators rely on patients to enroll and participate to generate the required clinical data to assess a treatment's performance. However, on average across a wide range of therapeutic areas, almost half of clinical trials fail to recruit patients within their target timelines,[2] and more than half of the patients become non-adherent or drop out throughout the course of the trial.[3] These enrollment and adherence challenges often result in a multimillion-dollar increase in direct trial costs and potentially hundreds of millions in lost revenue due to trial delays (see Figure 6-1).[4] More importantly, the intense focus of trials on science and product performance frequently results in a lack of attention from the clinical team to the patient experience.

In this chapter, we discuss the need for a paradigm shift in clinical research from the traditional, product-centered approach to one that focuses on improving the patient experience and ensuring that patients are treated as true partners in clinical trials. This shift can, in turn, improve the performance and impact of clinical trials and reduce the time required for drugs to get to market.

Figure 6-1: Historical Clinical Trial Enrollment and Challenges to Adherence[5]

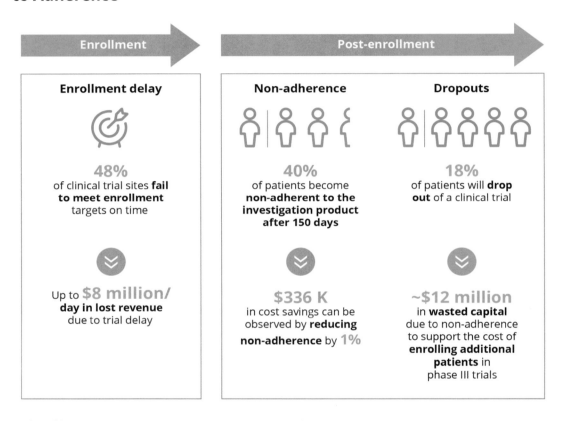

Challenges in Patient-Focused R&D

The traditional view of R&D considers drug development and clinical trials as scientific research studies to determine the clinical performance of a medical intervention or to answer specific health questions.[6] Such an approach, if not balanced by inclusion of the patient perspective, can lead to an engrained product-centric mindset in R&D organizations. As a senior R&D leader at a top-20 biopharma company bluntly put it: "Science trumps patient convenience … every time!" This traditional view is often a contributing factor in the underperformance of clinical trials across the industry. As we will detail below, there are a number of fundamental oversights that can result in the lack of a patient-focused R&D mindset at pharma companies, including:

- Failing to understand the patient

- Neglecting to consider the patient experience or level of trust

- Forgetting to engage patients as partners

The Consequences of Failing to Understand the Patient

R&D organizations often focus their efforts on the methodological and technical aspects of clinical research in an effort to maximize the chances to demonstrate product efficacy and safety. This mindset can preclude the integration of insights from patients about their journey through the disease, the day-to-day challenges they face and the outcomes they prioritize (i.e., better quality of life rather than clinical outcomes).

Subtle trial design elements may significantly impact patients' perceptions when they are choosing to enroll in a trial or their experience while participating during a trial. Elements that could deter patients from participating or negatively affect their experience might include procedures that exert an excessive burden on patients, overly restrictive inclusion criteria or a failure to include endpoints that are meaningful to patients. Without engagement of patients to review and flag such issues during trial design, complex trial protocols can cause significant trial delays when patients fail to enroll, leading to costly root-cause analyses.

A recent heart failure (HF) clinical trial offers a clear example of a non-patient-friendly trial design. The initial trial protocol asked for advanced HF patients to both exercise and come in for multiple visits as part of the trial commitments. While scientifically sound and reasonable from a trial logistics perspective, such requirements did not consider the unique situation of the target patients for the trial—stage IV HF patients—who often find it difficult to walk or get out of the house. Requirements to exercise and come in for regular visits created major challenges for patients to commit to during recruitment and to sustain during trial participation, resulting in substantial delays in patient recruitment and suboptimal trial efficiency. Such oversights could easily have been avoided had the R&D team adopted a more patient-focused mindset and considered what was realistic for the trial participants.

The Consequences of Neglecting to Consider the Patient Experience or Level of Trust

A product-centric mindset also often assumes an intrinsic commitment to product success from all stakeholders involved in the trial and sometimes overlooks the experiences of patient volunteers. While the protocol design dictates the individual steps within a trial, a range of additional components affect the overall experience of the participants, influencing their levels of engagement and decisions about whether to adhere to trial protocol or drop out. Such factors include the patient-site relationship, patient trust in the trial, how easy it is for patients to access trial sites and manage the required logistics, and the level of support available to help patients cope with the physical and mental burden of the trial, especially for patients from underrepresented and underserved communities.

The ProtecT Prostate Cancer study, which compared the benefits of proactive surgery versus active monitoring for patients with slow-growing cancers, serves as a clear example of how a lack of patient trust in the trial and investigators can hinder a study. For the non-surgery cohort, the trial used the term "watchful waiting." It turned out that prostate cancer patients, even with slowly progressing tumors, interpreted "watchful waiting" as "watch while I die," leading to a breakdown of trust between the patients and site. These impressions resulted in substantial challenges in patient recruitment for the trial. By changing language from "watchful waiting" to "active monitoring," the trial was able to almost double its successful recruitment rate (increasing from 40 to 70%).[7]

The Consequences of Forgetting to Engage Patients as Partners

Investigators will often refer to patients enrolled in a trial as "trial subjects." While the topic of the most appropriate terminology has been under debate for over 20 years,[8] such terminology is mostly driven by federal regulations and guidelines ("patients" receive care that is in their best health interest, while "subjects" follow a defined protocol for an intervention with the purpose of generating data).[9] However, in addition to dehumanizing trial participants, referring to them as "subjects" may prevent the engagement of patients as true partners in trial efforts. Considering trial participants merely as "subjects that follow the protocol" encourages a myopic view among the members of the trial team and damages their chances of establishing trust with participants and soliciting invaluable patient input throughout the trial design and implementation. One alternative for sponsors to consider is using the word "participant," as the FDA suggests that the terms "subject" and "participant" may be used interchangeably.[10] The shift in terminology can help reinforce a shift in mindset, from viewing patients enrolled in trials as passive subjects to viewing them as active partners whose engagement is imperative.

And it's crucial that trial teams maintain contact with participants even after the trial is complete. It's frequently the case that patients benefit from the therapy they receive during the trial, and so they are eager to advocate for the company's products when the trial concludes. But, more often than not, post-trial communications with the patients stop completely, with trial teams sometimes failing to provide the participants with even the most basic information, such as the product name, the names of the sponsors or when the product will be available on the market. Following up with patients is especially important in trials for products that treat chronic conditions; for participants with lifelong diseases, access to a novel medication could mean a once-in-a-lifetime opportunity to substantially improve their lives. Take, for example, the post-trial experience of patients in a clinical trial for type 2 diabetes, where an investigational product demonstrated potential to enhance the participants' quality of life by increasing their energy levels and ability to control their weight. However, following conclusion of the trial, the investigators abruptly cut off communication with the participants. As described by a patient: "[They would] check my sugar and goodbye—that's about it. Told me to go back to what I was on. Within a couple months, all of the weight I had lost was back on me. They never told me anything like [the trial sponsor or drug name]." Not providing participants with the necessary information to pursue ongoing therapy is a lost opportunity for the sponsors to cultivate loyal customers and, most importantly, can lead to significant deterioration in patient quality of life.

The Value of Patient-Focused Drug Development

In contrast to a product-centric approach, patient-focused drug development (PFDD) ensures that patients' perspectives, needs and experiences are meaningfully considered in any and all drug development activities.[11] While PFDD is intrinsically the right thing to do and needs to be a priority for biopharma and life sciences companies on the basis of ethics alone, this approach also results in a positive business impact for companies through improved trial performance, expedited clinical trial timelines and reduced costs.

Maximizing the Value of Clinical Research for Patients

First, PFDD serves pharma's core mission of improving patients' lives. Pre-trial, PFDD involves actively listening to patients' needs to identify treatments, formulations and indications that truly make a difference for them. During trials, patient engagement enhances the trials' chances of success, thus increasing the likelihood that companies will be able to bring new treatments to market and benefit the broader patient population. This, in turn, fuels a positive view of drug manufacturers as partners to patients on their healthcare journeys. Post-trial, patient engagement enables trial participants to spread awareness of the new medications and healthcare advances, helping other patients improve their lives. It is these values and aspirations that should be driving patient-focused efforts by pharma R&D teams.

Expediting Timelines Through Improved Recruitment Rates

In addition to patient value, the business value of PFDD is clear through improved recruitment and retention. The typical patient recruitment period comprises approximately 30 to 40% of the total clinical trial length (leading to recruitment periods of up to one-and-a-half years for a three- to four-year phase III clinical trial).[12] While the length of the recruitment period is highly dependent on patient response rates, consent and screening, multiple studies have shown that simple interventions, such as an easier consent process or consistently following up with potential participants, can improve patient response rates by between 30 to 60%.[13] This can ultimately reduce phase III trial duration by six months or more (see Figure 6-2).

Reduction in Trial Costs Through Reduced Patient Attrition

Patient-specific expenses often become a significant cost factor in clinical trials, with some analyses estimating per-patient costs of up to $35,000 (driven by the costs for trial procedures and laboratories as well as expenses for physicians and administrative staff).[14] Typical attrition rates of approximately 25%[15] suggest that these patient costs are expended for dozens or even hundreds of patients that ultimately don't complete the trial, translating into multimillion-dollar losses for sponsors. Patient-centric approaches, such as sustained contact between investigators and patients[16] or certain monetary incentives[17] (see Figure 6-2), can lead to the reduction of attrition by as much as 50%, translating to direct cost savings of about $1.5 million for a typical 500-patient phase III trial.[18]

Addressing the Challenges in Patient-Focused Drug Development

In the post-COVID-19 world, increasing levels of patient education in healthcare and pharmaceuticals, propelled by growing public awareness of healthcare generally and of the benefits of clinical trials more specifically, represent a unique opportunity to expand the role of patients as partners in clinical trials. It is crucial that PFDD be incorporated in all stages of clinical trial planning and implementation, from the initial pre-trial planning stage through trial implementation and post-trial follow up. In Figure 6-3, we summarize the key activities relevant to patient-focused clinical trials, all of which we will discuss in greater detail in this section.

Figure 6-2: Impact of Patient-Centric Interventions on Patient Recruitment and Retention[19]

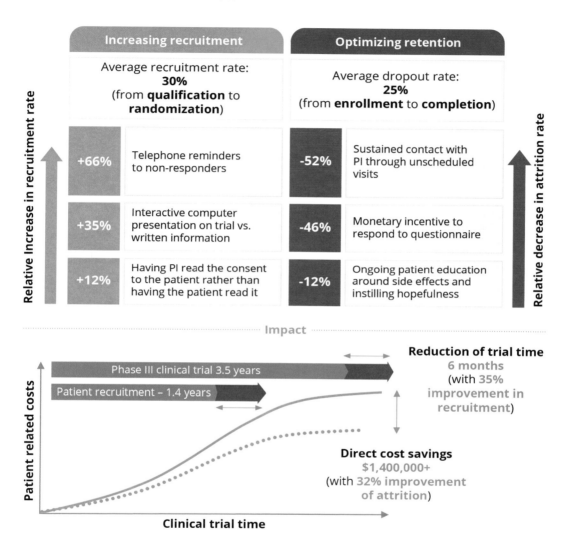

Figure 6-3: Key Patient-Focused Drug Development Activities Across the R&D Life Cycle

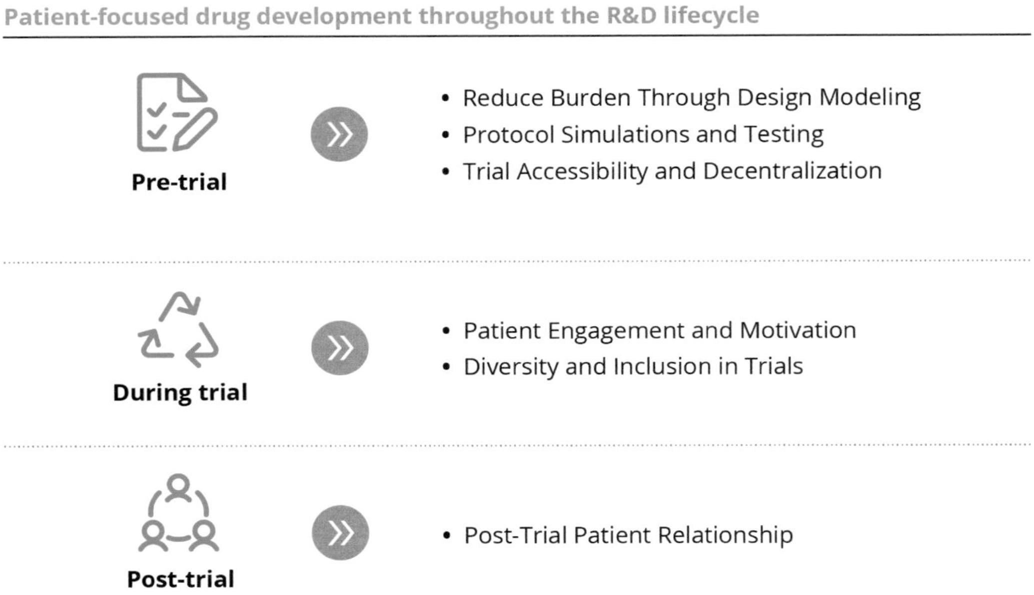

Patient-focused drug development throughout the R&D lifecycle

Pre-trial

- Reduce Burden Through Design Modeling
- Protocol Simulations and Testing
- Trial Accessibility and Decentralization

During trial

- Patient Engagement and Motivation
- Diversity and Inclusion in Trials

Post-trial

- Post-Trial Patient Relationship

Pre-Trial

Reduced Burden Through Design Modeling

The patient burden in clinical trials is often cited as the major source for patient recruitment and retention challenges. At the same time, there is a general lack of understanding about what constitutes a "burden"—the term is often vaguely defined and isn't easily quantifiable. Only a handful of studies have examined the relationship between patient burden and trial participation rates.[20]

Due to the limited tools to estimate and quantify patient burden in trial design, R&D teams may rely on qualitative and subjective perceptions of "overall trial burden." Even in a situation where the clinical team is aware that a protocol could be burdensome to patients, the team may lack the tools to objectively assess the burden and may not be aware of the available actions to take to alleviate it. When trial protocols prove to be too burdensome and unsustainable for patient engagement, clinical teams often have to resort to costly root-cause analyses, trial amendments and salvage techniques following trial launch.

Establishing a reliable, protocol-specific "trial burden composite score" is a key strategy for ensuring a patient-centric trial design and positive patient experience. In an effort to establish cross-indication burden assessment tools, ZS collaborated with Tufts Center for the Study of Drug Development (CSDD) to conduct a study with 3,000 clinical trial naïve and experienced participants across five therapeutic areas. We investigated the burden of over 50 individual trial procedures and a wide range of burden factors. The aim was to determine how particular clinical trial protocol elements and other relevant factors impact patient burden, study convenience and patients' ability to adhere to protocol requirements across different demographic groups (see Figure 6-4).[21]

The clinical trial burden score that we developed is highly predictive of clinical trial performance indicators, such as screening failure rates and overall trial duration, allowing us to quantitatively demonstrate the impact of patient burden on clinical trial performance. Furthermore, the global survey revealed that patient perception of trial burden depends on patient demographics (such as race, ethnicity and age) and healthcare experience (e.g., therapy area, caregiver reliance and previous participation in clinical trials).[22] For example, the burden of the same routine examination procedures will often be felt differently by a white patient versus a patient of color, by a patient suffering from cancer versus an autoimmune disease or by an independent patient versus a patient relying on the support of caregivers.

These findings clearly demonstrate not only the clear impact of patient burden on trial performance but also highlight that patient burden is not one-size-fits-all. Different patients experience trial procedures differently. Trial sponsors must establish a robust understanding of the burden of the upcoming trial protocol for their specific participant cohort during the protocol development phase in order to ensure a successful trial as well as a positive experience for the patient partners.

Figure 6-4: ZS/Tufts Patient Clinical Trial Burden Score Components

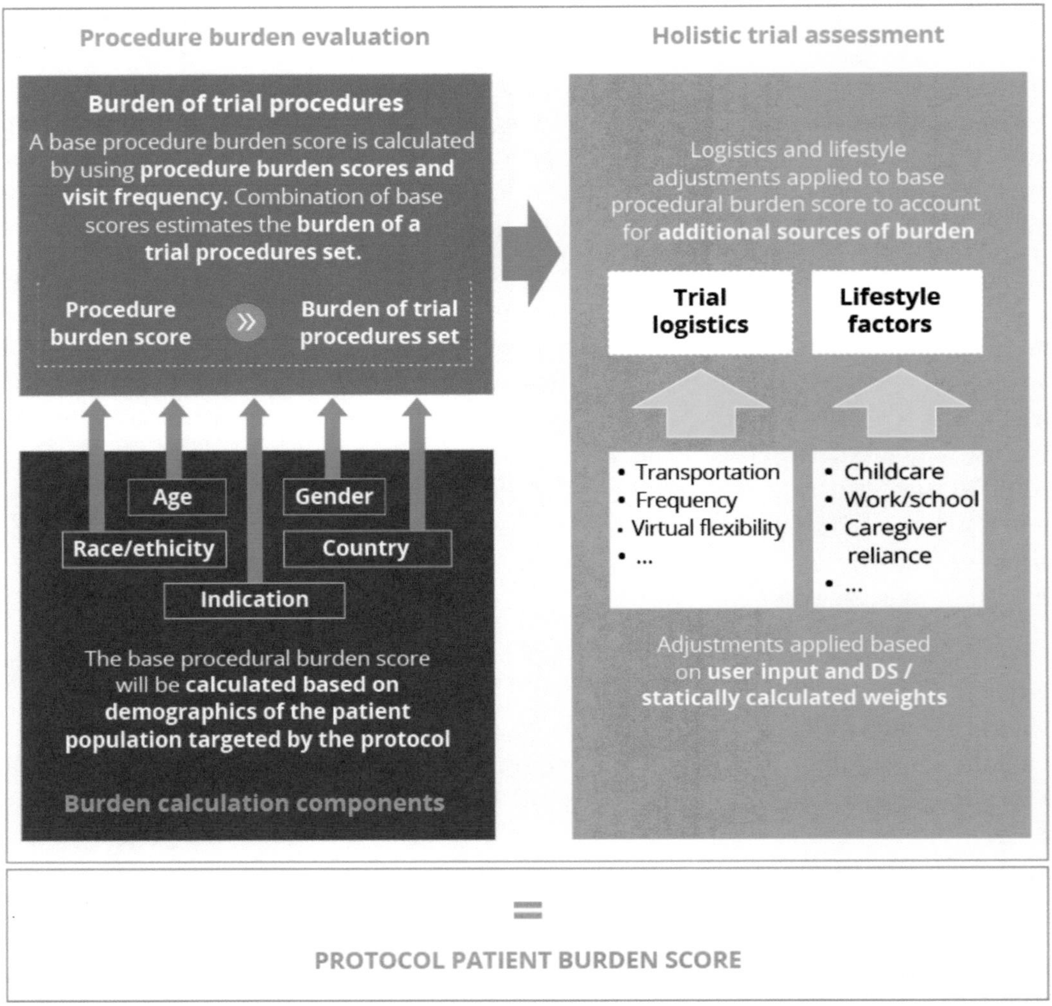

Procedure burden evaluation

Holistic trial assessment

Burden of trial procedures
A base procedure burden score is calculated by using **procedure burden scores and visit frequency.** Combination of base scores estimates the **burden of a trial procedures set.**

Logistics and lifestyle adjustments applied to base procedural burden score to account for **additional sources of burden**

Procedure burden score » Burden of trial procedures set

Trial logistics

Lifestyle factors

Age   Gender
Race/ethnicity   Country
Indication

The base procedural burden score will be **calculated based on demographics of the patient population targeted by the protocol**

Burden calculation components

- Transportation
- Frequency
- Virtual flexibility
- …

- Childcare
- Work/school
- Caregiver reliance
- …

Adjustments applied based on **user input and DS / statically calculated weights**

=

PROTOCOL PATIENT BURDEN SCORE

Protocol Simulations and Testing

Developing a full understanding of the barriers patients and caregivers face when confronting particular trial protocols is vital to optimizing the success of a trial. While we have highlighted some of the approaches to protocol modeling above, here we examine approaches to protocol testing in greater depth. We begin with the "tried-and-tested" methods on which the industry relies heavily today and then outline some of the "digitally innovative" methods currently on the rise.

"Tried and Tested": Trial Simulations

Trial testing through simulations has emerged over the past five to seven years as a means to provide patients with a more real-life experience of a trial, thus improving the reliability of the testing outcomes and helping investigators adjust the protocols to increase the likelihood of trial success. Typically, simulations have been used in R&D to understand and validate the patients' need for a drug and evaluate the trade-offs regarding risk and reward to cultivate a better understanding of future markets when choosing which drugs to develop. They also afford an opportunity to assess patients' interest in a clinical trial and their likelihood of enrolling, refine the recruitment and enrollment models, and evaluate patients' understanding of trial protocols and their related ability to be compliant or stay in the trial.

A recent inflammatory bowel disease (IBD) trial provides a stark example of how a mock-trial simulation helped sponsors validate and refine their hypotheses about key pain points and drivers in the patient journey throughout the trial. Initial patient focus groups during the trial design identified an overabundance of PROs as a key barrier to positive patient experience during the trial. During discussions, the focus group participants signaled that filling out up to 10 PROs was a key challenge that could affect the overall impact of a site visit; without actually filling out the questionnaires, they anticipated that dealing with that much paperwork would be time-consuming and overwhelming. However, upon simulating the site visit in a mock clinic setup, it turned out patients could easily fill out all the PROs in less than 15 minutes. Rather than flagging the number of PROs as a potential problem, participants in the simulation mostly expressed concerns over not knowing where and how to reach the bathroom, due to the nature of their condition. This logistical point never came up during the patient focus group discussions. Through co-creation of solutions with patients after the simulation, investigators recognized that the development of a basic visitation and logistics guide was a simple yet impactful mitigation strategy to address the patients' concerns. Patient interviews or focus groups can fail to identify such site-specific challenges and solutions due to the intrinsic limitation of a lack of experience.

"Digitally Innovative": Virtual Reality Trial Simulations

In an effort to overcome some of the limitations with live simulations (such as extended setup times for mock trial environments and the inability to efficiently scale the simulation across multiple geographies and patient groups), the industry is turning to technology. Virtual reality (VR) trial and procedure simulations are attracting interest from both clinical development and clinical operations teams. VR has already seen successful implementation in medical and therapeutic settings. For instance, VR is commonly used to train medical students and residents in surgery and anatomy.[23] To aid the patient experience, VR has also become an important therapeutic tool in psychology and rehabilitation medicine.[24]

Given the effective application of VR in these settings, it's easy to see how VR might be adapted to R&D.

For patient-focused R&D and trial protocol testing, VR-assisted exposure to protocol elements helps patients visualize complex procedures, enables investigators to more reliably predict patient concerns during the trials and simulates a real-life patient-to-investigator interaction to test communication strategies. Importantly, a VR simulation can be rapidly deployed across countries in the study universe, capturing more patient views and increasing the reliability of input to the protocol.

Virtual reality can take many forms that allow for customization, from simple to highly sophisticated. A simple approach is a web-based design that allows multiple users to interact in a created space, such as the ZS VITA platform (see Figure 6-5). This approach allows for swift deployment once the environment is created. A more sophisticated approach would involve both the creation of an environment and the ability to explore and interact with the environment through VR headsets, handsets and other body sensors. The VR assets developed during the trial recruitment phase can often be re-used during the actual trial as patient support and education tools to re-familiarize participants with trial procedures, reduce patient apprehension and alleviate some of the onsite patient education burden. In addition, VR can supplement or replace some in-person trial visits and thus reduce patient, site and caregiver burden. Those of us in the industry need to begin to think about building our expertise in VR for trial introduction, recruitment and retention as one of the most powerful tools in protocol development and decentralized trials.

Figure 6-5: ZS VITA Web-Based VR Trial Simulation[25]

Trial Accessibility and Decentralization

The traditional approach to clinical trials relies heavily on in-person site visits for data collection and intervention administration, both increasing the burden on the patients and introducing challenges with patient access to trial sites, especially in rural and underrepresented communities.[26] The COVID-19 pandemic has further exacerbated the burden of in-person site visits, due to increased health risks, mobility challenges and the disproportionate impact of COVID-19 on minority patient populations. Decentralized trials (DCTs) aim to reduce or eliminate clinical trial reliance on in-person site visits to alleviate patient burden and access challenges.

DCTs offer the opportunity to both optimize trial efficiency and increase patient comfort. Although still a new and evolving field, the feasibility and applicability of DCTs have been steadily improving with a maturing technological landscape and increasing digital technology components across trials. Meanwhile, the mobility restrictions imposed by the COVID-19 pandemic have resulted in patients across all demographics becoming more comfortable with digital technologies in their day-to-day lives.

In addition to decentralizing full trial protocols (i.e., designing fully decentralized trials), it's also possible to create individual trial components that are decentralized. A good example of a trial with individual decentralized components is Sanofi's Admelog Ph IV study, which used a virtual collection of consent and electronic PROs to provide better access and engage a diverse patient population.[27] As an example of a fully siteless trial, the Janssen CHIEF-HF study leveraged mobile technologies instead of site visits,[28] allowing the investigators to continue patient recruitment despite the COVID-19 pandemic. R&D teams need to determine the appropriate level of trial decentralization by considering an array of factors specific to each trial, such as the trial assessment procedures, the type of intervention, the nature of the disease (e.g., acute versus chronic), the target patient demographic and the demographic's comfort with and access to technology.

The COVID-19 vaccine trials of the Pfizer/BioNTech vaccine by ICON PLC (as Pfizer's CRO partner) offer one of the more recent examples of the opportunities available in trial decentralization. The urgency for the development of COVID-19 vaccines required the trials to be conducted at a previously never attempted speed and agility—the Pfizer/BioNTech vaccine trial enrolled 44,000 patients across 155 global locations and submitted results for emergency authorization of the vaccine in just 248 days.[29] One of the key digital strategies for managing this vast scale and expedited timeline was remote monitoring of the trial. The decentralization of monitoring capabilities by ICON enabled teams across the globe to rapidly scale up the study, and a limited number of centralized monitoring teams could monitor multiple sites across different parts of the globe remotely.[30] Ultimately, decentralization permitted more patients to enroll and led to faster trial completion.

While it should be noted that decentralization can add complexity to trial protocols and operations and will require additional time to fully mature,[31] there can be little doubt that DCTs are the way of pharma's future. As companies and patients become more comfortable with remote and decentralized trials,[32] the flexibility of fit-for-purpose trial design will facilitate striking the right balance between the reduction of patient burden, improvement of patient access and rigor of trial data collection.

During Trial

Patient Engagement and Motivation

Trial and protocol design and testing comprise the first steps in clinical trial implementation, setting the foundation for patient-focused clinical research. After the initial design, patient motivation to enroll and participate in the trial is what drives success. Patient engagement hinges on key strategic questions that define the patient experience during the journey through a clinical trial:

- Who are the stakeholders that impact patients' decisions about enrolling in a trial?

- What is the value of the trial to the stakeholders?

- How to best communicate the appropriate value to the stakeholders?

Identification of Decision-Making and Influencing of Stakeholders

While the individual patients are ultimately the decision-making stakeholders when it comes to trial enrollment, it is important to consider the full range of other stakeholders who might influence the patients' decisions. This concept is not new; trial sponsors often consider conversations that occur between patients, caregivers and physicians and prepare appropriate materials to support such discussions. ZS studies found that over 40% of these conversations involve doctors, and more than 35% of patients include spouses in making their clinical-trial-related decisions. However, stakeholders outside of the "direct decision-making" sphere, such as nurses, administrators and other hospital support staff, can also have an influence, which trial sponsors may not always consider. As an example of indirect influence on trial recruitment, in trials that require the skilled preparation of an interventional product, pushback from an overburdened hospital pharmacist may substantially impact the decision of an investigator to enroll patients into a trial, especially if other, less site-burdensome trials may be available for the patient.

Stakeholder Value and Barriers

Successful engagement and buy-in requires clear understanding of the value proposition and the barriers for each decision-making and influencing stakeholder. Highlighting the value through targeted stakeholder "value stories" while also providing clear explanations to preempt the most common concerns can help the patients and the influencing stakeholders in the patients' orbit assess the benefits of enrollment in a trial. As a typical example, simplified and visual trial materials and consent forms can supply the much-sought motivation for trial participants through straightforward communication of the value of the trial (such as improved health outcomes for the participant or the opportunity to help advance drug development for the benefit of others).

At the same time, simply eliminating barriers for enrollment can be just as crucial for trial success. Enrollment barriers may be directly related to protocol burden but may also involve "beyond-the-protocol" challenges. A common example of such a challenge is patient hesitancy to enroll due to apprehension about being assigned to the control group and administered a placebo. Throughout ZS's history of work on trial protocol testing and messaging projects, we have observed how such concerns can be alleviated through clear communication about the value of receiving "close care" from trial staff and having the opportunity to cross over to the test group in the future. In fact, in a recent ZS study on clinical trial participation, 73% of surveyed patients mentioned "opportunity for treatment by experts who focus on my disease" as a key motivator for enrolling. Providing reassurance that the trial will offer value to all patients who volunteer, including those receiving the placebo, helps potential participants become comfortable with the trial protocol.

Tailored Communication and Messaging

Identifying stakeholders who influence patients' decisions and then tailoring persuasive value stories for each of those individual stakeholder groups allows sponsors to create more impactful clinical trial materials. But ensuring effective communication with influencing stakeholders is generally overlooked, as communication and awareness materials often aren't customized for specific stakeholder groups and types. Typically, these materials focus on detailing the trial components rather than describing the value of the trial for each of the different stakeholder groups. Sponsors also don't always consider the method of communication (e.g., how an HCP or trial coordinator will present a trial brochure to the patient).

As a result, inefficient communication may itself become a barrier to trial enrollment, a challenge that is especially difficult to identify in a root-cause analysis. For example, a study investigating a product's testicular toxicity effects was beset by significant challenges in patient recruitment. Originally, the investigators believed the patients' reluctance was due to a protocol requirement for semen sample collection. However, in-depth research revealed that patients actually didn't find the requirement overly burdensome. Rather, it was the staff's lack of comfort and awkwardness in discussing the procedure that turned a large number of patients away. Education of staff on the topics of fertility and semen sample collection helped improve the trial recruitment rate by more than six times in the first quarter after implementation of the education campaign.

Diversity and Inclusion in Clinical Trials

Pharma has a duty to ensure equitable access to modern healthcare, enable better science, improve trust of minority communities in the healthcare system and mitigate engrained biases that permeate the system. Diversifying the patient populations involved in clinical trials is of paramount importance for securing healthcare equity, improving patients' well-being and facilitating the success of clinical trials. Engagement of diverse patient demographics allows a trial to shed light on different products' performance and relevance for patient subpopulations and to inform development of demographic-specific indications and labels.

Even as ensuring appropriate diversity in clinical trials is an acute social responsibility, it also presents an opportunity for pharmaceutical companies to optimize research and commercial performance. Through the engagement of historically underrepresented patient groups and better alignment of clinical trials with real-world outcomes, manu-facturers can expedite patient recruitment into clinical trials, improve product relevance across patient groups and inspire greater confidence among HCPs.

However, patient diversity remains a significant area of improvement for clinical trials, a challenge that is especially stark in therapeutic areas that are on the forefront of healthcare innovation, such as oncology and cardiovascular disease (see Figure 6-6).[33] The lack of clinical trial diversity (CTD), with trial participants not accurately representing the real-world population that will be using the product, precludes true understanding of a product's efficacy, safety and overall impact on patients.[34] Furthermore, a lack of adequate patient representation can undermine the confidence of physicians in trials and contribute to ongoing mistrust and lack of engagement from diverse patient populations.

Figure 6-6: The Current Landscape of Clinical Trial Racial Distribution Across Therapeutic Areas

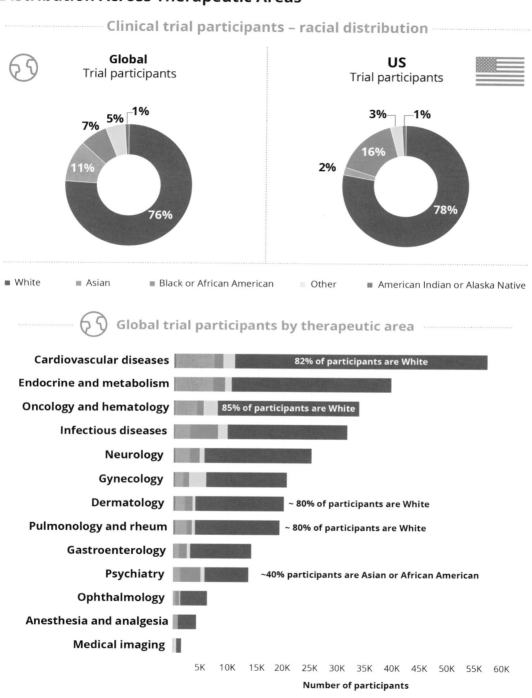

Some of the trials for well-known erectile dysfunction (ED) medications offer striking examples of the consequences of insufficient patient diversity. Initial trials for GSK's Levitra, such as the RELY-II trial,[35] relied on a Sexual Encounter Profile (SEP) questionnaire to assess product efficacy. Question 2 on the SEP questionnaire asked about heterosexual sexual encounters ("Were you able to insert your penis into your partner's vagina?"). The specific endpoint and lack of inclusion of men who have sex with men (MSM) as participants in the trial translated into Levitra's label, which described the drug's efficacy according to "the ability to achieve vaginal penetration."[36] The failure to consider MSM participants was not only an exclusionary practice but also prevented efficient marketing of Levitra for the MSM community, where the product found a certain level of popularity. Because sales representatives' communications are typically restricted to specific language on the label, the opportunity to discuss the drug's effectiveness for activities beyond vaginal penetration was significantly limited. The commercial performance of Levitra would likely have been improved by inclusion of MSM participants in the trial to allow the broader promotion of the product by GSK.

Over the past decade, a wide range of biopharma and healthcare stakeholders have engaged in initiatives to improve clinical trial diversity, equity and inclusion, with a noted increase in activity in 2020 and 2021. Such initiatives include individual activities by pharmaceutical companies and advocacy organizations (such as initiatives to diversify trial investigator pools and boost community outreach), as well as the issuance of position and guidance documents by industry and medical organizations (such as PhRMA[37] and ASCO[38]). Additional efforts by regulatory bodies (such as the FDA)[39] have also focused on promoting clinical trial diversity. The FDA Office of Minority Health and Health Equity has published awareness materials (such as brochures and infographics)[40] and a Clinical Trial Diversity Communications Toolkit,[41] including videos and social media promotion materials. Unfortunately, despite these efforts, the enrollment of underrepresented patient populations in clinical trials has not significantly improved over the past five years.[42]

Through our research at ZS, we have uncovered a wide range of challenges preventing the engagement of underrepresented and underserved populations, which we can roughly break down into four categories:

- **Communication and awareness:** Such challenges might include language barriers for non-native English speakers as well as limited health literacy and the difficulty of navigating complex healthcare systems.

- **Culture and community:** Patients may lack social and family support when deciding whether to enroll in a clinical trial, and there is often cultural incongruence between participants and physicians/trial teams.

- **Trust in the healthcare system:** There is widespread mistrust of the healthcare system among minority populations; meanwhile, some HCPs hold the belief that minority patients will not understand or adhere to specific protocols.

- **Logistics and financial burden:** Many patients contend with time and resource constraints (e.g., transportation time, loss of wages) associated with trial participation, feel concerned about related costs (e.g., getting to the study site, arranging childcare) and aren't sure how to ascertain if they will require health insurance to cover their trial participation.

Patients from minority and underrepresented groups often exhibit an intersectionality of identities (such as being both transgender and Black). Factors such as age and gender were shown to add to race and ethnicity, forming a compounded experience that leads to different paths on the patient journey. Studies of behavior for highly specific, underrepresented patient groups, which often require advanced behavioral research methodologies, can serve as robust examples of patient journeys and lend insight on how to better meet those patients where they are. Figure 6-7 demonstrates how different solutions and interventions may be necessary to engage diverse patient populations, ranging from financial assistance for low-income patients in oncology trials to decentralized approaches in respiratory trials to ease access restrictions for patients living outside of major urban areas. A deep understanding of the challenges particular groups of patients face and the factors driving their decision-making are absolute requirements to avoid a blanket approach to solutioning, which limits the impact of interventions to improve patient representativeness.

Successful design and implementation of CTD initiatives requires a collaboration between key healthcare players to change the mindset of patients and HCPs and dispel long-engrained biases. First of all, a truly effective partnership across the healthcare ecosystem will require active leadership from pharma; pharma companies are in a position to ensure equitable access to clinical trials and have the data power to elucidate the key challenges and relevant interventions needed to engage different patient communities. In addition, patient advocacy groups and community organizations can directly communicate with patient communities to spread awareness on the ground, debunk common myths and misconceptions, and mobilize community practice HCPs to encourage clinical trial referrals. Finally, medical societies and key opinion leaders can contribute by informing HCPs and trial investigators about the importance of including diverse populations in clinical trials and tackling the common biases within the HCP community. Efficient collaboration between pharma, patient advocacy groups and medical societies will work to both improve diversity efforts in individual trials as well as to spur a broader transformation in healthcare.

Such collaboration could also include a wide variety of global stakeholders, ranging from healthcare provider champions, academic experts, NGOs and regulatory bodies, all united by a broad vision as well as a prioritized set of objectives. While such coalitions have yet to be established specifically to redress challenges around diversity, equity and inclusion in clinical development, global coalitions have demonstrated the capacity to tangibly impact patients' lives. An example of a successful initiative is the Global Patient Advocacy Coalition in Migraine, uniting over 30 migraine-focused organizations.[44] Aligned on a common initial objective to increase migraine support in the workplace, the coalition successfully secured commitments from major employers around the world to support employees with migraines (something individual industry organizations and medical societies could not achieve on their own). The group also engaged powerful global health-care organizations (WHO and the World Federation of Neurology) to advance access to migraine care worldwide.[45]

Imagine what a similar coalition of powerful global actors could achieve for the cause of diversity. Collaboration across a wide range of influential champions for the cause, united by a shared vision and commitment to act, would enable the scaling up of diversity initiatives from "point-in-time" individual improvements to a transformational shift, impelling an expectation of diversity in clinical trials and in the field of healthcare more broadly.

Figure 6-7: Notable Examples of Therapy Area Specific Solutions to Improve Diversity in Clinical Trials[43]

Therapy area specific challenges to diversity

Oncology	Vaccines	Respiratory
Low income is an established challenge for patient participation in oncology clinical trials	**Lack of trust** in government initiatives and healthcare systems precludes underrepresented groups engaging in COVID-19 vaccine trials	**Access restrictions** to sites due to geographic limitations and poor health of patients living outside of major urban areas
Assistance for patients has been identified as a driver to improve enrollment of diverse patient populations in oncology trials	**Community engagement, awareness** and targeted **education** efforts can increase community participation	**Decentralized** and on-remote trial approaches reach patients "where they are at"

Post-Trial

Post-Trial Patient Relationships

Pharmaceutical companies often consider PFDD as engagement that is limited to patient participation in the clinical trial. Indeed, most patient-centric initiatives at pharma companies focus only on patient experience at enrollment and during the trial. Following trial close-out, patients are often disengaged from the drug development process, eliminating the value of the partner relationship that may have been achieved during the study. This disengagement can lead to significant consequences for the patient. As we mentioned previously, patients often receive substantial benefit from the investigational product and are keen to stay on the product after the trial is complete. While the immediate continuation of treatment may not always be possible, sustained communication with participants about when the product may be available on the market can inspire hope. Furthermore, given the time, effort and possible risk involved in trial participation, patients are often invested in the trial's outcome. Many join trials due to an altruistic motivation. Their devotion to the trial's success and their contribution to the research deserve recognition.

The importance of engaging the patient and maintaining a relationship post-trial should also not be underestimated from the business perspective. A continued relationship with patients enables them to act as brand advocates if they so choose. By establishing an ongoing relationship with trial participants, pharma companies can:

- Decrease the costs for the brand associated with the development of the initial patient population pool through the natural progression of trial participants to post-trial and prescription use of the product

- Inspire loyalty among trial participants as future customers, as a positive experience in the trial will likely lead patients to continue taking the drug after launch with strong adherence, persistence and commitment to the brand

- Optimize trial participants' potential as brand promoters, bolstering positive brand recognition and association

The trial sponsor can establish sustained engagement and relationships with trial participants by focusing on what is most important to the patient partners after the trial:

- "How did I help?": Communicating trial results, outcomes and the positive impact of patient participation in the trial

- "Can I continue using the medication?": Supporting patients in getting access to the investigational medication pre- and post-launch in cases where the product improved the patient's life or disease management

- "Can I share my experience and help others?": Creating opportunities for participants to further engage with fellow trial alums and share their experiences

The Pfizer Link portal for Pfizer clinical trial alumni is a notable example of successful patient engagement post-trial (see Figure 6-8).[46] Registration is available for previous clinical trial participants, and the portal provides patient partners access to news, study results and opportunities to participate in registries and additional trials. Even more importantly, Pfizer Link gives patients the opportunity to stay connected and engaged with Pfizer's efforts long after their original trial is complete.

Figure 6-8: Pfizer Link Portal

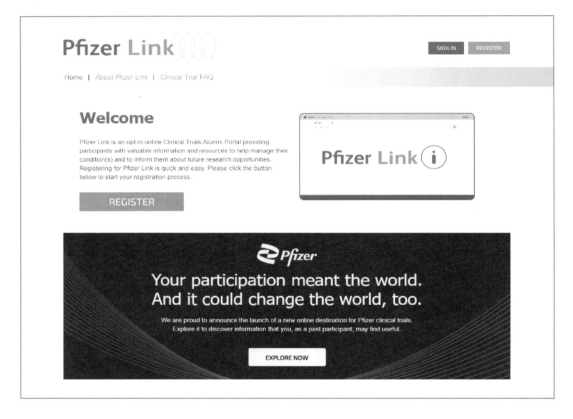

Pfizer Link has been featured as a case study for post-trial patient engagement and trial participant community multiple times across the industry. While Pfizer certainly deserves praise for its effort, it's our hope that such platforms and efforts to maintain the relationship with trial participants as partners will soon be considered an industry norm as a responsibility of all trial sponsor companies.

The ultimate pledge of the pharmaceutical industry is to improve patients' lives and well-being. Clinical trial participants are both patients whose well-being is pharma's responsibility and devoted partners striving to help fellow patients and incurring personal risk to advance healthcare. Sponsors of clinical trials have the responsibility and the duty to invest their utmost efforts to ensure the well-being of these patients before, during and after the trial. Adoption of a patient-focused mindset as the new norm across the industry will ensure that, rather than being relegated to the passive role of trial "subjects," patients will have the opportunity to become informed participants and active partners in every trial. Such a foundational shift will not only ensure the optimization of trial timelines and performance but also enable the robust and truly collaborative advancement of healthcare.

Key Takeaways

- While pharma companies strive to be patient centric, R&D activities within pharma companies traditionally focus on the product and the science of the clinical trial, positioning patient experience and engagement as a secondary priority.

- Patient-focused drug development has specific and measurable implications for both the patient and industry; it is both the right thing to do (to improve patient lives and experiences in clinical trials) and the smart thing to do (to improve clinical trial success and clinical development performance).

- A patient-focused mindset should be engrained across the full product development life cycle, focusing on both patient engagement and support during clinical trials as well as establishing patients as R&D partners in drug development.

- There are several innovative opportunities to support patient experience and engagement in the clinical development process, such as deeper patient burden calculations and better engagement of patients through virtual reality and decentralized trials.

- A wide range of challenges prevent the engagement of underrepresented and underserved populations (such as communication, trust and financial burden). A deep understanding of challenges and decision-making factors is required to avoid the typical blanket approach to the engagement of diverse patient populations that often limits the impact of interventions to improve patient representativeness.

- Impactful strategies and solutions will contribute to an overall baseline shift, establishing PFDD as the new normal in pharmaceutical R&D.

- In the post-COVID-19 world, increasing knowledge and awareness of healthcare and clinical research by patients represents a unique opportunity to enable significant change in the ways patients relate to and cooperate in clinical development.

Acknowledgments

The authors would like to thank the following for their help in the preparation of this chapter: Christopher Carney, Brian Dunn, Fan Gao, Irina Groysman, Sarah Jarvis, Sharon Karlsberg, Mike Martin, Aaron Mitchell, Bazgha Qutab, Victoria Summers and Ben Thomas.

Endnotes

1. Aaron Mitchel et al., "Pick Up the Pace on Patient Centricity in Drug Development," ZS, 2017, https://pages.zs.com/pick-up-the-pace-on-patient-centricity.html.

2. Tufts Center for the Study of Drug Development, Impact Report 15, no. 1 (January/February 2013), https://secure.touchnet.net/c21525_ustores/web/store_cat.jsp?catid=54&storeid=67.

3. Priya Tempkar, "Accelerating Study Start-Up: The Key to Avoiding Trial Delays," Clinical Researcher, February 1, 2017, https://acrpnet.org/2017/02/01/accelerating-study-start-up-the-key-to-avoiding-trial-delays/.

4. Moe Alsumidaie, "Non-Adherence: A Direct Influence on Clinical Trial Duration and Cost," Applied Clinical Trials, April 24, 2017, https://www.appliedclinicaltrialsonline.com/view/non-adherence-direct-influence-clinical-trial-duration-and-cost; Tempkar, "Accelerating Study Start-Up."

5. Tempkar, "Accelerating Study Start-Up"; Alsumidaie, "Non-Adherence"; Forte Research, "Retention in Clinical Trials: Keeping Patients on Protocols," January 23, 2020, https://forteresearch.com/news/infographic/infographic-retention-in-clinical-trials-keeping-patients-on-protocols/; Tufts Center for the Study of Drug Development, Impact Report 15; David B. Fogel, "Factors Associated With Clinical Trials That Fail and Opportunities for Improving the Likelihood of Success," in Contemporary Clinical Trials Communications 11 (August 2018): 156-164, https://doi.org/10.1016/j.conctc.2018.08.001; Terrence F. Blaschke et al., "Adherence to Medications: Insights Arising from Studies on the Unreliable Link Between Prescribed and Actual Drug Dosing Histories," in Annual Review of Pharmacology and Toxicology 52 (2011): 275-301, https://doi.org/10.1146/annurev-pharmtox-011711-113247.

6. European Medicines Agency (EMA), "Clinical Trials in Human Medicines," accessed September 30, 2021, https://www.ema.europa.eu/en/human-regulatory/research-development/clinical-trials-human-medicines; U.S. Food and Drug Administration (FDA), "Basics About Clinical Trials," last modified September 12, 2014, https://www.fda.gov/patients/clinical-trials-what-patients-need-know/basics-about-clinical-trials; U.S. National Institutes of Health (NIH), National Institute on Aging, "What Are Clinical Trials and Studies," last modified April 9, 2020, https://www.nia.nih.gov/health/what-are-clinical-trials-and-studies.

7. Jenny Donovan et al., "Improving Design and Conduct of Randomised Trials by Embedding Them in Qualitative Research: ProtecT (Prostate Testing for Cancer and Treatment) Study," in British Medical Journal 325, no. 7467 (2002): 766–770, https://doi.org/10.1136/bmj.325.7367.766; Sue Pavitt, "Clinical Trials and the Benefits of Patient Public Involvement," PowerPoint presentation, Slideshare, 2014, https://www.slideshare.net/nowgen/pavitt-ppi-impact-on-clinical-research-vs1.

8. Petra M. Boynton, "People Should Participate In, Not Be Subjects of, Research," in British Medical Journal 317, no. 7171 (1998): 1521, https://doi.org/10.1136/bmj.317.7171.1521a; Ali Hall, "What's in a Name? Research 'Participant' Versus Research 'Subject,' " PRIM&ER, January 6, 2014, https://blog.primr.org/whats-in-name-research-participan/#:~:text=while%20research%20%e2%80%9csubject%e2%80%9d%20is%20the,more%20respectful%20of%20research%20volunteers; Elisa A. Hurley, "From the Director: Why We Need to Keep the Term 'Research Subject' in Our Research Ethics Vocabulary," PRIM&ER, February 22, 2019, https://blog.primr.org/research-subject-vs-research-participant/.

9. FDA, "Glossary of Terms on Clinical Trials for Patient Engagement Advisory Committee Meeting," accessed July 29, 2021, https://www.fda.gov/media/108378/download; University of Arkansas for Medical Sciences Institutional Review Board, "The Difference Between a 'Patient' and a 'Subject,' " University of Arkansas for Medical Sciences Institutional Review Board, May 19, 2016, http://irb.uams.edu/2016/05/19/the-difference-between-a-patient-and-a-subject/#:~:text=when%20a%20person%20is%20a,is%20designed%20to%20create%20information.

10. FDA, "Glossary of Terms."

11. PhRMA, "Patient-Focused Drug Development," accessed September 30, 2021, http://phrma-docs.phrma.org/sites/default/files/pdf/patient-focused-drug-development.pdf.

12. Trialfacts, "Patient Recruitment Timelines—Why They Should Be Important to You," accessed September 30, 2021, https://trialfacts.com/patient-recruitment-timelines-why-they-should-be-important-to-you/); ZS Internal Analysis of Phase III Clinical Trials Data, 2000–2020.

13. Peter Bower et al., "Interventions to Improve Recruitment and Retention in Clinical Trials: A Survey and Workshop to Assess Current Practice and Future Priorities," in Trials 15 (2014): 399, https://doi.org/10.1186/1745-6215-15-399; Asuntha S. Karunaratne et al., "Improving Communication When Seeking Informed Consent: A Radomised Controlled Study of a Computer-Based Method for Providing Information to Prospective Clinical Trial Participants," in Medical Journal of Australia 192, no. 7 (2010): 388-392, https://doi.org/10.5694/j.1326-5377.2010.tb03561.x.

14. Batelle Technology Partnership Practice, "Biopharmaceutical Industry-Sponsored Clinical Trials: Impact on State Economies," PhRMA, March 2015, http://phrma-docs.phrma.org/sites/default/files/pdf/biopharmaceutical-industry-sponsored-clinical-trials-impact-on-state-economies.pdf; Aylin Sertkaya et al., "Key Cost Drivers of Pharmaceutical Clinical Trials in the United States," in Clinical Trials 13, no. 2 (2016): 117-126, https://doi.org/10.1177/1740774515625964.

15. CenterWatch Staff, "MediciGlobal Finds Fewer Trial Dropouts Among Participants Who Actively Pursue Enrollment Versus Those Recruited," CenterWatch, May 18, 2015, https://cms.centerwatch.com/articles/16609.

16. David C. Mohr et al., "Treatment Adherence and Patient Retention in the First Phase of a Phase-III Clinical Trial for the Treatment of Multiple Sclerosis," in Multiple Sclerosis Journal 5, no. 3 (June 1999): 192-197, https://doi.org/10.1177/135245859900500309.

17. Bower et al., "Interventions to Improve Recruitment."

18. Bower et al., "Interventions to Improve Recruitment"; Karunaratne et al., "Improving Communication"; Mohr et al., "Treatment Adherence and Patient Retention."

19. Bower et al., "Interventions to Improve Recruitment and Retention"; Mohr et al., "Treatment Adherence and Patient Retention"; Karunaratne et al., "Improving Communication When Seeking Informed Consent"; William C. Wadland et al., "Recruitment in a Primary Care Trial on Smoking Cessation," in Family Medicine 22, no. 3 (May-June 1990): 201-204; Batelle Technology Partnership Practice, "Biopharmaceutical Industry-Sponsored Clinical Trials"; Sertkaya et al., "Key Cost Drivers of Pharmaceutical Clinical Trials"; CenterWatch Staff, "MediciGlobal Finds Fewer Trial Dropouts Among Participants Who Actively Pursue Enrollment Versus Those Recruited," CenterWatch, May 18, 2015, https://www.centerwatch.com/articles/16609; Georg Kemmler et al., "Dropout Rates in Placebo-Controlled and Active-Control Clinical Trials of Antipsychotic Drugs: A Meta-Analysis," in Archives of General Psychiatry 62, no. 12 (December 2005): 1305-1312, https://doi.org/10.1001/archpsyc.62.12.1305.

20. Jennifer H. Lingler et al., "Perceived Research Burden Assessment (PeRBA): Instrument Development and Psychometric Evaluation," in Journal of Empirical Research on Hum Research Ethics 9, no. 4 (2014): 46–49, https://doi.org10.1177/1556264614545037; Connie M. Ulrich et al., "Development and Preliminary Testing of the Perceived Benefit and Burden Scales for Cancer Clinical Trial Participation," in Journal of Empirical Research on Hum Research Ethics 13, no. 3 (2018): 230–238, https://doi.org/10.1177/1556264618764730.

21. Kenneth Getz et al., "Assessing Patient Participation Burden Based on Protocol Design Characteristics," in Therapeutic Innovation & Regulatory Science, August 2019, https://doi.org/10.1177/2168479019867284; Zachary Smith et al., "Enhancing the Measure of Participation Burden in Protocol Design to Incorporate Logistics, Lifestyle, and Demographic Characteristics," in Therapeutic Innovation & Regulatory Science 55, no. 6 (November 2021): 1239-1249, https://doi.org/10.1007/s43441-021-00336-2.

22. Smith et al., "Enhancing the Measure."

23. Christine Moro et al., "The Effectiveness of Virtual and Augmented Reality in Health Sciences and Medical Anatomy," in Anatomical Sciences Education 10, no. 6 (2017): 549–559, https://doi.org/10.1002/ase.1696.

24. Andreas A. J. Wismeijer and Ad J. J. M. Vingerhoets, "The Use of Virtual Reality and Audiovisual Eyeglass Systems as Adjunct Analgesic Techniques: A Review of the Literature," in Annals of Behavioral Medicine 30, no. 3 (2005): 268–278, https://doi.org/10.1207/s15324796abm3003_11.

25. ZS VITA Virtual Reality Solution, 2020.

26. Fan Gao et al., "Why Decentralized Clinical Trials Are the Way of the Future," Applied Clinical Trials, April 5, 2021, https://www.appliedclinicaltrialsonline.com/view/why-decentralized-clinical-trials-are-the-way-of-the-future.

27. Eric Smalley, "Clinical Trials Go Virtual, Big Pharma Dives In," in Nature Biotechnology 36, no. 7 (2018): 561–562, https://doi.org/10.1038/nbt0718-561.

28. John A. Spertus et al., "Novel Trial Design: CHIEF-HF," in Circulation: Heart Failure 14, no. 3 (2021): e007767, https://doi.org/10.1161/circheartfailure.120.007767.

29. Rachel Arthur, "Inside the Pfizer/BioNTech COVID-19 Vaccine Trial: 'We Knew the World Was Watching and Waiting for Results,' " BioPharma Reporter, March 3, 2021, https://www.biopharma-reporter.com/article/2021/03/03/inside-the-pfizer-biontech-covid-19-vaccine-trial-insights-on-speed-agility-and-digital-development.

30.   Arthur, "Pfizer/BioNTech COVID-19 Vaccine Trial."

31.   Gao et al., "Decentralized Clinical Trials Are the Way."

32.   ICON, "What Does the Patient Want?" 2021, https://www.iconplc.com/insights/
       patient-centricity/patient-voice-survey-decentralised-and-hybrid-trials/.

33.   FDA, "Drug Trials Snapshots," April 9, 2021, https://www.fda.gov/drugs/
       drug-approvals-and-databases/drug-trials-snapshots.

34.   FDA, "Drug Trials Snapshots."

35.   Luc Valiquette, Francesco Montorsi and Stephen Auerbach, "Vardenafil
       Demonstrates First-Dose Success and Reliability of Penetration and Maintenance
       of Erection in Men with Erectile Dysfunction—RELY-II," in Canadian Urological
       Association Journal 2, no. 3 (2008): 187-195, https://doi.org/10.5489/cuaj.590.

36.   "LEVITRA (vardenafil HCl) Tablets," FDA, accessed July 30, 2021, https://www.
       accessdata.fda.gov/drugsatfda_docs/label/2003/21400_levitra_lbl.pdf.

37.   PhRMA, "PhRMA Announces First-Ever, Industry-Wide Principles on Clinical Trial
       Diversity," PhRMA, November 17, 2020, https://www.phrma.org/en/press-release/
       phrma-announces-first-ever-industry-wide-principles-on-clinical-trial-diversity.

38.   American Society of Clinical Oncology (ASCO), "Improving Diversity in Clinical
       Trial Participation," October 2020, https://www.asco.org/sites/new-www.asco.
       org/files/content-files/advocacy-and-policy/documents/2020-ctdiv-brief.pdf;
       Society for Clinical Research Sites (SCRS), "The SCRS Diversity Site Assessment
       Tool (DSAT)," October 2020, https://myscrs.org/downloads/download-id/13012/.

39.   Center for Drug Evaluation and Research (CDER) and Center for Biologics
       Evaluation and Research (CBER), "Enhancing the Diversity of Clinical Trial
       Populations—Eligibility Criteria, Enrollment Practices, and Trial Designs," FDA,
       November, 2020, https://www.fda.gov/media/127712/download.

40.   FDA, "Clinical Trial Diversity," July 23, 2021, https://www.fda.gov/consumers/
       minority-health-and-health-equity/clinical-trial-diversity.

41.   Office of Minority Health, "Clinical Trial Diversity Stakeholder Communications
       Toolkit," FDA, June, 2016, https://www.fda.gov/media/98497/download.

42.   FDA, "2015-2019 Drug Trials Snapshots: Summary Report," November, 2020,
       https://www.fda.gov/media/143592/download.

43. ASCO, "Improving Diversity in Clinical Trial Participation"; Beatrice Huang et al., "Strategies for Recruitment and Retention of Underrepresented Populations with Chronic Obstructive Pulmonary Disease for a Clinical Trial," in BMC Medical Research Methodology 19, no. 1 (2019): 39, https://doi.org/10.1186/s12874-019-0679-y; Joseph P. Williams, "From Tuskegee to a COVID Vaccine: Diversity and Racism are Hurdles in Drug Trials," U.S. News & World Report, November 19, 2020, https://www.usnews.com/news/health-news/articles/2020-11-19/from-tuskegee-to-covid-diversity-racism-are-hurdles-in-drug-trials.

44. David Dodick et al., "Vancouver Declaration on Global Headache Patient Advocacy 2018," in Cephalalgia 38, no. 13 (2018): 1899–1909, https://doi.org/10.1177/0333102418781644; International Headache Society and Global Patient Advocacy Coalition, "Who We Are," 2021, www.ihs-gpac.org.

45. David W. Dodick et al., "Vancouver Declaration II on Global Headache Patient Advocacy 2019," in Cephalalgia 40, no. 10 (2020): 1017–1025, https://doi.org/10.1177/0333102420921162.

46. Pfizer Link, Pfizer, 2021, https://www.pfizerlink.com/home.

Chapter 7:
If You Launch It, They Will Come ... Or Will They?

Greg Fry and Emily Mandell

Emily's Experience Starting Out in Pharma

When I started working in healthcare consulting, my first project was to help a pharmaceutical company identify appropriate patients for a new drug. I was young, eager and, frankly, floored! Why was I, a newly minted business major, tasked with something so important? Shouldn't a decision like that be left up to medical professionals, and why didn't the company already know the patient population most in need of its product?

If the manufacturer of a product has a hard time figuring out which patients are right for a specific drug, imagine how much harder it is for a patient to sort through all the information available about multiple diseases, treatment options and brands! The amount of information any individual or even any medical society has to process and act on is overwhelming. While some diagnoses are clear, others are incredibly complex. Some symptoms are easily identifiable, while others seem like they might just be "part of aging," "in your head" or "only a phase." (I've interviewed hundreds of women who report this in women's health and have tears in their eyes describing the frustration of not getting an answer or not being taken seriously, even when they know what condition they have.) The benefits and drawbacks of receiving some treatments are straightforward and well established, but, for novel, game-changing medications and therapies, the value is not always clear to the patients who will need to undergo the treatments and then pay for them. There are hundreds of conditions for which there is very little ongoing medical education and even a lack of key opinion leaders, as physicians tend to focus on areas in which there is proven science. While physicians can play a role in educating patients about complex conditions or new therapies, they often struggle to keep up with all the new developments themselves.

Helping a patient find and pursue the right medical care is an all-hands-on-deck endeavor, and life sciences companies have a critical role to play. Over the course of my career, I observed that, when faced with a therapeutic area that has low diagnosis rates, low treatment rates or for which there are novel and unfamiliar treatment paradigms, physicians and their patients need help. Life sciences companies often invest in physician education and awareness, but, in a market that's not yet established, it's not enough to stop there. Patients, caregivers, advocacy groups and physician organizations all need to be engaged to establish and develop a market so patients can receive timely diagnosis and treatment. I now see what my fresh-out-of-business-school self could not: that successful market shaping is truly critical to help patients get the right care. If done well, patient outcomes are better. If not, patients continue to swirl in the healthcare system, suffering for years without a clear diagnosis or without awareness of treatment options that can improve their lives.

In this chapter, we share critical success factors for three common market development needs we've observed across the industry: navigating a complex diagnosis, legitimizing an underdiagnosed health issue and communicating the value of novel treatments. We'll provide examples of companies that have handled the launch of a new product well by achieving success in these market development objectives, as well as an analysis of the pitfalls to avoid.

"I Need an Accurate Diagnosis Sooner": Navigating a Complex Diagnosis

Lindsey's Story

What would cause a healthy, typically developing eight-month-old baby to have a prolonged seizure? Would she have more seizures? And, if so, was there anything that could be done to prevent them?

These questions raced through the minds of James and Kate, two parents we interviewed about their daughter Lindsey's sudden development of seizures and the harrowing healthcare journey that ensued. "It was the first seizure I had ever witnessed, and I felt like I knew absolutely nothing about seizures, other than the warnings on TV shows and movies about flashing lights," said James. "After the first seizure, we were so scared and confused but also motivated. We were on a mission to understand why."

After a visit to the pediatrician, there was some relief. "The doctor explained febrile seizures, or convulsions in a child caused by a fever, were not uncommon. She explained it is often an isolated incident, and so we left the office thinking it would probably never happen again," Kate shared. "The fear and anxiety we had experienced started to subside, and life felt normal again. Until it wasn't."

After another prolonged seizure, the family visited a pediatric neurologist. The neurologist believed the second seizure was also febrile, and EEG testing returned normal results. "The doctor's perspective aligned with all of the information we could find online. There were tons of articles and parents sharing stories of children who had seizures brought on by high fevers as a baby who simply grew out of it," added Kate.

A few weeks later, Lindsey had another seizure that didn't stop, even after EMTs administered rescue medication, and she was airlifted to the hospital. James recalled: "Seeing about 15 doctors surrounding my baby is seared into my memory. My body went numb and I couldn't stop asking why. Why did these long seizures keep happening?"

In the days and months ahead, the parents continued to read information online, but most of it was what they already knew—babies who have febrile seizures often grow out of it. But the most recent seizure was different. It wasn't short, and it was extremely difficult to stop. James explained:

> *Thankfully, we were at a renowned children's hospital, and, after several neurologists discussed our case, we had genetic testing done, which eventually led to the diagnosis of Dravet syndrome. None of the doctors we saw in our five days in the hospital mentioned Dravet syndrome or explained why and how the results from the genetic test could be so crucial to our daughter's diagnosis. The doctor talked about how more people have epilepsy than we may realize, and that many of those patients have complete seizure control. It felt like we could still live a somewhat typical life, or at least that was the hope powering us through it all.*

When the family received the genetic results, they learned there was a genetic mutation in Lindsey's SCN1A gene, which is a key cause of Dravet syndrome. In this case, Lindsey received a correct diagnosis several months after the first seizure. Although it felt like an unbearably long time to James and Kate as they agonized about how to help their daughter, it is quite short relative to many other rare or difficult-to-diagnose diseases. For Dravet syndrome, and many other rare diseases, the path to diagnosis is too often measured in years, not months.

Although the genetic mutation was specific, it was difficult for the family to interpret exactly what this news meant. The neurologist suggested they not search for more information online, because they would find some "scary stuff." James stated: "I remember hanging up the phone and immediately rushing to the computer. The first words I saw after searching were 'a rare, catastrophic, lifelong form of epilepsy.' Again, I felt numbness throughout my body. I couldn't believe what was happening."

While that phone call with the doctor removed the uncertainty of lacking a diagnosis, simply hearing the test results and name of the disease was just the beginning. The parents kept reading everything they could find: information on prognosis, life expectancy and epilepsy medications from patient stories, support group notes and academic research papers. Kate described their frantic search for any and all information:

> *At the time of Lindsey's diagnosis, there were no approved treatments. The data on life expectancy was murky, but an estimated one in five children did not survive into adulthood. It was all so overwhelming and scary, but I couldn't stop. I was awake most nights staring at the baby monitor anyway. I needed*

to digest as much information as I could find. As we tried to process such a serious diagnosis, it felt like it was up to us to gather as much information as possible and plan our path forward.

Receiving a correct diagnosis for a disease can be an emotional, lengthy and winding journey. For many patients, an accurate diagnosis may never happen at all. Lindsey's story is not unique, as patients with a rare disease often visit a multitude of doctors and lack clear answers or receive conflicting opinions about their condition. Some doctors mistake their symptoms for more common conditions, while others inadvertently dismiss the possibility of a rare disease or may be unaware that the disease exists. It is not uncommon for patients to receive multiple misdiagnoses, spread out over many years, which can lead to discouragement about the likelihood of ever getting help and achieving symptom relief and skepticism about the healthcare system.

Critical Success Factors

While it's true that doctors are ultimately providing the formal diagnosis, life sciences organizations can play a key role in ensuring that patients get to the right diagnosis. Developing a deep understanding of the drivers and barriers along the patient journey is an initial step to helping more undiagnosed or misdiagnosed patients get to an accurate diagnosis sooner. From there, pharma can:

1. Increase disease awareness and diagnostic testing through collaboration with doctors, patients, patient advocacy groups and industry partners

2. Leverage real-world data and analytics to predict where there may be pockets of undiagnosed patients and identify the doctors they may be visiting to share information accordingly

The first critical success factor to help patients get an accurate diagnosis is increasing disease awareness. Pfizer's campaign to raise awareness about a rare and fatal heart disease called transthyretin amyloid cardiomyopathy (ATTR-CM) serves as a great example of how pharma companies can get information out to both doctors and patients about particular conditions and available treatments. In 2019, Pfizer received approval for Vyndaqel and Vyndamax, drug therapies to treat ATTR-CM.[1] The diagnosis of ATTR-CM is typically done through an expensive and invasive heart biopsy, leading to underdiagnosis of the condition. Walt, a patient diagnosed with wild-type ATTR-CM, reflected on his path to diagnosis, noting that, despite experiencing many of the early indicators of ATTR-CM, he didn't receive a diagnosis until 11 years after he first began experiencing symptoms. He expressed his hope that, even with a continuing lack of awareness about the condition, more physicians will begin to recognize the signs and symptoms so patients can receive the care they need earlier. Recognizing the need for increased awareness of the condition, Pfizer launched Suspect and Detect, a campaign to help doctors identify the disease and learn about tools for diagnosis.[2] The company also created Get the Message, an informational initiative that aimed to increase awareness among patients.[3] Pfizer estimates there are about 100,000 ATTR-CM patients in the U.S. and stated that the awareness campaigns have helped drive about 9,000 diagnoses.[4]

Increasing disease awareness is a significant mutual goal for both pharma and patient advocacy organizations. Patient advocacy groups can help co-develop and inform disease education content, ensuring it fills an unmet need. In addition, when advocacy groups collaborate in the content planning and development process, they can support the dissemination of resources and enable communication, like alerting patients about opportunities to participate in clinical trials. As one notable example, Pfizer collaborated with the Sickle Cell Disease Association of America to launch oneSCDvoice, a website developed with help from patients, advocates and medical experts.[5] It includes trusted resources, a smart social wall where patients can engage in conversation and a clinical trial educator tool that focuses on the importance of clinical trials to advance drug development.

Pharma companies can also take meaningful action to increase patient access to diagnostic testing. In Lindsey's story, when a team of neurologists conferred to discuss the pattern of Lindsey's seizures and other circumstances, their knowledge of Dravet syndrome led them to order a genetic epilepsy panel. It was these test results that allowed James and Kate to finally get the answers that had eluded them. Pharma can create opportunities to help patients and their families arrive at the right answers sooner. We've seen examples of industry collaboration where manufacturers have partnered to sponsor diagnostic testing for patients. Behind the Seizure is a free, 180-gene panel testing program for children sponsored by a group of pharma companies, including BioMarin, Stoke Therapeutics and Xenon Pharmaceuticals.[6] Several thousand children have been tested since the program began in 2017. Robert Nussbaum, chief medical officer at Invitae, a founding member of the initiative, said: "I see this as an absolute paradigm shift in genetics. It's a partnership that helps everybody. Because it's being sponsored, the physician essentially has no hassles to get the test done. There's no insurance billing, no co-pay for the patient. It's a seamless and effortless channel to get the genetic testing done." Biogen and Invitae also teamed up to lead another such initiative, designed to increase access to the SMA STAT test, a rapid-turnaround genetic test for spinal muscular atrophy (SMA) that doctors in the U.S. can offer to patients at no charge.[7] The test has reduced time to confirm a diagnosis of SMA by as much as 21 days, an incredibly valuable improvement for patients, as early diagnosis and treatment of SMA can slow disease progression.

For rare diseases without a strong advocacy organization or existing patient network, the level of difficulty in patient engagement and communications can be a major barrier. The second critical success factor we've identified is patient prediction using real-world data, which can associate patients with the physicians likely treating them to better target disease awareness efforts. The size of the patient population for which a novel treatment could have a positive impact may be unknown or undefined, as, depending on the disease, most patients may not yet have been diagnosed. In this case, pharma organizations can leverage data and analytics to look for patterns in diagnosed patients' health history and use the results to predict which touch points, specialists, tests and comorbidities may indicate a potential, undiagnosed patient. This data can help uncover the drivers that lead to patients receiving an accurate diagnosis as well as the barriers preventing diagnosis or leading to misdiagnosis. It can also enable better forecasting of the potential market size for a new treatment and allow for the creation of potential patient profiles across demographic, geographic and physician data dimensions, which can inform ideal clinical trial locations and future targeting.

"I Have Symptoms That Are Worth Treating": Legitimizing the Health Issue

Martha's Story

When Martha turned 60, she started to experience a dull, widespread aching pain all over her body. She had recently gone through a divorce, so she chalked the pain up to the significant stress she'd been under and tried to ignore it, hoping it would pass. It didn't. In the months that followed, the pain increased. She could no longer reach for a hanger in her closet without wincing. She used to be "go go go," but now she got so tired after doing one small activity that she found herself canceling plans all the time. When she did see people, her pain was so bad she had to refuse a hug.

Martha saw her general practitioner at her annual visit and described her symptoms. He attributed them to "aging and stress" and prescribed a muscle relaxer. Three months later, Martha's pain started to change. There was now some burning and tingling in addition to the dull ache, so Martha's friends told her to a see a neurologist. The neurologist put her through a series of tests, but, when the results were inconclusive, he told her the symptoms would likely resolve on their own and sent her on her way. Over the next two years, Martha saw six different doctors, ranging from another neurologist, to rheumatologists, to pain specialists. Meanwhile, the psychological effects of her pain and the limitations it imposed on her life took a toll emotionally. Not only did she find no symptom relief, but one doctor told her "it was all in her head," and another dismissed her experience as a result of depression and suggested she see a therapist.

One day, while watching TV, she saw a commercial where a woman described symptoms very similar to hers and called it "fibromyalgia." Martha immediately searched for the word online and came across a group chat among people who complained of the exact same symptoms. Their experiences were almost word for word what she had been describing to her doctors. She attested: "The relief I felt when I read those words is something I will never forget. I was not crazy—whatever this is, this is real." Martha went to see a new doctor recommended by a woman in the group. The new doctor eventually diagnosed Martha with fibromyalgia and prescribed Lyrica. This was the turning point in her story: "Little by little, I got my life back. On one hand, I had validation of what I had been experiencing. On the other, I genuinely had pain relief. It's amazing how much happier and more energetic you can feel when you're not living in constant chronic pain."

Critical Success Factors

Fibromyalgia is just one example of a condition that has had to be "legitimized" by the medical community for patients to get the right care. Depression, endometriosis and even chronic migraine all went through this evolution before patients received the care they desperately needed. We've identified two actions life sciences companies can take to speed up this process of legitimization:

1. Invest in a multi-pronged strategy to build awareness among patients and doctors, normalize the condition and help match patients with a knowledgeable doctor

2. Address dialogue gaps between doctors and patients, such that a patient's presentation of symptoms triggers the physician to think about an underdiagnosed condition, particularly in diseases that afflict groups that are underrepresented in medical research, such as women and people of color

In Martha's story, television and social channels eventually led her to the right doctor. Her breakthrough happened almost a year after companies such as Pfizer and Eli Lilly aired TV commercials for fibromyalgia medications like Lyrica and Cymbalta. So, what took so long? Awareness building among patients so that they feel empowered to go to a specialist and ask the right questions is important, but pharma won't move the needle unless doctors know what to do once the patient gets there. For a condition like fibromyalgia, there are 200,000 doctors across six specialties who could be seeing patients with those symptoms—so how can companies focus their efforts? The answer is to build a multi-pronged strategy: invest in getting patients to the right doctors who can recognize the symptoms as presented to them and are knowledgeable about treatment options, while also encouraging patients who have received successful treatment to refer others. Without the linkage between those two prongs, the effort can fail, which means patients will continue to swirl in the system without answers.

As an example of this dual approach in action, companies have used telehealth to facilitate patients' ability to find a doctor who is willing to give a condition the attention it deserves. Ironwood Pharmaceuticals and AbbVie were among the first companies to directly partner with a telehealth company to enable care for patients suffering from irritable bowel syndrome (IBS). The pharma organizations engaged with patients through digital channels and connected them with a telehealth provider so the patients could quickly and seamlessly speak to a doctor about their IBS symptoms and receive a diagnosis and treatment. The physicians who contracted with the telehealth company were already educated on the symptoms of IBS, how they differ from other conditions and what treatment options could be considered. The connection this telehealth strategy enabled between patients who needed care and doctors who were equipped to provide it is a great illustration of how the multipronged approach leads to better patient outcomes.

Figure 7-1: Prompt for Telehealth Treatment on Linzess.com, a Website for an IBS Treatment[8]

One of the most critical factors in a successful market development endeavor is addressing the dialogue gaps between doctors and patients. Dialogue gaps occur when a patient explains a particular set of symptoms but the doctor isn't triggered to investigate the associated condition. This is one of the major reasons for a delay in diagnosis: a genuine miscommunication. Endometriosis is a classic example of this. Prior to AbbVie's launch of Orlissa, endometriosis was a condition that could only be definitively diagnosed through a laparoscopic surgery or "empirically" diagnosed through a symptom assessment, which required ruling out several other conditions. Many women reported that, despite having described their symptoms to their gynecologist, it took years to get an answer about why they were experiencing severe abdominal pain and bleeding. Six months before AbbVie launched Orlissa, the company developed a year-long unbranded campaign, deployed through television commercials, a website and social media, called Speak Endo. The campaign aimed to give women tools to effectively communicate about their symptoms with their doctor. It included a discussion guide, which used the S.P.E.A.K. framework to encourage patients to forthrightly describe their symptoms and press for treatment.

Figure 7-2: Discussion Guide Tools for Endometriosis from AbbVie[9]

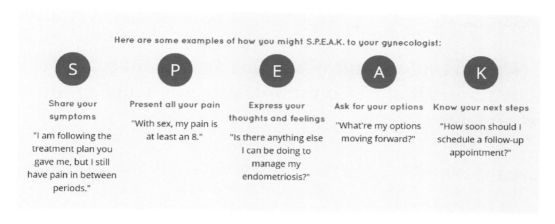

Marianne Sutcliffe, vice president of women's health at AbbVie, indicated that the health outcomes the company hoped to see from an unbranded campaign included promoting dialogue and awareness around this women's health disease and providing patients and doctors doing their best to treat it with new tools. She described this as a potential revolution in the dialogue around a disease which affects many of those around us. Dawn Carlson, AbbVie's vice president of general medicine, added her feeling that, even if the only effect of the campaign would be to enable greater awareness and dialogue, that would be a worthy outcome.[10]

Figure 7-3: Direct-to-Consumer Advertisement Encouraging Women to Use Specific Words with Doctors[11]

Since the launch of the campaign, several social hubs for women online have referenced it as a benefit. On bloominuterus.com, an endometriosis advocacy blog, one woman who had waited 20 years for a diagnosis expressed her belief that seeing a commercial like this one would have sped up the process considerably and could be of great help in getting other women to begin seeking answers.[12]

Equipping patients to speak up for themselves and insist to their doctors that their symptoms are worth treating (in a way that is credible and well supported by science) is critical to ensuring that those discussions lead to better patient care.

"I Need to Understand What This Treatment Is and Its Benefits and Risks": Communicating the Value of Novel Treatments

Suzanne's Story

Suzanne lived a very active lifestyle, running marathons and traveling around the world.[13] One day at the beach, Suzanne noticed her shoe kept slipping off. Soon after, she observed that her leg was shivering while seated at her computer. When her husband saw she was dragging her feet and expressed concern, Suzanne decided to mention these symptoms to her doctor at her next annual exam. The doctor told her it was probably a pinched nerve. However, after a subsequent visit to a neurologist for further evaluation, she was diagnosed with Parkinson's disease.

After her diagnosis, Suzanne shared that she went into "an emotional tailspin for about a year." While she strove to stay active as much as possible, the disease progressed, and her medicine was not consistently effective. Eventually, Suzanne could barely walk and decided that she had to find out if there were other options. She researched online and read about deep brain stimulation (DBS), a surgical procedure to address movement disorders that involves placing a medical device in the brain that sends out electrical impulses. However, when Suzanne asked her doctor about DBS, he dismissed it as being too drastic.

Suzanne proceeded to try multiple treatment options, but they didn't work and had adverse effects. She indicated her frustration at her inability to find a viable solution, having spent seven years waiting for an effective treatment but facing side effects with each new launch. She felt exasperated with this passing of time, vocalizing her disappointment at the inability to find a solution that worked for her. Suzanne noted that her doctor didn't seem comfortable talking to her about DBS, but she kept researching more about it online. Based on the information she was able to find, she ultimately decided to pursue DBS. She and her husband were thrilled with the results of the procedure. Suzanne attested that she no longer worries about whether her treatment will work. She's sleeping better, able to hike and, overall, much happier.

Suzanne expressed that she doesn't "understand why more doctors don't encourage DBS for their patients with Parkinson's disease," noting that, in her experience, many older people don't know anything about it, having never discussed it with their doctors. Suzanne and her husband readily share her positive experience with DBS with other patients. When Suzanne's husband detailed the positive changes he's seen in her life to a young, recently diagnosed patient, he recalled that the man began to cry on the phone. Suzanne's husband said the young man was crying tears of hope and happiness, overwhelmed at the prospect of being able to get his life back.

Critical Success Factors

As science advances rapidly and new treatment options are coming to market, patients and doctors alike may be hesitant to embrace therapies with which they have little familiarity or experience. But it's inappropriate and ineffective to prevent patients from having the opportunity to make an informed choice about whether they want to embrace a novel therapeutic option. Patient centricity in practice means empowering patients to learn about and evaluate options for their care. To do their part, pharma companies must acknowledge the hurdles complex treatments may face to "break through" with patients and doctors and find ways to provide trustworthy information to key stakeholders. When there is low acknowledgment of potentially transformative treatment benefits compared to current options, and patients and doctors feel they have limited ability to make informed decisions, companies can empower patients by:

1. Developing evidence-based tools and communication materials to help doctors educate and refer patients to appropriate treatment options

2. Facilitating the sharing of real patient stories, especially patient to patient

According to the CARE Monitor study, a high percentage of patients are reluctant to undergo DBS, despite it being one of the major breakthroughs in the treatment of Parkinson's disease.[14] Typically, a patient is preselected as a candidate for DBS by their neurologist, who refers them to a specialized DBS center, where specialists confirm whether surgery is appropriate based on a comprehensive diagnostic assessment. However, as highlighted in our patient story, some doctors may be reluctant to recommend DBS. Although Suzanne conducted extensive research on her own and felt confident in her ability to pursue this option, other patients can be more hesitant to take that initiative.

The CARE Monitor study shows that the decision to refer is difficult for many neurologists because they are not certain of what types of patients are the best suited to benefit. In the study, only 48 to 55% of the patients initially referred to DBS centers were assessed as appropriate candidates for surgery. Furthermore, even when the investigators introduced tools in the study materials to aid neurologists in preselecting patients, only 28% of patients with a referral actually went to the DBS center, mainly due to their reluctance to undergo surgery. The report states: "The study concluded that the consultation visit where information on DBS was provided played a key role in the patients' decision, yet mentioning negative aspects of DBS during the visit, such as the risks and complications of the surgery or side-effects of the stimulation, had no negative effect on patients' approval."[15] The study's authors indicated that doctors should not avoid discussing the risks of DBS or its possible side-effects with patients, because, interestingly, patients reported that having knowledge of the potential downsides of the treatment didn't deter them. Many actually felt that their initial fears were worse than the reality their neurologists described.

While doctors do their best to explain complex treatment options to patients, many questions naturally arise during and after the consultation. The DBS Select project aims to address such questions.[16] This innovative, interactive patient education platform is the result of a collaboration between KU Leven, Health House and University of Cologne in 2019, supported by neurologists, neurosurgeons and patients. Specialists can refer patients to the platform, where they can follow a storyline that offers information about DBS in an interactive way, leveraging patient testimonials about their experiences before and after surgery. For patients considering pursuing DBS, the platform offers an honest picture of what went well for others and where the reality diverged from their expectations. This tool facilitates communication between doctors and patients, as doctors can feel confident directing patients to the platform to access detailed, scientifically rigorous information presented in an accessible and engaging format that patients can easily comprehend.

Patient stories are also central to the website content of Medtronic and Boston Scientific,[17] both of which offer medical devices for DBS therapy. The websites highlight patient testimonials through both videos and text, bringing to life the considerations patients weighed when making their decisions. Medtronic provides the ability to "talk to someone who understands" and "connect with people who have had life-changing experiences with Medtronic DBS therapy."[18] Patients can request a call on the website and have a frank conversation with someone who has walked in their shoes. Brain surgery can be very frightening for patients and challenging for doctors to discuss, so content detailing treatment value from the patient perspective, including plainly stated benefits and risks, is essential to adopt. Making doctors aware that this content exists can also aid them in conversations with patients, as they can refer patients to hear what others like them have experienced.

Among the treatments that have seen recent progress, cell and gene therapies (CGT) are some of the most notable and promising. However, due to their novelty and unfamiliarity, manufacturers have noticed both patient and physician hesitancy in their adoption. Nicolas Garnier, director of patient advocacy for rare disease at Pfizer, indicated that discussing gene therapies with practitioners and doctors who don't specialize can be challenging, as reports have shown that general practitioners don't entirely understand gene therapy and how it works, leaving a clear area of opportunity for further education. Garnier further emphasized the difficulties doctors face in not knowing which patients are eligible, which specialists to refer patients to and how.[19] Kelly Hosmer, director of global marketing for bluebird bio, acknowledged that her firm, as a leader in the field, has the opportunity to help key stakeholders understand the opportunities and benefits as well as the background behind the technologies.[20] She further expressed her belief that the choice of a particular therapy is a crucial decision in the treatment process, and educating and addressing misconceptions can open up these potentially curative treatments to patients. Imagine how heavily the decision weighs on the parent of a child with a rare genetic disease and how valuable evidence-based information can be in that decision.

The examples in this chapter illustrate the importance of putting knowledge and power into patients' hands but also working with doctors to facilitate the right care. Taking a patient-centric approach to market development means providing patients with the knowledge they need to get to the right diagnosis, empowering them to insist that their symptoms are legitimate and worth treating, and offering them reliable, accessible information so they can evaluate whether a novel treatment is right for them.

Key Takeaways

- Getting patients the right care requires an "all-hands-on-deck" approach, and life science companies play a critical role in identifying market development needs, helping patients get to the right diagnosis and promoting novel treatment paradigms.

- To reduce delays in diagnosis, pharma has the power to leverage data, analytics and advocacy group engagement to enable patient identification through increased disease awareness and access to diagnostic testing.

- To prevent delays in willingness to treat, companies can invest in broad awareness-building among consumers and doctors and address dialogue gaps by equipping patients with the tools to communicate why their symptoms are worthy of intervention.

- For conditions with complex and novel treatments, it's crucial to empower patients and doctors to make informed choices by developing evidence-based tools and communication materials and facilitating the sharing of real patient experiences, especially between patients.

Acknowledgments

The authors would like to thank the following people for their contributions and input in writing this chapter: Katie Blodgett, Hensley Evans, Emily Kremens, Judith Kulich, Jay Lichtenstein, Lauren Mosadeghi, John Ryan, Sharon Suchotliff, Michael Thomas and Cecilia Zvosec.

Endnotes

1. Pfizer, "Delivering First-in-Class Science and Resources to Help People with a Rare, Underdiagnosed Heart Disease," accessed July 5, 2021, https://www.pfizer.com/sites/default/files/investors/financial_reports/annual_reports/2019/our-bold-moves/deliver-first-in-class-science/delivering-first-in-class-science-and-resources/index.html.

2. Suspect and Detect, Pfizer, January 2021, https://www.suspectanddetect.com/.

3. Get the Message, Pfizer, December 2020, https://www.yourheartsmessage.com/.

4. Eric Sagonowsky, "Pfizer's Heart Med Vyndaqel Off and Running Thanks to Diagnosis Push: Execs," Fierce Pharma, January 28, 2020, https://www.fiercepharma.com/pharma/pfizer-s-vyndaqel-off-and-running-9-diagnosis-rate-to-end-2019-execs.

5. Larry Luxner, "Sickle Cell Groups, Pfizer Work to Bring African-Americans into Clinical Trials," Sickle Cell Disease News, May 3, 2018, https://sicklecellanemianews.com/2018/05/03/pfizer-sickle-cell-groups-work-bring-african-americans-clinical-trials/.

6. Beth Snyder Bulik, "Biogen, PTC and More Back BioMarin's Genetic Seizure Testing Effort for Kids," Fierce Pharma, January 31, 2020, https://www.fiercepharma.com/marketing/more-pharma-sponsors-join-biomarin-and-invitae-genetic-testing-program-for-children.

7. "Biogen and Invitae Announce Availability of Rapid Results in Genetic Testing Program for Spinal Muscular Atrophy (SMA) to Improve Speed of Diagnosis for Patients," Globe Newswire, August 20, 2019, https://www.globenewswire.com/news-release/2019/08/20/1904049/0/en/biogen-and-invitae-announce-availability-of-rapid-results-in-genetic-testing-program-for-spinal-muscular-atrophy-sma-to-improve-speed-of-diagnosis-for-patients.html.

8. Prompt for Telehealth Treatment, http://www.linzess.com/.

9. Speak Endo, https://www.speakendo.com/.

10. AbbVie, "Endometriosis Treatment Is Grounded in Science, Driven by Commitment," September 11, 2018, https://stories.abbvie.com/stories/endometriosis-treatment-is-grounded-in-science-driven-by-commitment-2.htm.

11. Speak Endo, https://www.speakendo.com/.

12. "Have You Seen the Endometriosis Commercials on TV?" Bloomin' Uterus, February 3, 2018, https://bloominuterus.com/2018/02/03/have-you-seen-the-endometriosis-commercials-on-tv/.

13. "Punching Back at PD: Suzanne's DBS Story," Boston Scientific, 2021, https://www.dbsandme.com/en/dbs-therapy-success/dbs-patient-stories.html#suzannestory.

14. Lars Dinkelbach et al., "How to Improve Patient Education on Deep Brain Stimulation in Parkinson's Disease: The CARE Monitor Study," in BMC Neurology 17, no. 1 (February 2017): 36, https://doi.org/10.1186/s12883-017-0820-7.

15. Dinkelbach et al., "How to Improve Patient Education."

16. "Launch of a Patient Education Platform on Deep Brain Stimulation," EIT Health, September 19, 2019, https://eithealth.eu/news-article/launch-of-a-patient-education-platform-on-deep-brain-stimulation/.

17. DBSandMe, Boston Scientific, 2021, https://dbsandme.com/patientstories/.

18. "Karen and Jim's Story: DBS Therapy for Parkinson's Disease," Medtronic, accessed July 5, 2021, https://www.medtronic.com/us-en/patients/treatments-therapies/deep-brain-stimulation-parkinsons-disease/personal-stories/karen-and-jim.html.

19. Andrew Stone, "Breakthrough CGT Therapies are Coming Thick and Fast, Now Pharma Must Work on Multiple Fronts to Educate Non-Specialist Stakeholders About Their Exciting Possibilities," Reuters Events, September 16, 2020, https://www.reutersevents.com/pharma/patients-and-medical/complexity-clarity-cell-and-gene-therapy.

20. Stone, "Breakthrough CGT Therapies."

Chapter 8:
Activating and Reaching Patients in an Evolving Media Landscape[1]

Victoria Summers

In 2008, retired teacher Diane[2] was spending her newfound free time playing golf and volunteering. Then, blood tests for a minor foot surgery revealed that she had a chronic hepatitis C infection, and her relaxed mood quickly dissipated as anxiety about liver disease, cancer and eventual liver failure set in. She visited her physician and started a year-long course of Interferon, which, at the time, was the standard-of-care therapy for the disease. Unfortunately, the severe side effects—thinning hair, weight loss, nausea, vomiting, eczema and breathing problems—led her physician to halt all treatment. Diane learned of new medications for treating hepatitis C while watching TV, but she ignored the commercials at first because they reminded her of the terrible experiences she'd had on Interferon. However, as she continued to see ads in magazines and online when checking her Facebook page, her perspective began to shift: "I kept seeing these ads everywhere, and finally I just thought, 'Well, I might as well ask.' " She spoke to her physician about the new medications. Her physician explained that they had higher cure rates with far fewer side effects and initiated a two-month course of treatment with one of the new therapies. By the end of the treatment, Diane was cured.

Diane's story is a great example of how consumer messaging can help patients find treatments that improve their health. In 1997, the FDA issued guidance that allowed pharmaceutical companies to advertise products to consumers on all channels, including TV. Since that time, direct-to-consumer (DTC) ad spending in the U.S. has grown into a $6 billion dollar per year media industry, with an estimated $3.4 billion dollars per year spent on creative development. As you can see in Figure 8-1, TV ad spending has made up nearly 70% of pharma advertising budgets for the past several years.

Figure 8-1: Annual DTC Spend by Pharmaceutical Brands— Percentage of TV Spend Continues to Grow[3]

Annual spend in 2020 remained at $6.5B, with greater overall investment in TV

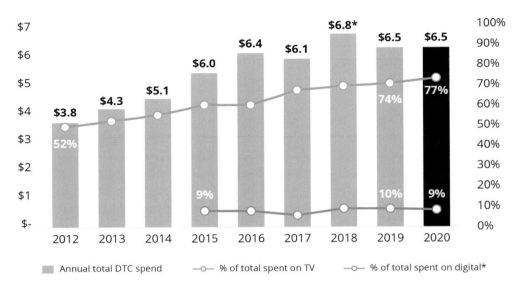

*Does not include programmatic spend

However, the tried-and-true formula of DTC broadcast TV and print is no longer the only way to reach patients. Consumers' increasing engagement with digital media has resulted in more activity online, as caregivers and patients seek out answers to their health questions instead of waiting for an appointment with a doctor. The COVID-19 pandemic's massive interruption of broadcast content, including live event coverage, has accelerated this trend toward on-demand digital content and streaming platforms, many of which have paid subscription models that allow consumers to opt out of advertising content.

As consumers are engaging in these new media channels at increasing rates, brand marketers are learning to think differently about how they reach patients. Pharma brands are turning to omnichannel strategies that integrate online and offline messaging to intersect consumers as they go about their day. A brand may place printed advertisements in magazines and doctors' offices that encourage patients to visit websites to find more information about treatment. Marketers are also tailoring digital content to consumers' online activity. For example, messages that appear while a consumer is searching for a particular treatment are different than those that appear while the consumer is searching for a disease term; a disease awareness ad may be served up to a consumer searching for a disease term, while a branded ad will be shown to a patient searching for a specific treatment. In this way, brands are creating a fuller, more personalized experience for patients. Using big data to drive digital messages, marketers are improving the way consumers get healthcare information—giving them the right messages, at the right time, in the right way.

Patient Insights: Improved Patient Outcomes Through Greater Understanding

"To engage anyone in a marketing message, you have to offer a solution to a problem they have," observed Rishad Tobaccowala, futurist and former chief strategy officer for Publicis Groupe, one of the top consumer media companies in the world and the largest health marketing agency network. People are grappling with a growing number of health problems as they live longer and contend with more chronic diseases than ever before. As discussed in Chapter 1, the advancements in pharmaceutical treatments for conditions that affect smaller patient populations (like specific types of cancer, rare conditions and genetic mutations), together with other advances in personalized medicine, mean patients have more complex information needs when seeking answers to their health questions. And rarely are patients managing just one condition—improved care also means people are living with an increasing number of comorbidities.

For a company wanting to raise awareness of a treatment or solution for a health condition, it's necessary to break through not only the clutter of advertising messages but also to connect with patients who have limited bandwidth as they try to manage multiple health issues while also going about their daily lives. Connecting with consumers in a meaningful way starts with a deep understanding of the drivers and barriers they face as they juggle their health priorities and the other demands on their time and energy. Consider, for example, Keshawn,[4] a computer programmer with psoriasis who's working to understand the nature of his autoimmune disorder and learning how to self-inject a new biologic treatment. Because he's focused on managing his psoriasis, he sometimes forgets to take his cholesterol medication. Controlling his high cholesterol feels like less of an immediate concern. Patients like Keshawn sometimes deprioritize serious but asymptomatic conditions and focus on conditions that cause more daily discomfort. As we discussed in Chapter 5, fully comprehending the patient experience means considering patients' total health as well as their environments, socioeconomic realities and mindsets to understand how to supply the right treatment information and empower them to take action.

Omnichannel Media Strategy and Channels: Reaching Patients Where They Are

Integrating messages and health information into patients' daily lives requires thinking about marketing differently—more personally. Omnichannel marketing and the growth of digital has enabled marketers to reach and engage patients at specific critical moments along their healthcare journeys.

The growth of digital has offset a decline in broadcast viewership. Pharma has traditionally relied on broadcast TV to connect with a wide number of patients and build awareness.

Years ago, the brands that were built by DTC TV had broad applicability across large patient populations. Heartburn, high cholesterol, migraine, allergies and other conditions had large patient populations that broadcast TV was effective in reaching. But that dynamic has shifted dramatically in recent years. Broadcast TV viewership has been steadily decreasing in every age demographic, except the 65 and over group, for the past several years (see Figure 8-2).

Figure 8-2: TV Viewership Is Declining in Each Age Group Except the 65+ Demographic[5]

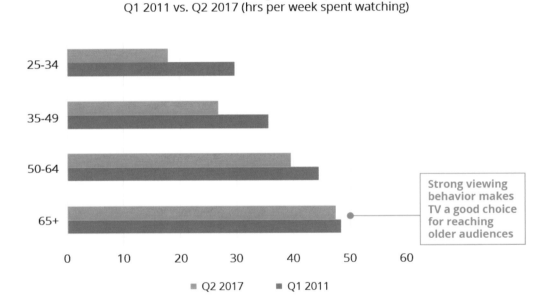

Traditional TV viewing trends by age group
Q1 2011 vs. Q2 2017 (hrs per week spent watching)

Strong viewing behavior makes TV a good choice for reaching older audiences

■ Q2 2017   ■ Q1 2011

At the same time, advances in treatments have brought new therapies to market that are often designed for smaller and younger patient populations. Specialty and oncology brands that are more expensive are still able to use TV to reach patients, because the opportunity to help one new patient balances the expense of reaching consumers who don't have the condition. Beyond those particular brands, though, more and more companies are moving to targeted, digital-driven omnichannel approaches, including social media, email, digital display advertising, and video and in-app mobile advertising. Rather than using TV to build awareness and then pull patients to a large, multi-page branded website, the focus is on getting content out to the digital and social platforms where patients are already engaging and then customizing the experience using AI and machine learning.

This multipronged strategy connects patients to the information they need to take the next step in their healthcare journeys. Tara[6] was dealing with a particularly bad ulcerative colitis flare-up just before her sister's wedding. She'd been noticing some advertising on social media that featured stories about people finding relief by using a type of medication called a "biologic." It sounded complicated, but Tara was ready to try something new. She found some information through WebMD and signed up on a brand's website for regular updates and information. It seemed she needed to talk to a specialist about her flare-ups, but she wasn't sure how to get to one. Did she ask her primary care doctor? Call her insurance company? Luckily, through the stream of emails she had signed up for on the brand website, she received information containing pointers on how to find the right doctor and what questions to ask. She was able to use this information to get a referral to a gastroenterologist in her town who was familiar with biologic treatments.

The growing emphasis on omnichannel marketing is starting to shift investment away from broadcast channels, like TV and print, and toward more targeted channels, like mobile, social and streaming video. "We spend more on social and digital than we do on television," explained Graham Goodrich, senior vice president of brand marketing for Biohaven. Goodrich directed the strategy for the launch of Biohaven's new migraine treatment, Nurtec, and said the company had discerned it was time to try out a new approach: "We see TV playing an important role to build overall awareness and brand integrity, but we realized we'd need to take a different approach to our consumer campaign." Goodrich focused on investing in digital channels, such as social media:

> Social is where patients are spending their time. What made it an obvious choice for us were the stories that happened on these platforms. Patients form informal communities where they find empathy and support. Their health problems are intense, and relief is transformational. With social, our strategy is to get out of the way and let patients talk about their experience.

Using a unique combination of social media influencer marketing, public relations, digital video, supported later by print and television ads, the Nurtec consumer campaign also connected patients with a telehealth option so patients could talk to a doctor immediately. Launched at brand approval, it was in market while the field force was still being prevented from reaching physicians due to COVID-19 restrictions. The patient-focused digital strategy enabled the brand to capture 50% market share in the first six months. Goodrich spoke about the difference Biohaven has been able to make in patients' lives: "We know from our research with patients that migraines make patients feel less than who they want to be. Our treatment allows them to live the life they always wanted to— what we want to do is help them share and amplify their experiences."

Evolution of Marketing Content

Customized Content

Omnichannel campaigns use a system of messages to tell bite-sized portions of a story over time. As consumers and patients interact with messages, automated, data-driven campaigns tailor the content and channel for each consumer. While this process will be impacted by the demise of third-party cookies, relevant content will continue to be the cornerstone of omnichannel marketing. First-party data and cohort data can help advertisers find and connect with consumers, but only if marketers are able to engage patients to opt in for content directly.

The use of digital and social media has given marketers a way to provide information in a highly personalized way. An important aspect of customized content is to create content that is designed to help patients at each point along their journey. Information a patient needs at the point of diagnosis is much different than the information they seek once they are starting treatment. Online tracking of search behavior is able to identify when a patient is likely early in their journey vs later and can be used to trigger the display of one piece of content over another. An effective omnichannel campaign moves patients along an educational journey, connecting them with relevant information that answers their questions at each stage.

This shift is easy to see when comparing the spend in digital over time. As the chart below shows, nearly every major pharma brand is investing in digital advertising—particularly display, search and mobile—and their emphasis on digital media spend continues to increase as the available media options grow.

Figure 8-3: Nearly All Pharma Brands Are Using Digital Channels to Reach Patients

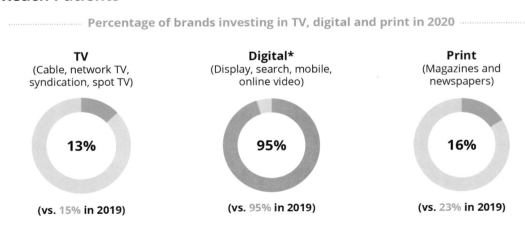

Percentage of brands investing in TV, digital and print in 2020

TV
(Cable, network TV, syndication, spot TV)

13%

(vs. 15% in 2019)

Digital*
(Display, search, mobile, online video)

95%

(vs. 95% in 2019)

Print
(Magazines and newspapers)

16%

(vs. 23% in 2019)

Source for data: Kantar StraDegy | *Does not include programmatic spend

In response to this trend, media companies are changing quickly. Tobaccowala has come up with a new name for the media company of the future: the "mongrel." Defined as a conglomeration of media, content and e-commerce, Tobaccowala pointed to seven mongrel media companies that are quickly taking share of mind away from the "pure bred" companies like CBS, ABC and NBC: "Mongrel companies (like Google, Facebook, Amazon, Twitter, TikTok, Pinterest and Snap) are quickly acquiring companies and talent to expand their offerings." Combining streaming content, e-commerce, social media, mobile apps and user-generated content, these companies are focused on creating spaces for consumers to have engaging experiences. "These new channels can integrate commerce and lead generation. They can be micro-targeted and scaled up. They can provide a blend of content creators and influencer networks to accelerate marketer's distribution footprints and storytelling—the content possibilities are endless," remarked Tobaccowala. There's an opportunity for pharma companies to use these new media spaces to craft campaigns that dynamically adapt and provide the information patients need, when and where they need it.

Patient-Friendly Content

Nearly half of smartphone owners use voice search at least once per day. The combined emergence of mongrel media conglomerates and the growth of speakable (audio-enabled) search prompted one company to take steps to ensure its content was more easily understood by patients. Barbara McCullough, director of cross channel operations and strategy at AstraZeneca, explained: "As we began to focus on the digital experience for our patients, we recognized the need to make our online content more accessible, understandable and reflective of how they talk." In an effort to make AstraZeneca's online content more accessible to users of voice search and audio assistants, McCullough led a multi-year project to establish guidelines for natural language content creation. Using the open-source Universal Patient Language as a foundation, McCullough's team created comprehensive guidelines and assessments for content development, which brand teams and agencies around the world are using. "We asked patients to compare different websites and how easily they could understand the information. Some of the websites were written in a way that was confusing and didn't connect patients to the answers they needed," McCullough explained. "We found through our research that by making our digital properties clearer and easier to understand, patients trusted us more and were able to find the information they needed."

Pharma marketers sometimes struggle with the need to use terms that are medically accurate, as these terms are often difficult for patients to parse. ZS conducted a review[7] of several pharma brand websites and found that, on average, content was written at an eighth-grade reading level, despite the recommendation from the Agency for Healthcare Research and Quality (AHRQ) that health content be written at a fifth-grade reading level.[8] Making patients work harder to interpret the information they are reading—especially at a time when they are coping with health issues—means they only comprehend a small percentage of the health content. To make information more impactful, it has to be accessible and understandable by different and diverse patients. As such, organizations such as the Centers for Disease Control and Prevention have developed publicly available resources and style guides to support inclusive communications.[9]

Pharma brands face regulatory hurdles when trying to get "patient-friendly" terms through the regulatory approval process. Many companies have overcome these obstacles by creating partnerships between marketing and regulatory review teams to create a standard glossary of patient-friendly terms that brand agencies can use to develop content that patients will easily understand.

Virtual Care and Telehealth Activation

Amid the proliferation of integrated omnichannel media companies across the globe, we've also seen rapid growth in the use of virtual options to provide care and information to patients. One of the biggest growth areas has been in telehealth. During the COVID-19 pandemic, all therapy areas saw a rise in telehealth use. Patients unable to go to in-person physician appointments—and some with conditions exacerbated by stress—reached out to their doctors through virtual care channels. Telehealth, at-home diagnostics and remote monitoring provided ways for patients to get the care they needed while remaining quarantined.

Talking to patients and physicians mid-2020 as part of our Telehealth Trends Study, ZS heard both groups express that they found value in this move to virtual care. Physicians appreciated being able to see more patients than is often possible in the office and even described having more effective care conversations due to not needing to conduct a physical exam. "Often the physical exam is unnecessary," noted an oncologist, "but patients expect it when they are in person. Without that pressure, I have more time to talk to patients [through telehealth]." Patients also told us they found value in the convenience and quality of their telehealth visits. "I knew I wouldn't be interrupted by the nurse," said one patient, "so I felt more comfortable talking about some of my concerns [than I would in person]."

Brand marketers can place messages in telehealth channels to increase patient awareness of products and programs. Point-of-care companies, like Populus, Phreesia and Patient Point, have all developed "virtual waiting room" experiences. These experiences take different formats—video, text, audio—and occur before a patient is connected to a physician as well as after the consult to provide patients more information. The messages are tailored based on the information the patient provides when initiating the virtual consultation. Data-driven programming matches content with each patient's interests and needs.

Many brands have also begun integrating access to virtual care into their own patient programs and communication campaigns to help patients. Providing "front-door" solutions, like access to telehealth before getting a prescription, brands are connecting patients to a doctor or health professional to ask about a treatment or condition. These solutions have proven effective at getting patients the education and information they need to make managing their health easier, more comfortable and more convenient—which ultimately leads to improved patient outcomes and reduced health costs.

Often used as a call-to-action (CTA) in consumer advertising, brand marketers are using telehealth to shorten the time between seeing an ad or message and talking to a doctor. During the COVID-19 pandemic, several DTC campaigns added virtual care "front-door" options as a CTA. The success of these efforts was mixed: some brands saw high use of the telehealth CTA, but others didn't.

ZS research found that, when brands intended the "front-door" options to only serve as an alternative to in-person physician visits, they did not consistently engage patients. However, when companies set up their telehealth channels to solve a specific patient problem, they got more use. For example, some brands designed telehealth channels to help users get answers to questions that patients are often reluctant to ask during in-person consultations. Other brands devised telehealth options to assist patients with getting started on treatment and to support them as they continued therapy. These telehealth offerings enjoyed more use from consumers. Instead of thinking about telehealth as another CTA, pharma brand marketers can improve results by treating telehealth as playing a role in the patient's journey and positioning it where it can help patients overcome a particular problem or challenge.

ZS also found that making telehealth one of several calls to action in a DTC campaign diluted the overall message and resulted in low volume through the channel. The value of telehealth got lost amid other treatment messages. But when a brand supported telehealth with a focused omnichannel campaign, using more of a direct-response strategy to draw patients to the channel, both the company and patients got more value: the brand got information out to patients faster, and more patients got the information they needed to make decisions about their care.

Figure 8-4: The Direct Response Approach to Building Awareness for Telehealth Options

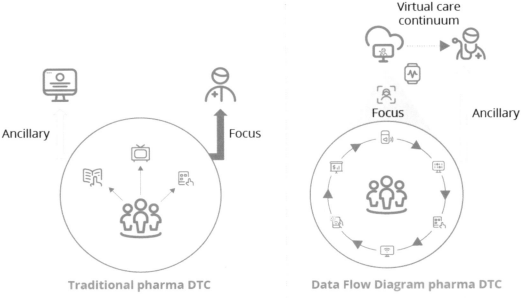

Traditional pharma DTC	Data Flow Diagram pharma DTC
Raises awareness in broad-reach channels to activate patients to go talk to their doctor in person	Raises awareness through targeted media channels that work together to activate patients to pursue telehealth

Telehealth tends to appeal first to "early adopter" consumers: those who are highly tech-literate and motivated to find a company's site and explore all its resources. As a campaign expands its reach and seeks to engage less motivated patients, it's important to identify and mitigate the deterrents that may dissuade such patients from engaging, such as digital literacy and concerns about privacy. Since telehealth requires patients to provide personal information and sometimes their payment information, it isn't unusual for patients to leave the site and abandon the process mid-way through. Marketers can improve the pull-through of these patients by taking an e-commerce approach. Capturing a small, bite-sized piece of personal information early in the process, such as patients' email addresses along with permission to contact them, marketers can follow up with information and education if a patient drops out of the process before pursuing a telehealth consultation. This relationship-building approach creates trust and helps patients navigate back to the telehealth site, should they decide to continue their journey. It is also important to offer patients options. The majority of patients would rather see their regular physician in person, so offering the option to help them navigate the health system and make an in-person appointment as part of the telehealth experience can be highly beneficial. It allows the patient to have the experience they want, while also getting some of their questions answered immediately.

Using Data and Analytics to Activate Patients

The use of data to drive patient marketing efforts has been expanding rapidly in the past 10 years. In the U.S., many pharma companies have implemented data-driven programs to align content with different groups of patients and consumers. Dynamic audience management systems are allowing pharma brands to create sub-segments of target audiences based on their propensity to take action and engage with content.

However, much of this data-driven marketing is set to change due to the planned elimination of third-party cookies by several digital giants. A "cookie" is a tiny piece of software code that gets installed on a web browser when a user visits a website. Cookies identify users and recognize them on subsequent visits. Large search engines and other sites gather third-party cookies and then sell them in an online marketplace, allowing pharma marketers to draw on the data about users' locations and online behaviors to programmatically deliver relevant content to particular patients. However, consumer privacy acts, like the EU's General Data Protection Regulation (2016) and the California Consumer Privacy Act (2018), are now requiring that cookie tracking happen transparently and with full consent of the consumer. This regulatory shift has caused companies like Apple, Mozilla, Facebook and Google to remove third-party cookies from their systems or to announce plans to do so in the next few years.

This means pharma marketers wanting to engage patients will need to adjust their data targeting strategy. One way to do this is to seek permission to gather cookie data directly from patients and consumers when they visit company websites. This allows companies to collect information on the visitors' interests and online behavior to use for future marketing efforts. While most retailers and CPG companies are already actively doing this, many pharma companies have yet to implement this method of data capture on their sites.

Looking ahead, there are emergent methods for gathering consumer information that could replace third-party cookies. Google is developing a new technology called Federated Learning of Cohorts (FLoC) that will allow pharma marketers to target groups of consumers who share similar behaviors while protecting individual privacy.[10] In addition, several ad tech companies are integrating online and offline data to create Universal IDs, which will enable programmatic targeting without third-party cookies. At the time of this writing, Universal IDs are still being developed and vary in efficiency.[11]

In addition to online behavior data, media consumption data is available in a variety of third-party shopper data sets. Pharma companies can combine this data with primary studies to create a full picture of patients' attitudes, behaviors and unmet needs. For instance, Kantar Health runs the National Health and Wellness Survey, one of the largest databases of nationally projectable, patient-reported information on health,[12] and the Kantar MARS Consumer Health Study, fielded each year to approximately 20,000 adults across the U.S.[13] These data sets capture key healthcare, pharma and media data that is projectable to the total adult population. Pharma marketers can match types of patients in primary research with similar patient types in these data sets. This allows marketing teams to augment primary research with a wide range of behavioral insights, including media consumption behavior, prevalence of OTC purchases, managed care coverage and other data points. Pharma companies can use these fuller patient profiles to develop messaging content and channel strategies that more closely align with patient behavior. Providing the right message for patients in the right medium and right channel at the right time enables manufacturers to better serve patients by making sure the information they need is at their fingertips when they need it.

In order to ensure messages are impacting patients, it's critical that companies track and measure their marketing programs. Brand marketers are using primary research surveys, conducted at different points in the life of the campaign (pre-campaign, mid-campaign and post-campaign, at a minimum), to track changes in patient awareness and perception. Frequent tracking reports show how people are engaging with online content, allowing marketers to make adjustments as the campaign is under way. Many pharma marketers are combining this tracking data with claims data to better understand how a campaign is performing. Audience quality, for example, can show how many patients that visit a website are diagnosed with a condition. This helps marketers understand which sites are drawing the patients the brand most wants to motivate. Integrated tracking across all channels can give marketers a clear view of what patients want and find helpful. This information can then be used to optimize the campaign and make it more relevant to patients.

Patient Activation Across the Globe

Pharma companies often consider patient marketing and activation to be U.S.-only concerns, but pharma can provide information, tools and resources to patients in many countries. The key is to understand the regulations. Many countries allow pharma to market directly to patients and consumers as long as the ad content is unbranded or the patient has opted in. These requirements still leave open opportunities for pharma to engage patients and help them access disease education and information.

Figure 8-5: DTC (Direct to Consumer) Marketing Is Allowed in Many Ex-U.S. Markets Across a Continuum of Regulatory Environments

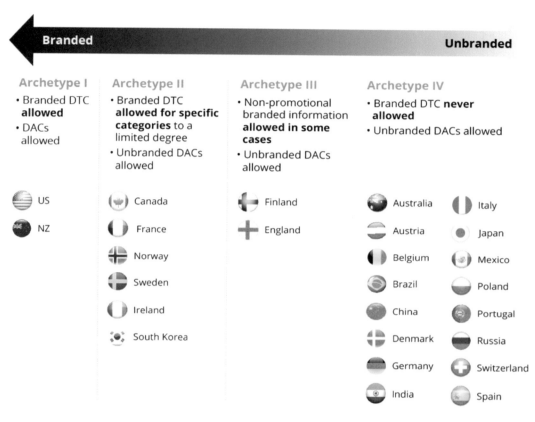

DTC: Direct to Consumer Advertising
DAC: Disease Awareness Campaign

The U.S. and New Zealand are the only two countries that allow branded DTC marketing. However, nearly every country allows unbranded disease awareness campaigns targeted to patients. These campaigns help patients understand their conditions and connect them to resources that enable them to make informed decisions about their care. Some examples of campaigns that have been targeted directly to patients outside the U.S. include:

- Pfizer's "Happy Eye" campaign in Japan, which sought to raise awareness among patients at risk for glaucoma. Pfizer promoted a mobile app that patients could download to understand how their eyesight might deteriorate without treatment. The app used the camera's functionality to let patients see their world through diminished eyesight and connected them with online resources to help them take action.

- As part of Novartis's Italian campaign for migraine awareness, the company partnered with Facebook to build an online community of migraine sufferers to help raise awareness for the condition.

- For an osteoporosis campaign in France, Amgen created a collection of porcelain plates with a high porosity, making them fragile and easily breakable, to call attention to the fragility of bones affected by osteoporosis. The company distributed these plates to influencers, accompanied with the following message: "Untreated, osteoporosis can make your bones as fragile as porcelain" (see Figure 8-6). The influencers could take the plate out of the packaging, see how easily it broke and share the experience with their followers.

- Japan's Meiji campaign used art to illustrate the complexity and beauty of the human immune system. The campaign raised awareness about immune functions and encouraged people to learn more about autoimmune disorders (see Figure 8-7).

Figure 8-6: This Award-Winning Consumer Print Ad Increased Awareness for Osteoporosis and Encouraged Patients to Take Action[14]

NON TRAITÉE, L'OSTÉOPOROSE PEUT RENDRE VOS OS
AUSSI FRAGILES QUE LA PORCELAINE.

Une femme sur trois est touchée après 50 ans.
Parlez-en à votre médecin et renseignez-vous sur
www.tout-sur-osteoporose.fr

Figure 8-7: Meiji's Use of Art to Illustrate the Beauty of the Human Immune System[15]

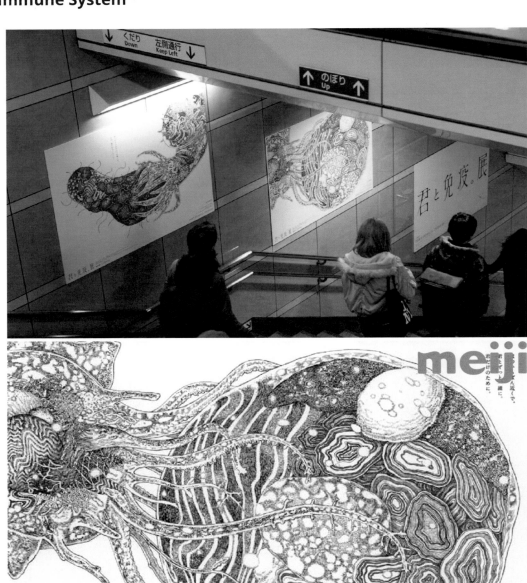

When expanding patient marketing into different geographies, it is important to consider how messaging can reach underrepresented and underserved communities of patients. Patient marketing has often focused on white, affluent, educated patients. However, more and more pharma brands are recognizing that the failure to expand message strategies to engage diverse patients negatively impacts patient health.

As a result, companies are incorporating health equity initiatives into patient marketing in many ways. The most common is to tailor marketing materials and channels for specific patient populations, a strategy often dubbed "multicultural marketing." Multicultural marketers reach out to patients from different ethnicities, races and socio-economic backgrounds, invite them to share their stories about their health journeys and then apply those patient insights in customized patient marketing materials in order to provide culturally and linguistically appropriate services (CLAS).[16] In addition to modifying existing creative materials, brands are finding new ways to connect with diverse populations through partnerships with community organizations, faith-based leaders, social service organizations and ethnic media outlets, among others. For instance, after noting particularly low breast cancer diagnosis rates among Black women in the Memphis, TN region, Genentech partnered with health systems, patient groups and others to create the Memphis Breast Cancer Consortium and, subsequently, the SisterPact program,[17] which aimed at increasing the number of Black women who sought mammograms. A survey revealed that four in five of the women in the SisterPact audience were extremely likely to get a mammogram, and three in four encouraged a friend to do so.[18] As the pharmaceutical industry strives to better serve diverse patient communities and improve health equity, we expect to see more initiatives like SisterPact, with brands bringing new patient-centric perspectives from diverse populations into the development of marketing messages, strategies and partnerships.

Conclusion

In our evolving media environment, patients are looking for information, guidance, advice, real-world evidence and empathy on more channels and platforms than ever before. The need for relevant, accurate content that informs and supports patients' decisions is high. Brands need to create data-driven, dynamic and tailored content for patients to buoy them on their journey to improved health and wellness. The methods of the past 15 years will not serve patients or brands in this new world of diverse media. Patient-focused content delivered through orchestrated, omnichannel strategies is the key to connecting with patients and providing value. Developing the skills, processes, tools and data necessary to support and connect with patients is an important investment for pharma marketers, and one that will result in benefits for both patients and pharma far into the future.

Key Takeaways

- Patient activation messaging, including DTC and disease awareness campaigns, is growing as more brands seek to engage and activate patients.

- However, patient messages don't just involve TV and print any longer. Digital channels, such as mobile, display, search and social, are all part of the new patient information ecosystem. Engaging patients at increasing rates means involving multiple channels in patient marketing plans.

- Brands are thinking more about omnichannel strategies and focusing on engaging patients by meeting them where they are—both in terms of content, by considering patients' unique needs, and in terms of placement, by delivering information using a wide array of channels.

- Advances in telehealth and mobile technology are changing how patients access care. Brands that recognize this potential and take action to develop ways to use these new tools can create greater opportunities to educate and activate patients. But this will require a different approach, one based on an omnichannel, direct-response media strategy that can anticipate patients' needs and questions at every step along their healthcare journey.

- DTC is a global tool to engage and inform patients. While there are restrictions for how to educate and inform patients in different markets, brands are working to help patients better understand their treatment options across the globe.

Acknowledgments

The author wishes to thank Graham Goodrich, Barbara McCullough and Rishad Tobaccowala.

Endnotes

1.   We recognize that "activating patients" is not the most patient-focused termi-
     nology. Few patients we spoke to want to feel like some outside organization is
     trying to "activate" them. In fact, much of the terminology we use in this chap-
     ter may not be very patient friendly. That's because we will be using standard
     advertising and promotional campaign terms. We may refer to consumers as a
     "target" or "end user" and discuss ways to measure their "lifetime value." It may
     sound off-putting to refer to patients in this transactional manner, but, because
     this language has become common, we use it with the intention of being clear
     and easily understood.

2.   Name changed for the purposes of this book.

3.   Kantar, Advertising Insights, 2021.

4.   Name changed for the purposes of this book.

5.   Analysis of Nielsen Data published December 2017, https://www.marketingc-
     harts.com/featured-24817.

6.   Name changed for the purposes of this book.

7.   ZS Digital Reading Level Analysis, 2018.

8.   Agency for Healthcare Research and Equality, "Assess, Select, and Create Easy-to-
     Understand Materials: Tool #11," in Health Literacy Universal Precautions Toolkit,
     2nd ed., published February 2015, last updated September 2020, https://www.
     ahrq.gov/health-literacy/improve/precautions/tool11.html.

9.   Centers for Disease Control and Prevention (CDC), "Resources & Style Guides for
     Framing Health Equity & Avoiding Stigmatizing Language," accessed January 21,
     2022, https://www.cdc.gov/healthcommunication/resources.html.

10. David Nield, "What's Google's FLoC and How Does It Affect Your
     Privacy?" Wired, May 9, 2021, https://www.wired.com/story/
     google-floc-privacy-ad-tracking-explainer/.

11. Zach Atlas, "The Ascension of Universal IDs in the Wake of Third Party Cookies,"
     SpotX Blog, March 25, 2021, https://www.spotx.tv/resources/blog/product-pulse/
     the-ascension-of-universal-ids/.

12. Kantar, "National Health and Wellness Survey," accessed
     October 8, 2021, https://www.kantar.com/expertise/health/
     da---real-world-data-pros-claims-and-health-records/
     national-health-and-wellness-survey-nhws.

13. Kantar, "Kantar MARS Consumer Health Study—2020 US Vaccine Willingness Report," accessed October 8, 2021, https://app.demyst.com/catalog/adx/kantar/kantar-mars-consumer-health-study---2020-us-vaccine-willingness-report.

14. Amgen, https://adsofbrands.net/en/ads/amgen-porcelain-bones/7184.

15. Branding in Asia Staff, "Meiji—You and the Immune System, by Dentsu," Branding in Asia, March 7, 2018, https://www.brandinginasia.com/meiji-immune-system-dentsu/.

16. U.S. Department of Health & Human Services, "What Is CLAS?" Think Cultural Health, accessed October 8, 2021, https://thinkculturalhealth.hhs.gov/clas/what-is-clas.

17. Lottie L. Joiner, "Sister Pact," Genentech, April 4, 2016, https://www.gene.com/stories/sister-pact.

18. Tanya Lewis, "Best Multicultural Campaign of 2016," Medical Marketing and Media, October 6, 2016, https://www.mmm-online.com/home/channel/agencies/best-multicultural-campaign-of-2016/.

Chapter 9:
Transforming the Treatment Experience

Tanya Shepley, Sophie Kondor and Mary Ann Godwin

The Problem

Consumers today have become accustomed to digital-first, customer-centric transaction models that take into consideration their preferences and prior activity. However, when these same consumers become "patients" managing their health, they are frustrated to find the healthcare industry does not live up to these standards. Healthcare and medical treatment is a major part of many peoples' lives—especially those with one or more chronic conditions. According to CDC analysis, in 2018, 52% of American adults had at least one chronic condition, and 27% had multiple chronic conditions.[1] For these people, it is critically important that the treatment journey be easy to navigate. But the healthcare ecosystem is fragmented, and the treatment journey can wind up being frustrating as a result. With disparate stakeholders participating in different parts of the treatment experience, it is difficult for any one stakeholder to see the full picture, and, inevitably, many patients are left behind. As Chapter 1 illustrated, it can take months or even years for patients to receive a diagnosis. Even after all that effort, some patients never start the treatment they're prescribed, and many more start therapy but discontinue prematurely.

Persistence (how long someone stays on therapy) is not the only issue. There are also substantial issues with compliance (how well patients follow their prescribed treatment protocol). Both fall under the umbrella of the term adherence (whether a patient takes treatment as prescribed, which includes both persistence and compliance). Specifying which aspect of adherence we are talking about can help us understand how to address the barriers patients are likely experiencing.

Pharmaceutical and life sciences companies, which manufacture the therapies patients rely on, have an opportunity and obligation to enhance the treatment experience—the part of the patient journey associated with starting and staying on therapy. Manufacturers are in a unique position to strengthen the connection points between patients, caregivers, advocacy groups, providers, payers and others involved in the treatment experience. An integrated treatment experience, driven by effective collaboration across these stakeholders, can make all the difference when it comes to patient outcomes. As an example, it can prevent the experience one ulcerative colitis patient shared:

I get a phone call from a brand representative every six weeks. They're nice, just not helpful. It's a very basic call asking how I'm feeling, do I need anything, whatever. The only time I said "yes, I need help" is when I had issues with my insurance company covering the drug. And they said, "I can't get involved with that." It was very hollow. They could've at least told me who to contact. The fact that they couldn't help me at all was kind of wasting my time.[2]

Figure 9-1: The Fragmented and Frustrating Treatment Experience

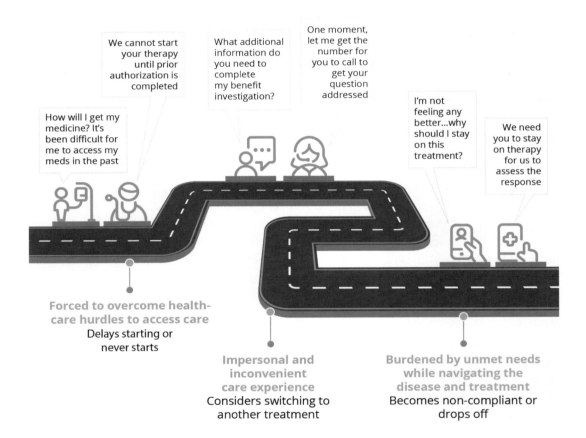

Patients today play an active role in their health management, and many follow a winding, arduous journey just to find the right diagnosis and treatment solutions. Unfortunately, from the moment they receive a prescription, patients and their caregivers often face a series of hurdles as they try to maneuver within a complex landscape of providers, health systems, payers, manufacturer support services, stand-alone digital services and advocacy groups. Furthermore, during the COVID-19 pandemic, many patients had to postpone non-essential medical appointments and quickly adapt to digital solutions, like telehealth. For some patients, digital engagement channels have enabled easier communication with providers, opening up new options for managing their treatment journey; for others, the sudden shift to digital engagement added additional complexity and difficulty to the process.

Poor patient experience has a staggering cost to society. Patients struggling as a result of socioeconomic factors and inconsistent care experiences are more likely to discontinue or become non-compliant with their treatments,[3] which can impact their health and their ability to realize the best possible outcome from therapy. Without proper treatment, patients can experience high rates of hospitalization, loss of work, worsening co-morbid conditions and poor quality of life. Even before COVID-19, on a national scale, patient non-adherence caused nearly 125,000 deaths annually, and the total costs of drug-related morbidity, patient non-adherence and failure to maintain treatment protocols was estimated at $528.4 billion.[4]

Despite these pressing reasons to improve cohesion across the healthcare ecosystem, the fragmentation of the treatment journey means service providers have many critical blind spots when it comes to the patient experience and the drivers of patient non-adherence. As a result, it's difficult to develop comprehensive, integrated and inclusive solutions for patients. In this chapter, we explore how pharmaceutical and life sciences organizations can transform their patient service model to partner across the ecosystem and improve both patient experience and adherence—a win-win solution for patients and manufacturers.

Building a More Inclusive Treatment Experience

For decades, manufacturers have focused on building and improving patient support services. Some organizations have developed truly innovative ways to reduce friction and enhance the patient experience. But, often, these resources only reach a small fraction of the patient population. To make a significant impact in the arena of patient support, those of us in the industry must view the problem through a lens of broader inclusion:

- **Inclusion at the start**: The steps for filling a first prescription are not always straightforward, and it can be challenging for patients to navigate access and affordability issues as well as the logistics associated with specialty or cell and gene therapies. These issues are exacerbated for patients who have to manage multiple prescriptions for more than one condition. Research shows that up to 30% of patients receiving a prescription never make it to their first fill.[5] It is critical to consider all patients when designing support offerings—not just those who make it to first fill or those who opt in to patient support programs.

- **Inclusion over time**: For patients with long-term health conditions, such as heart disease, cancer, diabetes, chronic obstructive pulmonary disease (COPD), arthritis or hepatitis, consistent treatment is a requirement to maintain their health. Unfortunately, however, treatment adherence tends to decline over time. It is estimated that half of patients being treated for chronic conditions miss doses, do not follow treatment protocols or drop off treatment within their first year.[6] Many programs focus on treatment initiation but fail to provide the ongoing support needed to help patients stay on therapy in the long term.

- **Inclusion of underserved patients:** In a 2018 ZS Patient Services study, fewer than 40% of patients were aware of any available support services to help them start and stay on therapy. Patients expressed confusion about their eligibility for support programs and were dubious about how helpful the programs really would be. In the Patient Experience Index survey ZS conducted in 2020, we found that patients with a household income (HHI) lower than $20,000 were half as likely to leverage support resources as those at the highest HHI levels. The patients who may be most in need of support are thus the least likely to get it. And, while in general we see a shift toward empowering patients to steer their own health decisions, low health literacy still creates a challenge for many patients, who find navigating the process themselves too great a challenge and may drop off therapy as a result. It is critical that patient service teams analyze data on social determinants of health (SDOH) in order to identify the needs of underserved patient populations and then tailor solutions to meet those needs.

The patients who are most often engaged with patient support programs are a small subset of the treatable patient market, which is itself a small portion of the total patient population. For example, out of 35 million migraine sufferers, it is estimated that only 4 million seek treatment, only 2 million receive a prescription for a branded treatment and, with a non-adherence rate of approximately 32%, only 1.4 million persist with treatment long term. If we assume (generously) that 20% of these 2 million patients on therapy are accessing patient services offered by manufacturers, it means pharma is reaching just 1% of the total treatable patient population! There is substantial opportunity to create value by building a more inclusive treatment experience.

Figure 9-2: Migraine Patient Journey

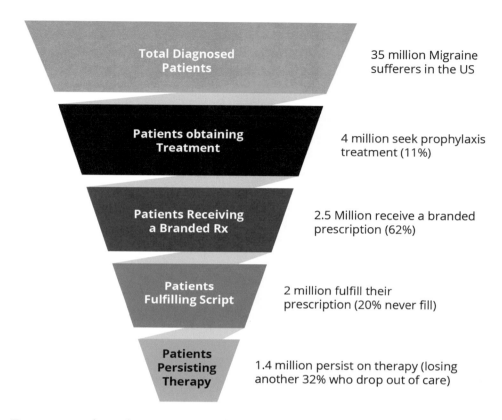

Total Diagnosed Patients — 35 million Migraine sufferers in the US

Patients obtaining Treatment — 4 million seek prophylaxis treatment (11%)

Patients Receiving a Branded Rx — 2.5 Million receive a branded prescription (62%)

Patients Fulfilling Script — 2 million fulfill their prescription (20% never fill)

Patients Persisting Therapy — 1.4 million persist on therapy (losing another 32% who drop out of care)

To support a broader patient population, healthcare stakeholders need to think outside the box to address issues associated with patient demographics, SDOH and other unique needs of individual patients. Until now, the healthcare industry has focused on pulling levers related to medical intervention, but it's crucial to design patient support services to address all determinants of health. Enhancing and expanding patient support services to reach a greater portion of the population is not only the right thing to do—it contributes to cost savings in the healthcare ecosystem by reducing non-adherence, thus mitigating the related risk factors patients face. Risk factors highlighted by the WHO Adherence Report include more intensive relapses, increased risk of dependence, increased risk of abstinence and rebound effects, increased risk of developing resistance to therapies, increased risk of toxicity and increased likelihood of accidents.[7] Providing better and broader patient support also represents long-term revenue potential for life sciences companies and opens avenues to new commercial opportunities. The need to transform the post-Rx treatment experience to make it inclusive and to improve therapy adherence for all patients is a mission critical for life sciences companies.

External Innovation: Rethinking Collaboration Models Across the Healthcare Ecosystem

Life sciences companies must recognize that they are not the only ones providing tools for patient support. In fact, most patients may not think of manufacturers as the primary providers of support services. While 56% of patients report using adherence tools (such as symptom trackers, medication reminders and prescription refill reminders), only 8% of that use is of tools created by a pharma manufacturer.[8] It's important to understand the landscape to find synergies and opportunities to partner with other stakeholders rather than continuing to try to build everything internally. ZS research found that about 50% of patient support resources offered by manufacturers are already being provided by others in the ecosystem, such as digital and connected health companies, patient groups, payers and providers.

Figure 9-3: Patients and Caregivers Are Often Unaware of Manufacturers' Role in Treatment Access and Financial Assistance[9]

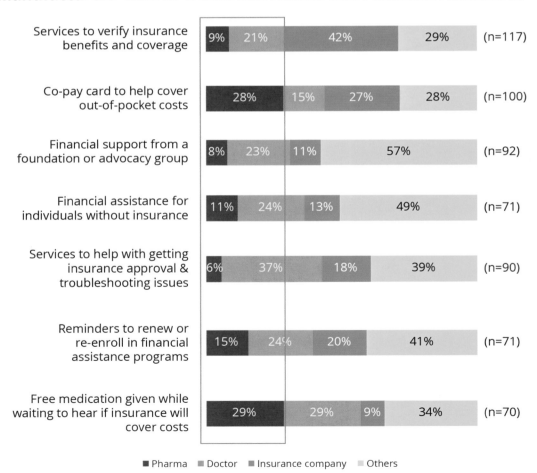

This duplication points to an important problem: a need for better coordination among healthcare ecosystem stakeholders to identify truly unmet needs and determine who is in the best position to address them. Crowded categories and a finite pool of patients mean that pharma organizations have incentives to compete against each other for patients and market share.[10] However, this prevents different stakeholders who are working in the same disease space from serving patients effectively. For example, life sciences firms conduct a lot of patient research and gain insights about patients' values, attitudes, beliefs about treatments and disease states. Too often, manufacturers hold onto this data as a competitive advantage instead of sharing it with patient advocacy groups and providers, even though sharing data could elevate the entire competitive class of products on the market and benefit patients. This tendency to hoard information creates a high degree of frustration and waste across multiple stakeholders in the ecosystem. The focus on competition within the healthcare ecosystem has also contributed to a lack of trust among consumers, with 47% of consumers believing the healthcare and life sciences industries are more focused on business needs than patient needs.

Manufacturers, payers, providers and advocacy groups have a common interest in facilitating positive patient outcomes. To build trust and achieve this collective goal, stakeholders need to start partnering effectively, sharing insights and data, and co-creating solutions. Transforming collaboration models between healthcare stakeholders isn't an easy task. But the role of the life sciences industry is critical in the path ahead, and other stakeholders are beginning to recognize that manufacturers have an important part to play in the overall patient support ecosystem. Pharma can offer:

- **Science expertise**: Pharma has the data and the analytic and scientific expertise to identify patients with specific needs and design validated patient experience enhancements that complement their medicines. For example, Abbott developed an FDA-approved app that allows patients with neurological conditions, including chronic pain and movement disorders, to manage therapy directly from their personal smartphones.[11] Using this app, patients can securely connect with their doctors in real time, and physicians can remotely adjust personalized treatment programs. Abbott's expertise in the disease state enabled them to develop a product to improve the treatment experience for this patient population.

- **Ability to scale**: Pharma has the resources to build and enable impactful solutions that can scale to include more of the patient population, but pharma companies are often only able to engage patients they can reach through HCPs and direct-to-consumer (DTC) advertising. Leveraging multi-stakeholder collaboration can enable these solutions to reach the entire patient population, which is where the industry should evolve in the future.

- **Stake in the game**: Non-adherence and poor patient outcomes are costly for pharmaceutical companies and payers looking to reduce healthcare utilization costs, so they share the same goals as other care providers seeking to improve patient experience and patient outcomes.

Today, more and more pharmaceutical companies are embracing patient centricity as a core part of their culture, and, as a result, these firms are earning the trust of other healthcare stakeholders. The life sciences industry played a critical role in the development of COVID-19 treatments and vaccines, casting the industry in a new light. There is an opportunity to continue the momentum of trust, collaboration, openness and patient centricity. Continuing to think innovatively about building relationships with other stakeholders will allow pharma to identify opportunities to better serve patients. There are several emerging examples of best practices in collaborations:

- **Engaging with community organizations to improve health equity**: Today, many manufacturers are taking a local market approach by engaging with local authorities and community leaders to tackle conditions affecting large, underserved populations. In the southern United States, Gilead engaged community leaders through the Gilead COMPASS Initiative. Launched in 2017, this 10-year partnership with over $100 million in funding is working to combat the HIV epidemic in the South using evidence-based solutions to meet the needs of people living with HIV/AIDS. The program aims to create collaborative partnerships to share knowledge on increasing organizational capacity, building awareness, reducing HIV-related stigma, promoting holistic wellness through mental health services and trauma-informed care, and building faith-based advocacy and spiritually integrated organizations to end the HIV epidemic.[12]

- **Engaging with employers and advocacy groups**: The stigma around certain health conditions, including mental health conditions, has resulted in diagnosis delays and impaired treatment for patients. To combat stigma, manufacturers have gotten involved in numerous initiatives to support public awareness of mental illness. As an example, Janssen Pharmaceutical's involvement in the mental health space began in the 1950s with the company's breakthrough treatment for schizophrenia, and Janssen continues to be dedicated to improving outcomes for those suffering from mental illness. Recently, Janssen partnered with the American Heart Association and more than 40 CEOs across the U.S. to offer employers strategies to support colleagues suffering from mental health conditions and to develop a "mental-health-friendly" environment.[13]

- **Engaging with hospitals**: Patients with Parkinson's disease need to take their medication at the same time every day, but, when they are hospitalized for other reasons, the hospitals often do not have the patients' prescribed Parkinson's medication readily available. This can result in intake delays, worsening symptoms and extended hospital stays. Belgian biopharmaceutical company UCB partnered with hospitals to ensure the availability of Parkinson's medication, resulting in a decrease of hospitalization duration for Parkinson's patients.[14]

By connecting different stakeholders, life sciences companies can elevate the quality of treatment and provide a win-win-win opportunity for all stakeholders: patients avoid interruption in their treatment and have better experiences, hospitals have better quality scores and fewer complications, and manufacturers retain patients on therapy. All stakeholders benefit when they collaborate in service of the patient.

Internal Transformation: Life Sciences Companies Must Commit to Making Lasting Changes

In addition to building and maintaining patient support programs, many pharma companies are investing in initiatives to expand their patient services capabilities overall. Companies must look beyond the scope of one-off initiatives to see the full potential of patient support programs. For an organization to meaningfully move the needle on non-adherence, it must transform its whole culture, mindset and structure.

From Analog Research to Data-Driven Research

In the age of big data, organizations need to break down barriers and rethink their data approach. Most patient support programs enroll less than 15% of the treating patient population,[15] which means organizations must look far beyond the scope of their opted-in or enrolled patient base to have a real impact. Few companies have tapped into the full potential of real-world data (RWD) and applied behavioral insights. The application of these tools can help identify drivers of non-adherence and offer clues about how to reach a more comprehensive set of patients.

As reflected in a 2021 ZS study on medication adherence by Albert Whangbo and Vaibhav Bansal,[16] RWD repeatedly demonstrates much lower medication adherence for newly initiated patients than what is observed in clinical trials. The authors noted that pharmaceutical companies lose up to 50% of patients within just two months of initiation and 70 to 80% within six months. This severely impacts both patient outcomes and product performance as compared against manufacturer expectations. The research reinforces the notion that medication adherence is informed by a myriad of factors, ranging from the disease and treatment complexity; systemic issues, such as racism; healthcare disparities; access to healthcare; education and awareness; a physician's or patient's individual approach to medication; and the available patient support. This means manufacturers need to identify the drivers of poor medication adherence and design targeted approaches to address them accordingly.

As mentioned earlier in this chapter, migraine is a debilitating condition that impacts millions of people, but most migraine sufferers do not receive acute or preventive treatment. In 2020, Eli Lilly and Company conducted a large, population-based, real-world study of migraine patients, including people who were both seeking and not seeking care, diagnosed and undiagnosed, and treated and untreated.[17] Using RWD, Eli Lilly was able to capture participants' experiences and yield insights that were not apparent in clinical trials or the company's patient support data. For example, the study found that less than one in five patients with migraines who were eligible for preventive treatment were prescribed such treatment. With this data, Eli Lilly can help educate the healthcare community about the real-world experience of migraine sufferers, which may help expand treatment to previously overlooked patients. The use of RWD is critical to achieving a complete understanding of the patient journey.

From Patient Service Silos to an Interconnected Network

Life sciences organizations need to harness high-quality insights to trigger the appropriate interventions. According to a recent ZS survey, only 5% of patient-focused marketing and services teams feel their services are responsive to patients' needs throughout the healthcare journey.[18] One way companies can remedy this is by tearing down silos; as discussed in Chapter 4, silos result in patient insights becoming trapped in one part of an organization, rather than circulating throughout the organization and thus informing all aspects of development and commercialization. Breaking down such barriers is essential to improving the connectivity of companies' data, processes and people. Patient centricity needs to permeate all parts of the organization. Organizations with a highly interconnected operating model will be most successful in their patient service transformation.

For example, Genentech is an organization that has made significant strides in adopting new ways of working to enhance patient centricity. The company set a new approach to uniting teams across the organization who were working directly and indirectly with patients. Establishing a dedicated and focused initiative on patient engagement operations helped the company define what a "great experience" for patients looks like and unify its teams around a "North-Star" outcome. One of the greatest hurdles observed by Genentech in this process was the lack of consensus for a definition of patient centricity and the experiences of patients who engaged with their organization. This central function helped break down silos and united the company's range of patient engagement efforts.

From "Checking Boxes" to Human-First Measurements

Life sciences firms must rethink their success metrics. Patient experience measures are often overlooked, even though they are leading indicators of success for patient support programs. Most organizations only track ROI in terms of enrollment, clinical indicators and activity. But measurement of activity often becomes a self-fulfilling prophecy, and it does not always translate to a positive experience for patients. For example, when a condition is stigmatized, as in cases of mental illness, sexually transmitted disease or obesity, patients may not want to actively engage with programs. The most patient-centric support program might not actually require engagement from patients at all.

AbbVie has exemplified patient-centric measurements in assessing the success of its industry-leading support program to assist patients using adalimumab (Humira) with medication costs, nurse support, injection training, pen disposal and medication reminders. The company conducted a 78-week observational study of patients with rheumatoid arthritis and found that the percentage of patients achieving MCID in HAQ-DI was higher among patient support program (PSP) users versus non-users (48.1 versus 37.8%), indicating participation in the PSP can have a positive effect on quality-of-life outcomes.[19] AbbVie also has an internal patient-centered research group that helps bring in the voice of the patient and understand the whole picture of patients' experiences. Katie Benjamin, director of health economics and outcomes research at AbbVie, stated: "Patient-reported outcomes (PROs), or data that comes directly from the patient, are an important way to measure their experience."[20]

Where to Begin: Transformation Inspiration

Moving large organizations to address deep-rooted problems is not an easy undertaking. Widespread change is often necessary to motivate leaders to explore new and transformative ideas. As pioneers in the movement toward a more inclusive treatment experience, pharmaceutical and biotechnology companies can pave the way for other healthcare ecosystem stakeholders who need to become more patient-centric. In striking off down this path, pharma can take inspiration from other industries and companies, borrowing key features that have created an improved consumer experience, such as customer service excellence, end-to-end support and empathetic leadership:

- **Zappos:** Pharma companies often overlook the importance of creating easy-to-navigate websites, informative phone lines and easily accessible channels to communicate with consumers. Zappos entered the online shoe retail market with a philosophy that providing excellent customer service over the phone is the key to growth marketing. In the early 2000s, Zappos relocated its entire business in order to staff a large 24-hour call center and make customer service a central part of the company's strategy. Unlike most online retailers, Zappos prominently displays a customer service telephone number on every page of its website. Additionally, Zappos offers customer-centric services, like free shipping and free 365-day returns, which cost more than many retailers are willing to spend. But Zappos looks at every customer interaction as a branding opportunity, and this approach has led to a 75% rate of return.[21] Similarly, pharma can unlock a lot of value through simple customer service best practices. There are parallels in the underlying goal of customer engagement. As expressed by

Zappos's director of customer loyalty: "It's about reducing customer anxiety and making it easy for them."[22] With this objective, Zappos empowers employees to provide daily "wow" moments that deliver above and beyond. Their call center employees are required to undergo a four-week training before they handle calls, and there's no phone tree process, meaning customers benefit from a single point of contact for call resolution.

- **Home Depot:** Pharma can also take inspiration from companies with traditional supply chains that have recently embraced digital trends to create a more seamless end-to-end experience for customers. For example, in 2017, Home Depot launched a multi-year culture and operations strategy shift called One Home Depot to "unlock a frictionless interconnected shopping experience" and "to seamlessly blend the digital and physical worlds."[23] The company rebuilt its supply chain network to allow for scale and flexibility. Home Depot also created an interconnected retail strategy to uncover a more comprehensive view of the customer and create deeper personalization. This strategy not only led to increased market share but also paid off during the COVID-19 pandemic, when demand for home improvement goods soared; the flexibility of Home Depot's IT software allowed the company to adapt and immediately support online sales. Similarly, life sciences companies that had invested in digital infrastructure were more agile in response to the COVID-19 pandemic. We've seen that integration of digital patient services in healthcare can enable a more cohesive end-to-end solution to patient treatment experience challenges.

- **Amazon PillPack:** Traditional manufacturers can also learn from new pharmaceutical and biotech brands that are making "customer obsession" a core part of their culture. In 2018, Amazon, the world's largest online retailer, acquired PillPack, an online pharmacy startup that offers convenient medication packaging and streamlined customer service for patients. With its user-friendly operations and 24/7 call center, PillPack has a Net Promoter Score (NPS) of 80, compared to the pharmacy average of 26.[24] Teams at PillPack are required to undergo "empathy training" by sorting pills while wearing bulky gloves and prescription glasses so that they experience the restricted mobility, limited eyesight and anxiety of older patients. With an emphasis on human-centered design to address the physical and emotional needs of patients, many teams co-create products and solutions with their customers. By embracing a similar approach to radical empathy, pharma companies can better understand what services and interventions would be truly meaningful to patients.

At ZS, to help our life sciences industry clients gain a reference point for where to start, we've developed a PSP maturity model across key elements of the patient journey to guide client teams through goal setting for patient support programs in order to drive long-term relevance and sustainability. Biotechnology and pharmaceutical companies can map their capabilities in four critical objectives at different phases along the patient treatment experience: "Activate," "Get," "Start" and "Stay."

Figure 9-4: Four Critical Objectives for Patient Support

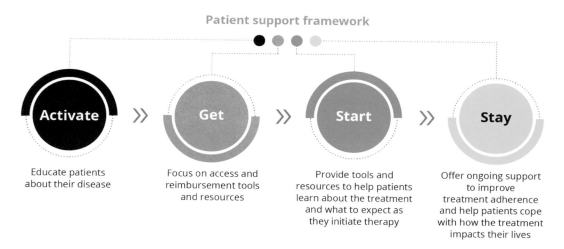

The ZS PSP framework outlines elements of successful patient support programs, from companies just starting to embrace patient support strategies to leaders in the space. Our clients use this framework to assess their organizations' strengths and identify growth opportunities as they begin their patient support transformation. From our work with clients across the spectrum of maturity, ZS has been able to learn what excellence looks like in patient support. Life sciences leaders offer dynamic and cutting-edge services for patients at each stage of the treatment journey.

Activate

This is the initial phase during which patients become educated on the disease, treatment options, support communities and PSPs. To facilitate this phase for patients, life sciences leaders with highly advanced PSPs actively collaborate with patient advocacy groups (PAGs) and community groups to raise awareness. These collaborations with PAGs aim to establish win-win awareness campaigns and avenues for content co-creation. More mature organizations also work to gather patient/HCP feedback on disease area solutions and opportunities that are most impactful to customers. Their use of social media and digital engagement through PSP "champions" (such as HCPs and patient volunteers) is also a critical element in spurring enrollment into the offered services.

The challenge for life sciences companies of generating enough enrollment volume in their support programs is often overlooked. The industry spends billions of dollars on support programs, but a vast majority of patients do not use them. According to a recent survey by Phreesia, the in-office patient intake software provider, only 8% of patients report ever having used patient support programs.[25] Awareness of tools, resources and services remains low throughout the patient and caregiver journey. With awareness, utilization follows. According to ZS's independent research, the average utilization for respondents who are aware of resources in the "Activate" stage was 74%.[26] Part of the design for patient support programs should include considerations for promotion and the inclusion of strategic channels to effectively reach the broader patient audience.

An example of a campaign that deftly combined these success factors was AstraZeneca's (AZ) "New Normal, Same Cancer" campaign,[27] which the company created in collaboration with seven patient coalitions[28] and with guidance from a behavioral psychologist. AZ initially posted the ad/spot on LinkedIn and Twitter globally, and members of the cancer community quickly began sharing it. The ad soon started appearing on additional digital channels, such as Facebook and Instagram.

Get

In the "Get" phase, the goal for healthcare providers is to enable patient access to therapy. Here, the most advanced life sciences organizations create two-way channels and feedback loops to address access hurdles. Leading organizations not only actively engage HCPs and local accounts to facilitate access support (inbound/outbound) for patients, but they also adapt their processes to include a multitude of channels based on patient preferences for engagement.

Many of these programs took center stage during the COVID-19 pandemic, as large numbers of patients lost or changed insurance coverage tied to their employment. For example, Merck and Genentech both offered new options (such as texting photos, instructional videos and online submission options, among others) for patients to enroll in access programs. Genentech also extended its communication platforms to include live chat, email and text. Meanwhile, Merck offered new options for collecting signatures on enrollment forms and created an instructional video available on YouTube that detailed how to download, print and sign the enrollment form and then mail it to Merck.

Start

During the "Start" phase of the treatment journey, the objective is for patients to have a positive customer experience starting therapy. The most advanced pharma organizations have their PSPs integrated into all patient/HCP promotional assets; patient support is a core part of their brands' value propositions. Such resources might include nurse/educator coaches, whose role is to streamline patient initiation and actively facilitate interactions between HCPs and patients, as well as support program nurses whose role is to connect patients with HCPs for action.

These offerings can be in person, as in the case of the support program BMS offers for patients on the MS drug Zeposia.[29] The program provides patients the option to receive home visits from a nurse to complete various tests in order to avoid the inconvenience of having to go into their physician's office. Companies can also offer support virtually, like the training videos Novartis created to help patients with relapsing MS learn how to administer Kesimpta via injection.[30] The videos include demonstrations and step-by-step instructions on how to use the Kesimpta pen and are available on the brand's website. Patients have the option to get a training pen, and they can schedule a one-on-one training demo online as well.

Stay

In the "Stay" phase, patients need ongoing support to facilitate therapy compliance and adherence. Industry leaders in this space provide tailored, outbound, multichannel communications using predictive analytics to proactively address needs across the treatment journey. The ability to anticipate patients' needs at different stages of therapy allows the intelligent targeting of services to enhance the patient experience throughout the treatment journey. Advanced analytic models can identify key patient requirements and predict which patients will have compliance issues leading to drop-offs, allowing companies to design support service interventions for those particular patients.

GAIA's online intervention, Elevida, which was clinically proven to effectively reduce fatigue in patients with MS,[31] is based on cognitive behavioral therapy and psychotherapeutic approaches, like mindfulness. Patients navigate through Elevida at their own pace and via multiple choice questions. The software serves as a guided therapy session and tailors how quickly a patient progresses according to the answers they provide, matching progress to each patient's specific needs.

The Future

The journey from initial prescription to optimal patient outcome has a number of friction points and gaps in connection to care, often resulting in patients discontinuing treatment. We've seen that the consequences and costs of this attrition are staggering. The solution is for the industry to come together to create a more inclusive and cohesive treatment journey to engage more patients that have been left behind and support them at every step.

Unfortunately, most manufacturers who have been trying to address patients' needs for a long time still find themselves stuck with a limited impact on a relatively narrow subset of the patient population. In this chapter, we've identified several ways in which manufacturers can reframe their position in the healthcare landscape, break out of old patterns and transform their patient support organization to drive inclusion and meaningful patient outcomes.

The future of healthcare will exist between two polarities: highly advanced technology will enable speed, efficiency and customization, even as human-centered care will be a critical differentiator and driver of long-term adherence. AI and machine learning will open the door to innovative new care and service models and allow us to know what patients need before they even need it. At the same time, across all industries, empathy will be a core competency to improve customer experience and retention. Both of these movements promise a more inclusive treatment experience across the healthcare industry. By transforming their patient service models and enhancing collaboration, life sciences companies have the power to improve quality of life and long-term outcomes for millions of patients.

Key Takeaways

- There is a need to improve the treatment experience for patients, but current efforts only reach a small portion of the patient population. Life sciences companies can take a more inclusive approach to patient support services by targeting adherence and persistence.

- External innovation, propelled by new collaboration models across the ecosystem, is the key to large-scale change. Biotech and pharma companies have several characteristics that make them uniquely suited to play a connector role in the treatment journey:

  - Scientific expertise to identify patients with specific needs and design effective solutions that complement their medicines

  - Resources to help other stakeholders reach a larger scale

  - Powerful incentives to improve patient outcomes

- Life sciences companies must commit to making lasting changes internally as well.

  - Many organizations are making the shift from analog to data-driven research, ramping up their data, AI and machine learning capabilities to better understand the broader patient population.

  - They're optimizing their resources and tightening the connection between patient needs and patient solutions by shifting from patient service silos to an interconnected network.

  - And they're changing how they measure impact from "checking boxes" to human-first measurements, gaining insight into patients' behaviors, preferences, socioeconomic conditions, relationships and quality of life.

- Now is the time for organizations to significantly improve the treatment journey by evolving from offering reactive, legacy services to proactive, digital-first, human-centric patient support programs.

Acknowledgments

The authors would like to thank the following people for their contributions and input in writing this chapter: Emily Kremens, Jordan Less, Daniel Ogletree, Asheesh Shukla, Alexander Tung and Albert Whangbo.

Endnotes

1.	Peter Boersma, Lindsey I. Black and Brian W. Ward, "Prevalence of Multiple Chronic Conditions Among US Adults, 2018," in Preventing Chronic Disease 17 (September 17, 2020): 1-4, https://doi.org/10.5888/pcd17.200130external icon.

2.	ZS Independent Research, 2018.

3.	Jan M. De Maeseneer et al., "Provider Continuity in Family Medicine: Does It Make a Difference for Total Health Care Costs?" in Annals of Family Medicine 1, no. 3 (September 2003): 144-148, https://doi.org/10.1370/afm.75.

4.	Jonathan H. Watanabe, Terry McInnis and Jan D. Hirsch, "Cost of Prescription Drug-Related Morbidity and Mortality," in Annals of Pharmacotherapy 52, no. 9 (2018): 829-837, https://doi.org/10.1177/1060028018765159.

5.	Meera Viswanathan et al., "Interventions to Improve Adherence to Self-Administered Medications for Chronic Diseases in the United States," in Annals of Internal Medicine 157, no. 11 (December 4, 2012): 785-795, https://doi.org/10.7326/0003-4819-157-11-201212040-00538.

6.	World Health Organization (WHO), "Adherence to Long-Term Therapies: Evidence for Action," 2003, https://www.who.int/chp/knowledge/publications/adherence_full_report.pdf?ua=1

7.	WHO, "Adherence to Long-Term Therapies."

8.	Hensley Evans and Rachael Pius, "Creating a Stronger Patient Support Program," ZS, accessed July 18, 2021, https://www.zs.com/insights/creating-a-stronger-patient-support-program.

9.	Delivering on the CART customer experience, 2019.

10.	Sophia Elson, "New Research Reveals Global Consumer Trends for Healthcare & Life Sciences," Salesforce, November 5, 2019, https://www.salesforce.com/news/stories/new-research-reveals-global-consumer-trends-for-healthcare-life-sciences/.

11.	Abbott, "Neurosphere Digital Care," accessed January 18, 2022, https://neuro-sphere.abbott/learn-more/.

12.	Gilead, "Questions About COMPASS," accessed January 18, 2022, https://www.gileadcompass.com/questions-about-compass/.

13. American Heart Association CEO Round Table, "American Heart Association CEO Roundtable Delivers Roadmap to Help Employers Confront America's Mental Health Crisis," March 5, 2019, https://ceoroundtable.heart.org/american-heart-association-ceo-roundtable-delivers-roadmap-to-help-employers-confront-americas-mental-health-crisis/.

14. Danie du Plessis et al., "Patient Centricity and Pharmaceutical Companies: Is It Feasible?" in Therapeutic Innovation & Regulatory Science 51, no. 4 (2017): 460-467, https://doi.org/10.1177/2168479017696268.

15. Arjit Ganguli, Jerry Clewell and Alicia C. Shillington, "The Impact of Patient Support Programs on Adherence, Clinical, Humanistic, and Economic Patient Outcomes: A Targeted Systematic Review," in Patient Preference and Adherence 10 (2016): 711-725, https://doi.org/10.2147/ppa.s101175.

16. Albert Whangbo and Vaibhav Bansal, "Mining Insights to Improve Patient Retention on Medication," ZS, June 15, 2021, https://www.zs.com/insights/mining-insights-to-improve-patient-retention-on-medication.

17. Eli Lilly and Company, "Real-World Evidence: The Role of Patient Population Surveys to Improve Care in Migraine," Eli Lilly, October 9, 2020, https://www.lilly.com/news/stories/real-world-evidence-improve-care-in-migraine.

18. ZS Optimizing Patient Experiences in Life Sciences Study, March 24, 2020.

19. Filip Van den Bosch et al., "Impact of Participation in the Adalimumab (Humira) Patient Support Program on Rheumatoid Arthritis Treatment Course: Results from the PASSION Study," in Rheumatology and Therapy 4, no. 1 (June 2017): 85-96, https://doi.org/10.1007/s40744-017-0061-7.

20. AbbVie, "How Patient Voices Are Changing Medicine: An AbbVie Leader in Patient-Centered Research Helps Us to Hear and Consider the Patient Voice," May 2, 2019, https://stories.abbvie.com/stories/how-patient-voices-are-changing-medicine.htm.

21. John Waldron, "How Zappos Wins at Customer Service Every Day," eTail, accessed January 18, 2022, https://etailwest.wbresearch.com/blog/how-zappos-wins-at-customer-service-every-day.

22. Zappos, "Why Zappos Is So Obsessed with Impressing Its Customers," September 11, 2018, https://www.zappos.com/about/stories/obsessed-customer-service.

23. Pamela A. Danziger, "Home Depot's Transformation to a Fully Interconnected Retailer Shows Record-Breaking Results," Forbes, February 26, 2020, https://www.forbes.com/sites/pamdanziger/2020/02/26/home-depots-transformation-to-a-fully-interconnected-retailer-shows-record-breaking-results/?sh=f31231573307.

24. Datex, "Amazon and the Transition to Patient-Centric Healthcare: Amazon Positions Its Brand in Move to Patient-Centric Healthcare," accessed July 18, 2021, https://www.datexcorp.com/amazon-and-the-transition-to-patient-centric-healthcare/.

25. Phreesia Life Sciences, "Expanding Awareness of Patient Support Programs," 2021, https://www.phreesia.com/industry-perspectives-support/.

26. ZS Independent Research, 2018.

27. AstraZeneca, "New Normal Same Cancer," December, 2020, https://www.astrazeneca.com/our-therapy-areas/oncology/new-normal-same-cancer.html; AstraZeneca, "New Normal, Same Cancer: Our Commitment to the Cancer Community During the Pandemic," October 1, 2020, https://www.astrazeneca-us.com/media/astrazeneca-us-blog/2020/new-normal-same-cancer-our-commitment-to-the-cancer-community-during-the-pandemic-10012020.html.

28. These included ABC Global Alliance, Lung Cancer Europe, the World Ovarian Cancer Coalition, the World Pancreatic Cancer Coalition, the International Kidney Cancer Coalition, the Global Colon Cancer Coalition and the European Cancer Patient Coalition.

29. Zeposia, "Getting Started," accessed July 18, 2021, https://www.zeposia.com/starting-relapsing-ms-treatment/.

30. Kesimpta, "Kesimpta® Resources: Info at Your Fingertips," 2021, https://www.kesimpta.com/patient-support/resources/.

31. MS-UK, "Clinical Study Shows Online Therapy Elevida Helps Manage MS Fatigue," June 4, 2018, https://www.ms-uk.org/clinical-study-shows-online-therapy-elevida-helps-manage-ms-fatigue.

SECTION THREE INTRODUCTION: Making Patient Centricity a Reality

So, you've read Chapters 1 through 9 in this book and are persuaded that you want to make your organization patient-centric. But how do you get there? What will it take to pull this off?

Being serious about patient-centricity will necessitate a major transformation of each individual organization's ways of working, culture and operating model. Therefore, it needs to be driven from the top. This cannot be a grassroots effort. It cannot be driven just by one function or by a few enthusiastic evangelists. Each organization needs to build a patient-centric organizational ecosystem where people interact with an evolved organizational environment in new ways to create better outcomes. This will require that many functions of the organization change together, in a coordinated way. Leaders will need to shift their mindset from seeing change as an implementation problem to understanding change as a way of working—in other words, change is just what we do.

In this last section of the book, we examine what patient-centric transformation looks like, demonstrate that we should and can measure the impact of patient centricity for patients and the business, and imagine what the future could look like for patient-centric pharmaceutical companies.

So how can you make it happen? How can you change your organization into a patient-centric ecosystem? What needs to evolve in your organization's capabilities, ways of working, culture, structure and governance? How do you pull these changes through, winning the hearts, minds—and hands—of all your stakeholders? These are the questions we consider in Chapter 10. One example we discuss shows how one pharma organization created ambassadors among the ranks of its front-line managers and equipped them with coaching guides to help support their teams in making the transition to more patient-centered ways of working.

How do you ensure your actions are translating into meaningful impact? What data can you tap into? Collect? Combine? In Chapter 11, we detail the ways in which organizations can forge a link between patient-centric activities, the patient experience and, ultimately, outcomes. We look at both real-world data sources that can provide feedback on how specific programs are working, and examples of companies forging relationships with organizations like 23andMe to uncover better insights about patient needs as they live with specific diseases.

Finally, as an entire industry, we should start thinking about what comes next. How do we sustain patient-centric change? How do we continue to innovate and evolve? In Chapter 12, we examine some examples of innovation outside the pharma industry that may just give us some ideas for the future of patient centricity, including Northwell Health, which took a page out of Ritz Carlton's book (whoever heard of good hospital food?), Netflix and Delta Airlines.

Patient-centric transformation will involve many interdependent parts and many stakeholders; the change effort will be highly complex. It will require alignment, commitment and leadership from the top. If that's where you're at, read on. You have a key role to play, well beyond blessing the endeavor. If you're a patient centricity evangelist, you must first and foremost evangelize up before rallying the people around and under you.

Let's get started. To patient centricity—and beyond!

Chapter 10:
Transforming to a Patient-Centric Organization

Torsten Bernewitz

Change is hardest at the beginning, messiest in the middle and best at the end.

– Robin Sharma, author and leadership expert[1]

Announcing a vision for becoming patient centric can energize the people in an organization. But, like any change, it can also produce uncertainty and anxiety. Chapters 5 through 9 discussed the need to transform the pharma industry's approach to specific organizational functions—insights, ecosystem partnerships, R&D and marketing. Those aspects encompass one part of the patient-centric ecosystem: the operating model and governance.

Equally important is the other part of the patient-centric ecosystem: the people who transform the vision into a reality and make the operating model work. Here, it's important to consider the various stakeholders in patient centricity. First and foremost, there are those of us who work in the industry and endeavor to serve patients in our daily performance of our jobs. Then, there are our shareholders who want to see value from the patient-centric approach. Next, there are the healthcare providers, who are an integral part of shaping the patient experience and thus need to be with us. There are also "bystanders," like the media, who keep score and influence public perceptions of what we do. And, finally, there are the patients and their caregivers with whom we will need to partner in order to deliver on this new approach. We must win the hearts, minds and hands of all these stakeholders in order to make patient centricity a reality. That's the job before us!

This will not be a small feat, but it is not impossible if done right. This chapter will discuss what "doing it right" means. It addresses three areas that are essential to make patient centricity a reality in an organization: 1) how to shift mindsets, skills and behaviors; 2) how to set up an organizational structure that facilitates patient-centric ways of working; and 3) how to organize and orchestrate the change process itself.

Shifting Mindsets, Skills and Behaviors

We all know that major organizational transformations tend to fail, or at least disappoint, more frequently than they succeed. As an industry, we must be careful to navigate the change process with diligence and rigor, using evidence-based approaches. Thankfully, over the last two decades, the cognitive sciences have supplied valuable insights into why people act the way they act and feel the way they feel. Behavioral psychologists have dissected what makes people embrace some changes while rejecting others. We can use this body of research to facilitate our process of transformation.

Why Change Resistance Is a Myth but Change Failure Remains a Reality

It's a widely held belief that people are inherently resistant to change. Yet, upon closer examination, a more nuanced picture emerges. In fact, we all make fundamental changes in our lives all the time and do so voluntarily and, for the most part, happily. We go off to college, enter the work force, switch jobs, get married, have children. We move to a new house, a new city, sometimes even a new country. We embrace new media and entertainment options. We demand constant upgrades to our gadgets. We elect politicians in a landslide—and then can't get rid of them fast enough just a few years later. Sure sounds like a lot of change! The common belief about our latent aversion to change appears to be a myth.

But the difficulty of bringing about effective organizational change is still very real. Why is that? There is an impressive body of research exploring this question. In the end, the answer boils down to this: we adopt a new idea, like patient centricity, when we *understand* it, *like* it, *can act* on it and *want* to act *now*! These are the four conditions that need to be in place to bring about change. If one or more of these elements is weak or missing, the chances for successful change are slim.

Unfortunately, that is often the case. Having witnessed many change initiatives play out in practice, it seems to us at ZS that "understanding the change" is probably the most overplayed among these conditions, "liking it" the most underplayed, "being able to act" the most underestimated and "wanting to act" the most overlooked. To enable a patient-centric shift in pharma, the industry needs to unite to create all four conditions in a synergistic, systematic and diligent way. In order to do that, we need to think about change management as a marketing campaign to our stakeholders. And, like a marketing campaign, we must craft an exciting pitch for our proposal, understand our stakeholders' motivations and behaviors, and then create compelling experiences that shift attitudes and trigger actions.

Let's examine what it takes to plan and execute a great campaign for patient-centric ways of working and consider what challenges might crop up along the way. Step by step, a successful campaign involves:

- Pitching the change with a clear and persuasive case for patient centricity

- Ensuring that the leaders in the organization are aligned and committed

- Analyzing the different stakeholder groups and their motivations and behaviors

- Designing the what's-in-it-for-me (WIIFM) and change experience for the stakeholders

- Building momentum and ensuring sustained adoption of patient-centric ways of working

Pitching the Change: Where Are We Going, Why and How?

As an industry, we must articulate a clear and compelling case for embracing patient centricity. Why are we making this change? And why now? How is this all going to work? What is our collective vision for the industry's future, and what does it mean for each of us in our different roles?

The first section of this book thoroughly explored both the why and the what of patient centricity. But one important consideration we have not yet discussed is how to bring the why and the what to life for pharma's stakeholders. We need to create a sense of urgency to overcome the inertia that prevails in many organizations. Chapter 2 of this book detailed the forces driving the industry's move toward patient centricity. To recap, shifts in consumer, payer and healthcare professional (HCP) expectations and demands—both within an ever-intensifying competitive environment and together with diminishing R&D productivity—have created the *necessity* to do better. Meanwhile, advances in technology, data and analytics offer the *opportunity* to do better. Together, these trends make healthcare ripe for disruptive innovation. Patient centricity will be the future; it is just a question of whether pharma can claim a proactive position as a "change-shaper," or whether the industry will be relegated to the role of a bystander with limited differentiation and relevance.

This may sound harsh, and it is. We're being purposely blunt here to emphasize that pharmaceutical leaders must make sharp, punchy statements to communicate the urgency of this change and spur transformation throughout their organizations. This is not the time to be nuanced and subtle. Psychology teaches us a lot about the right framing of the case for change. We can either frame it as a way to avoid a significant risk to our business (loss aversion framing) or as a positive and exciting new development (opportunity framing). Loss-aversion framing is typically more effective for organizations that are established and doing reasonably well. As incumbents, many pharma organizations will fall into this camp. Opportunity framing, on the other hand, is typically more effective for organizations

187

that are relatively young and have strong growth expectations. This is the framing for an organization to use when it has nothing to lose—ideal for an industry disrupter.

Our stakeholders are the "customers" of our transformation to patient centricity: we must "sell" the change to them, and they need to "buy in." As stated earlier, we can think of the change effort as a campaign that we carefully plan and execute. To make a strong pitch to our stakeholders, we need to understand their motivations and pain points. We need to orchestrate a compelling experience for them that pulls them in emotionally. We need to do the change *with* them, not *to* them. We need to close the deal!

Admittedly, most organizations do a reasonable job of making the case for change and describing what they want to achieve with it. This is important, but it isn't sufficient in itself to propel the change. With our eyes set on our destination—our North Star—we must chart our course. What is our path to achieving our vision? What are our waypoints on this journey? Where do we want to be in 90 days? How close to our destination do we want to be after 12 months, in two years, in five years? Delineating a clear and attractive vision is essential, but now we must also make it feel real for our stakeholders.

Here's a great example how this can be done. To make their patient-centric vision tangible, cross-functional teams at a mid-sized pharmaceutical manufacturer co-created "destination postcards." They used the postcards to cast themselves two to three years into the future, imagining having completed a successful patient-centric transformation. In notes from their future selves, they described the new ways of working they had adopted and the benefits they had derived from those changes. Then they put posters of the postcards on the walls around the office to remind themselves: "This is what we are striving for. This is what we will create. This is our mission."

For ambitious transformations—and patient centricity most certainly fits that bill—it may be useful to "shrink the change" by chunking down the overall vision into smaller, more achievable pieces. This approach will also make organizational capability development more agile, as managing the change one step at a time makes it easier to adapt the approach as we learn. And it reduces the temptation to make "jam tomorrow" promises, i.e., good things that are promised for the future but never happen.

For instance, the same organization that created the destination postcards then laid out a "Future 1.0, 2.0 and 3.0," the stages of a patient-centric maturity model that the company would realize over time. While maintaining the overarching ambition and vision of patient centricity, the company leaders detailed the capabilities they would build and the outcomes they would achieve with each stage. With a playful nod to software development, they called these stages "releases of the future." This is the mindset and "learn-as-you-go" approach of the Agile methodology that has expanded in the last decade from information technology into the mainstream of organizational capability development, arriving in pharma over the last five years or so. We will revisit the Agile approach later in this chapter.

In all of this, we must be careful not to be prone to what psychologists call "positivity bias"—underestimating the difficulties we may encounter on our path toward realizing the vision or the time it may take to get there. This is a common pitfall. If our assumptions are too optimistic, we may over-promise and create anxiety and frustration when some unforeseen issues emerge, as they invariably will in a complex transformation. We must be realistic about the challenges in order to develop effective risk mitigation strategies, and we need to make sure that we resource the change initiative appropriately to be able to deal with setbacks.

For instance, when ZS worked with a biopharmaceutical organization on the planning of one of its key change programs, our team purposefully set up "red cap" thinking sessions as part of the process, during which we encouraged the company leaders to play devil's advocate. The team borrowed "red cap" from the Six Thinking Hats framework devised by Dr. Edward de Bono.[2] The red color stands for fire and emotions. When people participating in a discussion put on their imaginary red hats, this signifies that they have granted each other free range to express their true feelings and make critical statements without fear of causing offense. In ZS's work with this client, deploying red cap thinking made criticism of plan elements part of the change process, rather than a disruption that could potentially derail it. This allowed our team to be realistic about risks and obstacles and proactively develop mitigation strategies and contingency plans. The team also maintained a risk log alongside the implementation plan, regularly rating the overall risk level on a color-coded scale ranging from green to yellow to deep red.

Both the pressure testing with red cap thinking and maintaining a risk log helped our client avoid blind spots and surprises that could have hampered or disrupted the change process. By anticipating challenges and providing an arena where productive tension could play out safely, our client was able to proactively mitigate obstacles and steer the organization to a successful outcome in its change efforts.

To sum up, pitching the change entails crafting a credible and motivating narrative about the what, why and how of patient centricity: what do we want to achieve, why is this necessary, and how will we make it happen? In this, we must strike the right balance between audacity and feasibility, between speed and practicality, and between inspiring and critiquing.

The Leaders: Gathering Sponsors and Guides

Ok, almost ready. We have clarity about the reason behind, vision for and path to patient centricity. We have identified the risks along that path and have a mitigation plan. Now we must ensure that senior leadership and the sponsors of patient centricity are fully aligned with what we have presented. And we need more than buy-in—we need their proactive and visible commitment and support, not just at the beginning, but throughout the journey, and in both words and actions. The leaders need to model that new way. They must be honest about both the benefits as well as the difficulties and limitations.

At this stage, "bless and delegate" is a pitfall we at ZS have observed frequently. If leadership endorses the initiative but then steps away into the background—usually out of the benign motivation not to micromanage—this allows other agendas and distorted versions of the change vision to proliferate. This does not mean that leadership should be driving and involved in everything, but there needs to be consistent signaling to the organization that its leaders share a unified vision and are fully committed to seeing it through. Sponsors of patient centricity and the senior leaders in the organization must set the conditions for success, ensuring the leaders are—and stay—committed, that timing and pace are appropriate, and that the right change management resources are present.

Underestimating and underfunding the change effort is another common mistake to which too many organizations fall prey. At ZS, we recommend looking at the costs of managing change as the "insurance premium" for the success of the initiative. It's important that organizations view these costs not as a separate budget item but rather in relation to the value they are protecting. Based on ZS's experience, we recommend that companies dedicate about 15% of the overall investment in patient centricity to stakeholder engagement and communication—and potentially even more than 15% if the company is contending with deeply entrenched, old behaviors or significant pushback.

Change management is not just managing down or managing center-out. We need to manage up as well. And we need to ensure that honesty is brought to the table and that we don't avoid conflicts, ignore red flags or allow ambiguity or misalignment at the leadership level. Often, we need to make the case not just for change but also for change management. Leadership teams that don't see the need are most likely not ready to embed patient centricity in their organizations.

The Players: Who's in the Story, and What Happens to Them?

Once leaders are aligned and committed, we can plan how to translate our patient-centric vision into meaning for all the stakeholders who are directly or indirectly involved and affected. And there will be many—when it comes to patient centricity, almost all functions in an organization will be impacted in significant ways, if we consider the changes in resources, operating model and conditions that we discussed earlier in the book. We will have to assess change readiness, identify potential barriers and develop effective stakeholder engagement plans.

At ZS, we recommend taking a person-centric approach. In fact, a person-centric approach is consistent with—and models—patient centricity. Thus, the way we manage the transformation begins to shape the culture. We can start by creating a stakeholder map or stakeholder registry in order to comprehensively identify all internal and external stakeholders who will be impacted by the change or take part in the patient-centric transformation effort. Who are the people in our story, and how are they connected? What are their motivations, and what are their roles? Then, having identified the stakeholders, we need to walk a mile in their shoes. This allows us to develop the what's-in-it-for-me (WIIFM) and to design a cohesive and positive stakeholder experience. When change fails, it is almost always because of emotions. To be successful, we need to fully understand and master the emotional impact. What do the stakeholders think and feel?

Here's an example how a smaller pharma company navigated this challenge when the organization started to align core business processes with a patient-centric vision. At the outset, the vision of patient centricity sounded compelling and very positive. Who wouldn't like it? Who wouldn't agree that an organization creating products for patients should be patient centric? But as soon as the company began to think about the practical implications, concerns bubbled up that made some of the company leaders hesitate and dial back their enthusiasm. For example, they realized that a patient-centric pharma organization must be willing to accept a certain amount of new risk. Immediately, many legal, compliance and regulatory issues arose, all of which had the potential to drag the organization back to the status quo. There was a lot of nervousness and fear of getting into trouble, as an organization and maybe even individually. Also, as the company was engaging more with patients, its leaders had to be willing and able to act on what they heard. Raising expectations without follow-through would lead to disappointment and then disengagement—the opposite of what they wanted to achieve. With these potential headwinds, it was even more important to keep the leaders firmly aligned with the strategic North Star to avoid the organizational drag that could significantly slow down or even kill the vision.

What worked in the company's favor was its smaller size. With a nimbler, less complex political organization, the leaders succeeded in at least neutralizing the major naysayers through pushing and nudging, combined with a lot of patience. It was also an approach of picking battles and tolerating some imperfections in the patient-centric ways of working—at least for some time—in order to create momentum. Larger organizations may struggle with this even more, and it's all the more important for them to ensure full and sincere leadership alignment on the patient-centric vision and to be hyper-vigilant about spotting and addressing instances of ambiguity and diverging agendas.

In a transformation like patient centricity, as with all major changes, we must meet our stakeholders' concerns and fears with empathy. We cannot just plow on—any unresolved concerns could derail the movement later. We should empathize with the stressors associated with new ways of working, which can include anxiety about perceived risk, loss of existing relationships and affiliations, reduced control and influence, less transparency, higher complexity, reduced job security, increased ambiguity, increased workload, reduced resources and reduced variety.

After accounting for stakeholders' concerns, barriers and fears, it's now possible to focus on the elements of patient centricity that will make stakeholders excited about the change. What are unmet needs that we can leverage as we construct the WIIFM, the stakeholder-specific value proposition for the change? We can allay stakeholders' fears and anxieties by detailing the benefits the shift may hold for them; these "exciters" could include reduced risk, higher predictability, more decision rights and influence, higher clarity, lower complexity, reduced workload, increased resources and more variety. Depending on the stakeholders' mindsets, they may perceive some implications of the transformation as positive or negative; for instance, a change of status quo, the need for new knowledge and skills, and increased collaboration are developments that may hold appeal for some but not for others.

It's a good practice to evaluate the impact of the change on each stakeholder group and establish an "anxiety score." When ZS was working with a biopharmaceutical company undergoing a major transformation of ways of working and culture, the team created an "anxiety score" by giving each stressor and exciter across all initiatives impacting each stakeholder group a point value based on significance and then evaluating the cumulative effect. This helped the team spot where stakeholder groups were impacted by too many changes at the same time, risking change overload and change fatigue. To avoid such situations, the team re-prioritized and reordered the planned change initiatives and associated workstreams across the firm.

At another pharma company that ZS supported at some waypoints along its patient-centric quest, company leaders surfaced concerns, fears and exciters about the pending change by hosting "deep listening" sessions in interviews and workshops with representatives of each stakeholder group; this was paired with attitudinal stakeholder engagement surveys across the organization. Similar to the biopharmaceutical company mentioned above, this client also put anxiety scores and excitement scores together on an "emotional balance sheet" to measure the overall change load for each stakeholder group, which was a useful input in prioritizing stakeholders and sequencing the rollout over time. The leaders realized that doing this "deep listening" well would be an important foundation for the change strategy. Messaging for communication about the changes, design of touch points to interact with the stakeholders and creation of effective collateral to support these touch points all flowed from an unbiased, deep understanding of the stakeholder audiences. Accordingly, the leaders resisted the temptation to press ahead with the change program and allowed two months to fully understand the stakeholder groups before creating the change plan, which took another month. Let's now examine what it takes to build an impactful change plan.

Designing the WIIFM and Change Experience

Marketers have long known that customer experience is paramount. Since we are "marketing" our change, the same is true for the experiences of our stakeholders. These experiences will make or break the transformation to patient centricity. We must be purposeful and diligent in designing them.

Two elements will shape the stakeholder experience: content and stage set. Content is what is communicated in stakeholder engagement events; stage sets are where and how the engagement events happen. At ZS, we often liken change management to a theater production. The content is analogous to the play with the scenes and lines for the actors, while the stage set encompasses the set design, props and lighting. Together, they create an experience for the audience that is (hopefully) engaging and illuminating. Depending on its emotional resonance, the experience may even change the audience members' perspectives.

Let's focus on content first. With an enhanced understanding of the stakeholders' concerns, fears and exciters, we can now construct the stakeholder-specific value propositions for the change. This is not the same as the case for change for the company as a whole. Here, the questions are: "What do I lose?" (the WDIL), and "What's in it for me?" (the WIIFM). We must create stakeholder-specific narratives and messages that address fears and disarm barriers while also emphasizing and demonstrating the WIIFM. The relevance and credibility of the WIIFM are paramount—no spin! Figure 10-1 contains an example of a message set for one stakeholder group, showing how the messages ladder up to the value proposition and the overall case for change.

Figure 10-1: Example of a Core Message Set

Goal	Enabling cross-functional collaboration and innovation to drive impact through patient centricity
Overarching message	The Patient Lighthouse enables swift and powerful cross-functional decision making around patient centricity
Message 1	**Message 1: What** • We are setting up a data environment to put the right data at your fingertips in near real time. • The Patient Lighthouse is the **one-stop analytics solution** to track progress and impact of patient-related activities across our portfolio in a dynamic and transparent manner. • The Patient Lighthouse provides high quality data that can be trusted. It serves as our **single source of truth to provide a consistent and transparent understanding of the patient experience and the associated opportunities and risks across the organization.**
Detailed topics (separate briefing sheets)	• What is happening? • What is different? • What is the same? • Who will be impacted? • What is the timeline of the changes?
Goal	Enabling cross-functional collaboration and innovation to drive impact through patient centricity
Overarching message	The Patient Lighthouse enables swift and powerful cross-functional decision making around patient centricity
Message 2	**Message 2: Why** • Benchmarking shows that our patient experiences are less impactful than those of many of our competitors. We need to be in a much stronger competitive position versus our industry peers. • Our goal is to be a recognized and respected leader in the area of patient centricity by 2025. • This means we need to **optimize, streamline and pioneer new ways to look at all our available data** in order to fully understand how our activities are linked to patient experiences and identify and prioritize all levers to create better outcomes.
Detailed topics (separate briefing sheets)	• What brought about this change? • Why now? • What happens if we don't change? • WIIFM?

Goal	Enabling cross-functional collaboration and innovation to drive impact through patient centricity
Overarching message	The Patient Lighthouse enables swift and powerful cross-functional decision making around patient centricity
Message 3	**Message 3: Impact** • We envision a future where our people are working cross-functionally in an agile, innovative and collaborative environment. • This requires an investment in technology. But this is really **an investment in our people**—in the opportunity for accelerated professional growth, for participating in important innovations and for making new connections across the organization. • **The future is fast, cross-functional and data-driven**, and the Patient Lighthouse is designed to help you excel in this future through **swift, efficient and powerful decision making and planning.**
Detailed topics (separate briefing sheets)	• How will we shrink the change? • How will we support you in the transition? • How can you help and contribute? • What is the ask from stakeholders? • What are the next steps?

Equipped with stakeholder narratives and message sets, the next step is to design and then execute a compelling stakeholder experience. This requires more than communication and certainly more than training, although of course these elements are part of the overall experience. How can we tap into exciters and motivators, and what experiences should we avoid? How will we give the stakeholders some agency in the change, so that we can enact the change *with* them, not *to* them? Agency goes a long way in helping stakeholders embrace the change, any change.

An effective stakeholder engagement program involves change ambassadors (i.e., employees charged with supporting the change and helping to drive it forward) and consists of communications (multi-channel, multi-media, push-and-pull), workshops, learning sessions, co-creation opportunities and Q&A/FAQ support, among other elements. Figure 10-2 shows what such an engagement journey might look like.

Consider this example of how one pharma company designed a stakeholder journey. The company was building a new analytics platform to optimize its approach to clinical trials with an eye to creating better investigator and patient experiences. So, the change management team tasked with driving organization-wide adoption of the new platform ran four engagement sprints to shift stakeholders' mindsets, develop skills, and create new behaviors and habits. The stakeholders included a vast array of employee groups, such as therapy area leads, project delivery and asset leads, clinical trial managers,

Figure 10-2: Example of a Stakeholder Journey Design

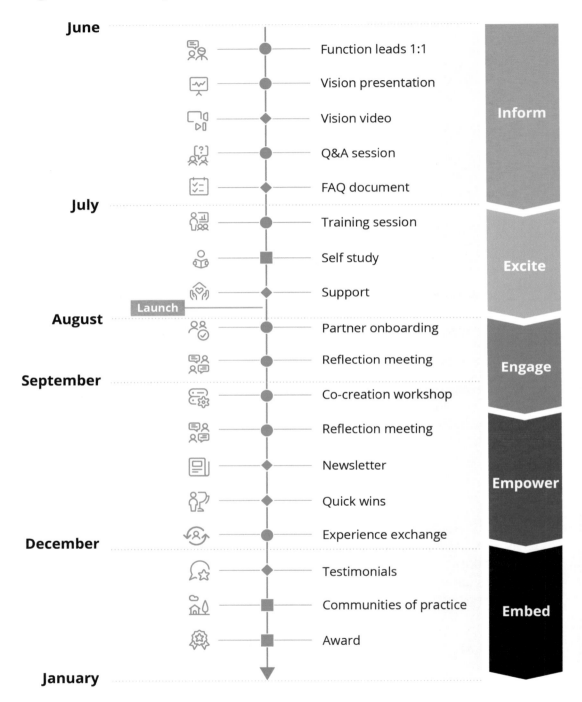

analytic leads, data owners and R&D technology owners, to name just a few. Each sprint had a particular focus in moving the stakeholders forward on the change journey: Excite, Engage, Empower and Embed. Each sprint had specific objectives regarding what the stakeholders should feel, know and do (again, concepts borrowed from marketing).

The Excite sprint took three weeks and was all about instilling desire and urgency to make the change by helping the stakeholders feel informed and understand why this change was necessary and beneficial. The change management team orchestrated a series of townhall meetings with discussions and Q&A sessions, facilitated the creation of vision videos and posters about the analytics platform and disseminated market research and benchmarking findings highlighting the shortcomings of the current approach, which was highly siloed and disconnected. The goal of the next sprint, Engage, was to ensure that the stakeholders felt valued and involved in the change process; believed the WIIFM, which had been tailored for each employee group; and made time to provide input and support for the new approach. The change management team achieved these objectives through a month-long series of workshops, feedback sessions and work-team deep dives about the functional implications. The subsequent sprint, Empower, took another six weeks and aimed at helping the stakeholders to feel well supported throughout the change process, embrace learning to become competent in the new way of working and start to work in this way with confidence. This sprint consisted of training sessions, self-study and a change ambassador program that included office hours with ambassadors during which fellow employees could pose questions or discuss any challenges. Finally, the Embed sprint was two months long and was designed to ensure that the stakeholders felt successful, never wanted to go back, and adopted and advocated the new patient-centric ways of working. This final sprint involved distribution of an internal company newsletter featuring success stories and testimonials from peers, healthcare providers and patients about their clinical trial experiences. The sprint also included workshops for each company function involved in clinical trials to share and discuss the realization and successes of the new patient-centric ways of working.

Momentum and Last Mile

With our stakeholders on board, we are now on the way, and we need to build and sustain the momentum. We can turn the patient-centric transformation into a movement by leveraging a key aspect of human behavior: not many people want to go first, but no one wants to be left behind. The pharma company mentioned above identified early adopters of the new approach and onboarded and proactively supported them so that they could be effective ambassadors for the change. These ambassadors built a growing inventory of stories and testimonials of early wins that they then disseminated during their efforts to promote the change.

Other organizations that ZS has accompanied on their transformation journeys even gamified the roll-out process, creating excitement and momentum about change initiatives through contests and adoption leaderboards. Numerous gamification companies have demonstrated that almost any task in the world can be gamified.[3] And, indeed, gamification can be a useful arrow in pharma's change management quiver; it can be an excellent way to make boring, routine tasks more engaging and to re-program engrained behaviors. The software company SAP, for example, used games to turn the thankless task of data scrubbing into an engaging challenge and to incentivize sales representatives to study the plethora of new documents and materials that they usually pushed down to the bottom of their to-do lists.[4]

Of course, we cannot expect that navigating a complex change program will always be smooth sailing. As the saying goes, no plan survives first contact. That's the reason why we must continue to monitor the "chatter" and sentiments throughout the organization. This helps us make the necessary course corrections in our stakeholder engagement events. We must be agile in our change management approach.

The leaders at the biopharmaceutical company mentioned earlier realized that it would be critical to monitor sentiments throughout the company's patient-centric transformation to identify and track the success of the mindset shift. Thus, they captured both qualitative and quantitative feedback through one-on-one leader discussions, Agile-style biweekly or monthly retrospectives of workstream teams, reports from a group of change ambassadors who acted as a bridge between the core change team and the functional communities, senior leadership townhalls and Q&As, and regular six-month employee engagement surveys to gauge enthusiasm about the direction the company was taking.

We've now reached the last mile of the journey. This is where we enable the team leaders on the frontlines to work with their people to make the change meaningful for them and adapt it to their specific environments and situations. For instance, at a biopharmaceutical company that wanted to bolster its commitment to patient centricity, leaders realized that the approach would not stick without mobilizing the frontline managers to act as ambassadors and coaches for their teams of individual contributors. To onboard the managers and equip them with tactics they could use with their teams, the company leaders created coaching guides for the heads of all the teams, ran coaching sessions as role plays and conducted a series of reflection calls and coach-the-coach interactions. They sustained these initiatives for several months until the roll-out was complete.

Finally, and crucially, we must not declare victory too early. This is where we "close the deal." As some organizations have learned the hard way, it's absolutely vital to sustain change management support until the new ways of working have been firmly implanted and cannot be uprooted again. Transformation strategists like John Kotter have been pointing this out at least since the mid-1990s, but time and again organizations fall into the premature victory trap. Only last year, a ZS client experienced this. Having just launched a new system designed to accelerate and enhance data-driven decision-making around the company's clinical trial strategy and implemented extensive training to help employees acclimate to the system, early usage data indicated good user adoption. This was appropriately celebrated and reported to senior leadership—a job well done. Management attention could now be allocated to other challenges, and so it was. However, after only a few months, usage appeared to be waning. Interviews revealed that users had been curious to learn about the new system and try it out—hence the strong uptick in the beginning. But then the novelty effect wore off, and the old habits and shortcuts re-emerged. Those engrained behaviors seemed easier and more familiar, while the knowledge users had acquired about the intricacies of navigating the new system faded through lack of practice. It took a substantial re-launch and sustained coaching effort to re-invigorate and then maintain usage of the new system. The company got there in the end but had lost valuable time because it had taken its eye off the ball too soon.

Shaping the Organizational Structure

Silos build the wall in people's minds and create the barrier in organizations' hearts.

– Pearl Zhu, author and corporate global executive[5]

So far, this chapter has focused on the people power necessary to make the transformation to patient centricity. The prominence of this discussion is justified, because, in the end, it will be people who deliver the patient-centric experience. But this work can be easy, or it can be unnecessarily hard. And that is where organizational structure comes in. Unfortunately, most healthcare organizations are structured in a way that is not conducive to patient-centric ways of working.

Companies may have become victims of their own success when it comes to structure. Most healthcare companies, like those in many other industries, are structured to maximize functional efficiency through specialization—and it works! But specialization creates disconnection between the functions, which results in poor patient centricity. Here's why: a company might have a sales team doing great in sales, a marketing team doing great in marketing, a medical team doing great in medical and an R&D team doing great in development. But rarely do they meet! It's impossible to create a holistic, end-to-end patient experience this way. It's the blind-men-and-the-elephant problem.

How to create a holistic patient experience then? There are a number of options, ranging from careful tweaking of the existing organizational model to the creation of Agile structural overlays to the radical approach of dissolving (most of) the existing structures and rebuilding a new operating model from the ground up.

In the healthcare sector, many companies have business cultures that lean toward the conservative, risk-avoidant end of the spectrum, so most have so far chosen an evolutionary approach and eschewed the more radical approaches we will describe later in this chapter. We will see in a moment that the more common incremental approaches have limitations, but they can still be useful stepping stones to create momentum and start embedding patient-centric thinking across an organization. This is the shrinking-the-change strategy that we discussed earlier in this chapter. Companies just need to ensure that they're not getting stuck at Future 1.0 and never move further—this would only lead to disillusionment and the perception that patient centricity is overhyped.

A Starting Point

In our research at ZS, we have come across four types of organizational structures aimed at fostering patient centricity:

- **Brand/Therapeutic-Area-Led (TA-Led) Model:** This model is typically found on the commercial side of the organization, where marketing teams often take the lead on patient-centric activities.

- **Distributed Universe Model:** Under this model, patient centricity is everyone's job, meaning that all (or most) functions within the organization hold some responsibility for patient centricity.

- **Center of Excellence (CoE) or Hub Model:** In this structure, a distinct functional group comprised of specialists focusing on varying aspects of patient centricity leads the organization's patient-centric efforts.

- **Federated Model:** This model is a hybrid of the CoE and distributed universe models, with a specialized core group that establishes best practices for patient centricity but with some responsibilities also falling under the aegis of various teams across the organization.

Figure 10-3: Example Patient-Centric Organizational Models[6]

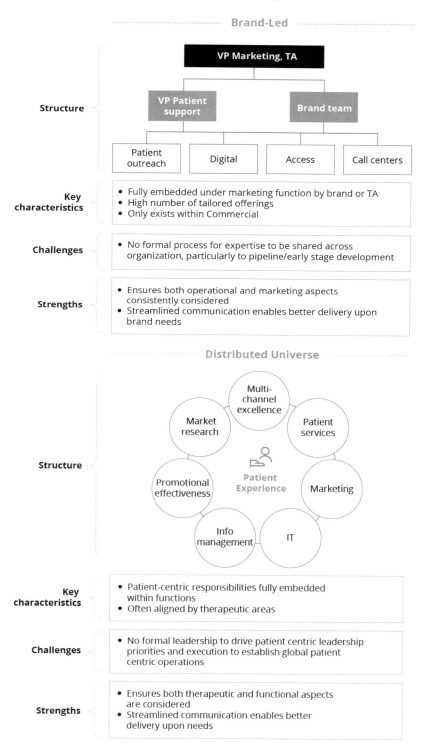

Figure 10-3 (continued)

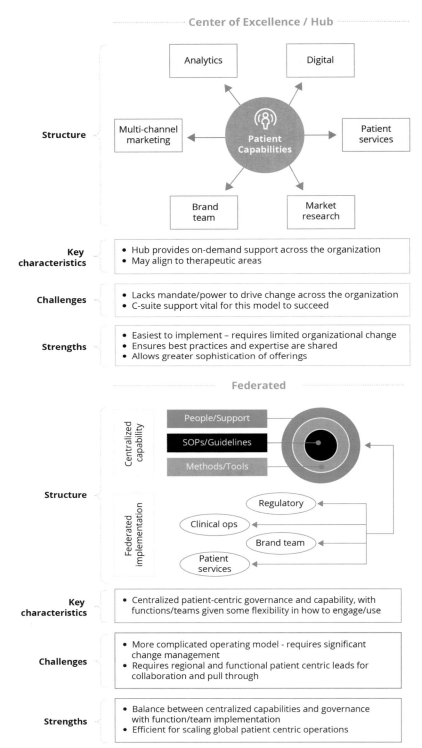

Center of Excellence / Hub

Structure

Analytics · Digital · Multi-channel marketing · Patient Capabilities · Patient services · Brand team · Market research

Key characteristics
- Hub provides on-demand support across the organization
- May align to therapeutic areas

Challenges
- Lacks mandate/power to drive change across the organization
- C-suite support vital for this model to succeed

Strengths
- Easiest to implement – requires limited organizational change
- Ensures best practices and expertise are shared
- Allows greater sophistication of offerings

Federated

Structure

Centralized capability: People/Support · SOPs/Guidelines · Methods/Tools

Federated implementation: Regulatory · Clinical ops · Brand team · Patient services

Key characteristics
- Centralized patient-centric governance and capability, with functions/teams given some flexibility in how to engage/use

Challenges
- More complicated operating model - requires significant change management
- Requires regional and functional patient centric leads for collaboration and pull through

Strengths
- Balance between centralized capabilities and governance with function/team implementation
- Efficient for scaling global patient centric operations

Figure 10-3 outlines the strengths and challenges for each of these models. What they all have in common, though, is that they are fairly cautious attempts to push toward patient centricity while keeping one foot in the old world. This hesitancy may be one of the reasons that, for many pharma organizations, patient centricity has not yet fulfilled its promise. One of the risks in adopting a tentative approach, then, is providing fodder for the skeptics and naysayers of patient centricity.

To start, the Brand/TA-Led Model, while maintaining proximity to the business and often to patient insights, does almost nothing to address the silo problem, which is one of the most common root causes when patient-centric initiatives fail. On the other end of the spectrum, the Distributed Universe approach is well intended, making patient centricity a key component of every function; however, without formalization through restructuring or Agile teams (as we will discuss later on) everyone's job quickly becomes no one's job. The Center of Excellence (CoE) approach is closely aligned with pharma's historical tendency toward specialization but relies on the goodwill of the other functions and has no teeth without a clear mandate and the associated authority. The Federated model, finally, is the most advanced and aspires to the ideal of balancing expertise and focus with the fluidity required to make meaningful and lasting change. But, as long as the underlying organizational structure itself remains unchanged, an overlay is required to enable effective cross-functional collaboration. This overlay can come in two forms: a) an additional layer of multi-functional task forces, work teams or committees, or b) a clear and achievable delineation of cross-functional workflows and associated decision rights. Unfortunately, this approach is complicated to run. Without clear governance, the approach can quickly be mired in ambiguity. At the same time, if organizations regulate too much, they run the risk of creating a Frankenstein's monster in terms of oversight and micro-management. In either case, these approaches may be slowing the organization down instead of making it faster and more agile.

The limitations aside, we have seen more advanced patient-centric organizations successfully employ CoEs and the Federated model to embed patient centricity. This is not to say that Brand-Led or Distributed Universe models can't work at all, but, to find traction, they require a well-established culture that's already steeped in patient focus to supersede the structural limitations mentioned above. Not many pharma organizations have that yet.

These approaches can be a useful first step. But, in order to realize and sustain the full promise of patient centricity, organizations need to incur more risk. If we really want transformation in the industry, we may need to break some things. That is why a few pharma companies have started to embark on more audacious—and also more disruptive—endeavors.

Achieving Superfluidity

These companies—pioneers at the forefront of the industry—have built their organizational structure around dexterous cross-functional teams. In this approach, individuals have a home in their respective function but perform almost all of the work cross-functionally. As a useful analogy, think about a soccer team: different players have different skills (while a few positions are versatile by design), but they all play together on one field in the same game. What does this mean? It means that these organizations no longer have marketing strategies that are developed exclusively by marketing teams, sales plans created exclusively by sales teams or future portfolio strategies developed exclusively by R&D teams. Instead, these companies' patient solutions strategies are co-created—and co-owned—by all these functions together. And, importantly, this co-ownership is formalized through governance.

Critics of this approach might balk at the significant costs and inefficiencies of collaboration, and, yes, these detractions do come with the territory. To move forward, some old behaviors and approaches must be left behind. If companies have the discipline to stop doing some of the things they are doing today, like brand-centered strategic planning, push action tactics and relentless ROI quantification,[7] the net effect of adopting a collaborative model may not be as big as it might seem.

This approach is a super-charged version of the structural overlays described in the federated model. In the federated model, most of the work is performed in the business functions, and some of the work is in cross-functional teams. Organizations that strive for superfluidity flip this balance: the norm is cross-functional work; the exception is functional work. Cross-functional teams are no longer just an overlay; rather, they are integral to the organization's structure. Furthermore, the cross-functional teams remain fluid—or Agile—in the sense that their composition and mission can, and will, change frequently to respond to new business challenges or opportunities.

One of the healthcare trailblazers in organizing and managing in more Agile ways in both the R&D and commercial arenas is Genentech. In an effort to improve patient experience and outcomes, Genentech has been transitioning over the last three to four years from a traditional siloed organizational model to Agile, cross-functional, team-based ways of working.[8] The leadership team felt that the organization had built up internal structures and processes that distanced people from the purpose of serving patients with life-threatening and life-altering diseases. Genentech introduced Agile ways of working to remove a lot of the complexity in the organization so that the link to the patient became a lot clearer and more direct, helping the company bring innovative medicines to patients faster. Key principles Genentech adopted from the Agile approach were greater empowerment, a fit-for-purpose evolutionary design over perfectionism, advice seeking and, of course, patient centricity.

In a similar vein, with a view to delivering a positive end-to-end clinical trial experience for patients, Pfizer's Global Clinical Supply (GCS) organization has created new decision-making bodies, cross-functional committees the company has dubbed "tetrads." Each tetrad is comprised of talent from GCS's line functions and is collectively accountable for all of the clinical supply teams within a single therapeutic area.[9] This organizational feature, which started as an experiment, was one of the factors contributing to the extraordinary speed of the clinical trial execution for Pfizer's COVID-19 vaccine. Keeping cross-functional teams with decision-making authority working closely together turned out to be a key factor of success in this instance.

The move toward nimble, fluid organizational structures is not easy, however, even for leading firms in fast-paced industries. For instance, Cisco and Microsoft both explored a number of organizational changes to improve their flexibility and agility, only to find that, despite the best of intentions, these changes proved difficult to implement and were only partially effective.[10] But superfluidity is still possible at such organizations, as the example of Chinese tech giant Huawei illustrates. Huawei's structural design ensures the customer is at the center of everything the company does. Its support functions are built around flexible platforms that are shared across business groups, and management-level employees continually rotate between different jobs. The company's culture embraces a constant pace of change as a key operating principle. All of these elements together make Huawei one of the most fluid organizations in the world, despite its size and complexity.[11]

These examples show that finding ways to create a more customer-centric—or, in the pharma world, patient-centric—organization that is fast and adaptable is a fairly universal challenge across industries. And that's good news: pharma companies can learn how to do it well and what pitfalls to avoid from the trailblazers within the pharma industry and also from the successes and failures of companies in other industries.

Restructuring and Rebuilding

One drawback of the Agile ways of operating described above is they can become unnerving and create change fatigue. While some may enjoy change, most people crave stability and may not be able to sustain the relentless flux that leaves them feeling unmoored. The alternative would be to dissolve (most of) the existing structures and rebuild a new operating model from the ground up. In a way, this involves forging the fluid structure that comes with Agile cross-functional teams into a more permanent structure. There would no longer be marketing, sales and R&D divisions. Instead, a company might have patient research, patient experience design and patient experience delivery as its externally-facing core functions supported by production functions, such as product development and communication collateral development, to make and supply what the core functions need (see Figure 10-4).

Figure 10-4: Illustrative Model of the Ideal Patient-Centric Organizational Structure, Built Around Patient Needs and Deliberately Designed Experiences

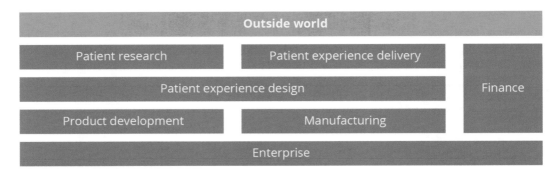

If there is still a need for therapeutic specialization, a company might move these behind the scenes and, for example, subdivide product development by therapy area. However, this approach is likely not palatable to most healthcare organizations right now; it is too radical, too disruptive. It will be next to impossible to align everyone on a common vision of what the new structure should look like, and thus industry incumbents will find it hard to do. However, this is how a disrupter in healthcare, unencumbered by a legacy structure—say Apple, Google or Amazon—might organize a patient-centric healthcare business, thus achieving potential competitive advantage. And these new healthcare players are coming—and they will likely be able to make a strong claim on patient centricity!

Best Practices

Regardless of the structure selected for fostering patient centricity, ZS has observed a few best practices that successful organizations employ:

- **Accountability at the top**: Having a member of the senior leadership who is accountable for instilling patient centricity across the organization is critical. This is not to say that a chief patient officer is necessary, but, whether it's the chief marketing officer, the senior vice president of customer experience or another function, it's crucial that the patient have an advocate with a position at the top. Otherwise, patient-centric initiatives tend to flounder without authority behind them.

- **Balancing proximity to the business and functional expertise**: Successful companies will ensure that patient-focused functional expertise is balanced with knowledge specific to each therapeutic area and connection to the business needs. This can be accomplished in multiple ways, depending on the organizational structure and culture; for instance, achieving this balance might mean embedding patient engagement functional experts in TA, program or brands teams.

- **Measurement and accountability**: As the old adage goes, you can't change what you can't measure. High-performing patient-centric organizations set clear objectives with measurable KPIs to create accountability for the path forward and understand the impact for the patient and the organization (more about metrics and KPI in the next chapter).

Orchestrating the Transformation Process Itself

The conductor of an orchestra doesn't make a sound. He depends, for his power, on his ability to make other people powerful.

– Benjamin Zander, conductor of the Boston Philharmonic and the Boston Philharmonic Youth Orchestras[12]

To reiterate, the transformation to patient centricity is a journey with many waypoints, and leadership commitment is critical for it to succeed. But, not only do we need leaders, we also need a navigator or conductor. As we are shaping new patient-centric capabilities in the ways outlined in Chapters 5 through 9 and also shifting stakeholders' mindsets, skills and behaviors as discussed above, we need to ensure that both the organizational capabilities and the people making them a reality remain aligned to our North Star for the patient-centric ecosystem.

This is very important. If one part of the ecosystem gets out of sync with the other, that could jeopardize the overall initiative. We could do an excellent job of shaping the operating model, but if we leave the stakeholders behind and don't win their hearts and minds, all of our investment in the organizational infrastructure goes to waste—it's a we-built-it-but-they-didn't-come situation. This risk is universal across industries: customer centricity fails if the power of the status quo is ignored. Consider the example of Best Buy: despite the best efforts of the CEO and senior leaders, the company's success got derailed by competing visions of the future. What did customer centricity even mean for Best Buy? What was the best path to take to get there? Some store leaders understood that achieving true customer centricity would require a broad shift at the level of company culture, while others were narrowly focused on the financial implications. These competing internal forces got in the way of long-term growth, and, without a strong North Star, customer centricity collapsed, at least for a while, when the CEO who had been the main proponent of the customer-centric vision left.[13]

The opposite is also true. If we create a lot of excitement and promise around patient centricity, but we are unable or unwilling to design an operating model to live up to the promise, all we have created is hype. If the hype proves empty, stakeholders will be disappointed and become cynical, and there may not be a second chance to get it right. Already, some industry insiders put patient centricity somewhere between the "peak of inflated expectations" and the "trough of disillusionment" on Gartner's hype cycle.[14] They ask questions like, "A dream deferred, or a promise denied?"[15] and state that "patient centricity is not enough."[16]

The processes of shaping the operating model and shifting mindsets, skills and behaviors must therefore be well synchronized and orchestrated. This is a job of constant steering, communicating, listening, facilitating, experimenting and tracking. Companies looking to make the move to patient centricity need an orchestrator—usually not a single person but rather a team of program management experts with experience not just in project management but also in change and communication strategy.

And beyond the conductor, we still have all the individual musicians (stakeholders) who are virtuosos on their respective instruments (their roles). While all the musicians excel at playing their own instruments, they still need to have sheet music (plans) to know how to play in harmony. The conductor is there to hold it all together, to energize and synchronize the musicians and to get the best out of all the performers, molding a collection of talented individuals into a unified ensemble that is more than the sum of its parts.

Governance and Metrics

The governance of the transformation includes the transformation team structure, decision rights and escalation paths. It's important to keep governance simple, clear and without ambiguity. A good practice is to leverage transformation playbooks that include guidelines and templates for transformation governance, team charters, RACI and recommendations regarding the engagement between the center and affiliates.

One word of warning: we need to ensure that we don't allow a "shadow" governance model to emerge, one that entails backchannelling and ambiguous decision-making processes. As discussed above in the subsection titled "The Leaders: Gathering Sponsors and Guides," inconvenient truths must be brought up, and politicking must be avoided or called out when it happens. Backchanneling can be a pitfall in any type of organization. While side conversations can be valuable by facilitating collaboration and promoting change, they can also be the source of a lot of trouble: encouraging political maneuvering, marginalizing members with key expertise, fostering inappropriate alliances and leading to poor decisions. This is a particular risk in initiatives like patient centricity, which can be ambiguous and require a strong effort to gain and sustain leadership alignment.

We also need to align on how we want to track progress of our transformation journey. Transformation metrics must not be confused with the metrics around patient centricity (more on that in Chapter 11). Transformation metrics measure and track the progress and success of the transformation itself. We should configure a set of leading and lagging performance indicators for the "inner game" (internal stakeholder engagement, enthusiasm for the change and progress in adopting the new patient-centric ways of working) as well as the "outer game" (customer reactions, net promoter scores and improvement of our business results).

The metrics should be configured into a transformation dashboard to assess change readiness and to monitor and report progress. It's important that we track not just how the program advances, but also if and how the mindset shift happens. Are we winning the stakeholders' hearts and minds? What is the "chatter" in the organization? Who are the supporters? Where may there be pockets of active or passive discontent? Most organizations track these metrics by administering surveys, monitoring participation in events, analyzing feedback and questions, and considering qualitative feedback from the change ambassadors. In some (but rarer) cases, organizations also use social listening.

Methods

Finally, we have to determine which approach we want to use to build the data flows, tools and processes for the new patient-centric ecosystem. Many organizations these days use Agile for most workstreams (though not all). The Agile methodology is a superior choice when we are initially uncertain about requirements of what exactly needs to be built, when timelines are short, and when we want rapid delivery. For example, Agile is a great fit for online applications for patients or healthcare providers, where the solution can be released to the users as a so-called "minimum viable product" (MVP) as soon as it can provide some value, and is then continually evolved and optimized based on user behavior and feedback. Internal examples where an Agile development approach may be preferred are reporting and analytic systems running on top of the data management architecture and ecosystem. Waterfall, on the other hand, is superior when there are complex interdependencies between components of the solutions that we need to manage. This approach is best suited for solutions where the functionality can't be delivered in pieces or released as a minimum viable product, for example a medical device or healthcare app that must be fully functional, proven to be safe and effective, and have received regulatory approval before delivery. Internally, Waterfall is preferred for enterprise applications and the data management ecosystem that have low uncertainty in both the requirements and the solution, but are highly complex and difficult to change once set up. To develop technical solutions, companies have been turning to early experience teams—cross-functional teams that develop and refine a solution in a real environment and with real customers. For one ZS client, a multinational agrochemical organization, early experience teams have become the go-to approach for almost any type of major change. ZS Principal Mike Moorman describes the approach thus:

> Successful organizations … start with a small team of superstars and a high-quality account list and over-support them while they figure out Key Account Management (KAM) and demonstrate the impact that it can have. These early experience teams are not pilots. Pilots tend to be run as lightly supported experiments. With early experience teams, the focus isn't, "Will it [this effort] succeed?" but rather, "How do we make it successful and scalable?"[17]

Deploying early experience teams differs from the conventional piloting approach in terms of objectives, methodology and level of support. The objective is to co-create or at least refine a process, develop material, win advocates and enable coaches for the broader roll-out. Early experience teams receive a high level of support and coaching in the form of just-in-time manuals, ad hoc materials and tools that can be standardized and automated at a later stage.

At ZS, we often recommend using the Double Diamond design process model developed by the British Design Council. Divided into four phases—Discover, Define, Develop and Deliver—the main feature of the Double Diamond is its emphasis on "divergent" and "convergent thinking," where a team first proposes an array of ideas before refining and narrowing down the list to identify the best idea. This process of refinement happens twice in this model—once to confirm the problem definition and once to create the solution.

As discussed earlier, the change experience must be congruent with key tenets of patient centricity, which is why we at ZS recommend a person-centric approach to the transformation process itself. In a similar way, the change management approach must be consistent with the selected development methodology—a Waterfall-like, sequential change process does not work with Agile. When deploying Agile, it is best to use an approach with sprints, scrums and retrospectives to engage the stakeholders.

And now we're off to the races! Achieving patient centricity offers a lot of reward but comes at the price of effort and disruption. But if it were easy, we wouldn't have written a whole book about it (and you wouldn't have made it to this chapter)! In Chapter 2, we talked about the perfect storm that is propelling the industry toward patient centricity: seismic shifts in consumer behavior and expectations, competition, technology, data, analytics and regulatory oversight, among others. There is both challenge and opportunity as the industry sails into this storm. We hope that the suggestions in this book will help you harness the energy of the perfect storm and steer your organization toward new levels of performance and relevance.

If you can find a path with no obstacles, it probably doesn't lead anywhere.

– Frank A. Clark, American lawyer and politician[18]

Key Takeaways

- Transforming to patient centricity can be exciting but also produce uncertainty and anxiety. We must be careful to navigate the change process with diligence and rigor, using evidence-based approaches from behavioral science.

- People will adopt patient centricity when they *understand* it, *like* it, *can act* on it and *want* to act *now*! We must create these four conditions in a systematic way through a "marketing campaign" to our stakeholders.

- We must take a person-centric approach and meet our stakeholders' concerns and fears with empathy. The way we manage the transformation will begin to shape the culture.

- An effective stakeholder engagement program involves change ambassadors and consists of communications (multi-channel, multi-media, push-and-pull), workshops, learning sessions, co-creation opportunities and Q&A/FAQ support, among other elements.

- Change management is not just managing down or managing center-out. We need to manage up as well. And we need to ensure that "the truth" is brought to the table.

- We must have a robust change plan, but we also must stay agile in our change management approach. We must continue to monitor the chatter and sentiments throughout the organization and make necessary course corrections.

- We must not declare victory too early. It's vital to sustain the change management support until the new ways of working have been firmly implanted and cannot be uprooted again.

- Most healthcare organizations are structured in a way that is not conducive to patient-centric ways of working. There are many options to remedy this, ranging from careful tweaking of the existing organization model, to Agile structural overlays, to the radical approach of dissolving existing structures and rebuilding a new operating model from the ground up.

- Current approaches to the structure question have limitations but can be useful stepping-stones to create momentum and start embedding patient-centric thinking across the organization. We just need to ensure that we don't stop there.

- The processes of shaping the operating model and shifting stakeholders' mindsets, skills and behaviors must be well synchronized and orchestrated. This is a job of constant steering, communicating, listening, facilitating, experimenting and tracking. It requires a team of specialists with experience not just in project management but also in change and communication strategy.

- The governance of the transformation process itself must be simple, clear and without ambiguity. A good practice is to leverage transformation playbooks that include guidelines and templates for transformation governance, team charters, RACI and recommendations regarding the engagement between the center and affiliates.

Acknowledgments

The following people helped or advised in the writing of this chapter: Hensley Evans, Sharon Suchotliff and Maria Whitman.

Endnotes

1. Robin Sharma, "The Leader Who Had No Title: A Modern Fable on Real Success in Business" (New York: Free Press, 2010).

2. Edward de Bono, "Six Thinking Hats" (Boston: Little, Brown and Company, 1985).

3. Yu-Kai Chou, "The 10 Best Examples of Using Gamification in the Enterprise, Corporate Workplace," Yukaichou, accessed August 15, 2021, https://yukaichou.com/gamification-examples/top-10-enterprise-gamification-cases-employees-pro-ductive/#.wvhl91spnyu.

4. Chou, "The 10 Best Examples."

5. Pearl Zhu, "Digitizing Boardroom: The Multifaceted Aspects of Digital Ready Boards," 2nd ed. (self-pub., Pearl Zhu, 2018).

6. ZS Associates, external industry interviews, completed June 2018.

7. Tim Lebrecht, "If You Really Want to Be Customer-Centric, Stop Doing What You're Doing," Inc., July 9, 2019, https://www.inc.com/tim-leberecht/if-you-really-want-to-be-customer-centric-stop-doing-what-youre-doing.html.

8. Frank Duff and Malte Schutz, "Agile: The New Active Ingredient in Pharma Development," interview with Aliza Apple and Steven Aronowitz, McKinsey & Company, July 7, 2019, https://www.mckinsey.com/business-functions/organi-zation/our-insights/agile-the-new-active-ingredient-in-pharma-development; Nancy Oak and Jamie Freedman, "Pioneering a New Customer Engagement Model During COVID-19," Genentech, July 17, 2020, https://www.gene.com/stories/pioneering-a-new-customer-engagement-model-during-covid-19.

9. Linda A. Hill and Emily Tedards, "Michael Ku and Global Clinical Supply at Pfizer Inc: Bringing Hope to Patients," in Harvard Business School Supplement 421, no. 37 (December 2020, revised February 2021), https://www.hbs.edu/faculty/pages/item.aspx?num=59377.

10. Peter J. Williamson, Xiaobo Wu and Eden Yin, "Super-Fluidity: Creating an Organisation That Flexes with the Market," Centre for Chinese Management, University of Cambridge Judge Business School, 2019, https://www.jbs.cam.ac.uk/wp-content/uploads/2020/08/wp1901.pdf.

11. Peter J. Williamson, Xiaobo Wu and Eden Yin, "Learning from Huawei's Superfluidity," Ivy Business Journal, May/June 2019, https://iveybusinessjournal.com/learning-from-huaweis-superfluidity/.

12. Benjamin Zander, "The Transformative Power of Classical Music," filmed February 2008, TED video, 17:17, https://www.ted.com/talks/benjamin_zander_the_transformative_power_of_classical_music/transcript?language=en.

13. James Damian, " 'Customer Centricity' Is Misunderstood," Retail Dive, May 24, 2018, https://www.retaildive.com/news/customer-centricity-is-misunderstood/524103/.

14. Paul Tunnah, "Tunnah's Musings: Hope Over Hype for Pharma in Patient Centricity, Multichannel and Beyond the Pill," Pharmaphorum, December 20, 2016, https://pharmaphorum.com/views-and-analysis/tunnahs-musings-hope-hype-pharma-patient-centricity-multichannel-beyond-pill/.

15. Virgil Simons, "Patient Centricity: A Dream Deferred or a Promise Denied?" LinkedIn, April 6, 2021, https://www.linkedin.com/pulse/patient-centricity-dream-deferred-promise-denied-virgil-simons-mpa/.

16. Marc Lafleur, "The End of Patient Centricity," Gemic, March 16, 2018, https://gemic.com/the-end-of-patient-centricity/.

17. Pretap Khedkar, "Achieve KAM Success by Overcoming the 'Challenge from Within,' " BioPharma Dive, May 29, 2018, https://www.biopharmadive.com/spons/achieve-kam-success-by-overcoming-the-challenge-from-within/524101/.

18. Forbes, "Thoughts on the Business of Life," accessed January 21, 2022, https://www.forbes.com/quotes/3054/.

Chapter 11:
Forging the Link Between Patient Experience and Outcomes

Fiona Taylor and Albert Whangbo

Chapter 4 outlined several hypotheses for why pharma companies have been slow to adopt patient-centric approaches. One of the primary reasons is the fact that their key performance indicators (KPIs) and incentives are not aligned with achieving patient-centric outcomes. While we would expect most of today's core business measures—product development times, number of patients on therapy, prescriptions, sales, etc.—to continue to guide business decision-making, adopting enterprise-level patient centricity will require linking patient-centric activities directly to indicators of business impact. But, for many companies, this link has been tricky to demonstrate convincingly. How can pharma companies be sure that their patient-centric actions are translating into impact for their own businesses? The answer, to put it simply, is more and better measurement. Three steps are required to establish a measurement capability that ties patient-centric outcomes to business impact:

1. Create a measurement-driven culture around patient impact
2. Put a mechanism in place to quantify and connect the three pillars of patient centricity:
   a. Activity
   b. Experience
   c. Impact
3. Gather or generate the data needed for measurement

Establish a Measurement Culture

Most pharma organizations are adept at measuring the impact of their core business activities. Take sales force promotion as an example: estimating the sales lift associated with field-based promotion has long been an essential element of the marketing mix analyses that insights teams conduct for the annual business planning process. Many pharma companies have now taken this data-driven approach to evaluate and optimize their promotional efforts even further, investing in automated next-best-action capabilities that use artificial intelligence to predict which content, channels and cadence of customer engagement will drive the highest incremental gains. Of course, achieving today's level of sophistication in sales planning and operations did not happen overnight—it took years of advances in data, technology and analytical methods to become possible. It also required a cultural shift in sales leadership to embrace the role that data and measurement could play in augmenting the intelligence and effectiveness of field professionals.

Data-driven clinical trial execution provides another example of how measurement is meaningfully impacting business outcomes. Historically, relationships with investigators drove trial site selection. Now, however, careful assessment of the local prevalent patient population and the likelihood of successful recruitment at each candidate site are the major determinants. Methodically identifying the best trial locations is helping pharma companies accelerate the time to market while reducing overall trial costs. Closely monitoring trial recruitment rates and leveraging data to predict and prevent dropouts is also helping accelerate trial completion, with huge implications for brands' commercial opportunities.

The same kind of data-driven cultural shift that has transformed product development and commercial operations is required to activate patient-centric measurement that will lead to virtuous action-to-impact cycles. As David Waller pointed out in his Harvard Business Review article, a new measurement culture starts at the top with leadership, values and communication.[1] Leadership's objective should be to challenge, encourage and empower employees to demonstrate—using data—how their decisions and actions positively impact both patients and the business. Pfizer Innovative Health is a leading example of a company that has instituted a patient-centric measurement culture. Back in 2017, while he was senior vice president of patient and health impact at Pfizer, Andy Schmeltz integrated patient benefit metrics, such as the number of patients helped, into the standard business outcomes. Schmeltz exemplified the ideal leadership vision for integrating patient centricity and consistently lived up to his promise of putting the patient first: "Patients link together the interests of pharmaceutical companies, healthcare systems and society. If we can align around what's best for the patients, everyone wins."[2]

The Three Pillars of Patient-Centric Measurement

With the right data-driven culture in place, we can turn our attention next to the kinds of measurements that need to happen to keep organizations consistently aligned with their patient-centric objectives. In a 2020 literature review, ZS identified three pillars of measurement for patient-centric organizations: activity, experience and impact[3] (see Figure 11-1). Measurement of activity refers to both internal enabler metrics (such as organizational effort, time, capital and communications around patient-centric programs) and patient engagement metrics (including website visits, emails opened and program registrations). Experience refers to patients' perspectives of their overall experience, from taking their medications to using beyond-the-pill solutions to interacting with the pharma company or its representatives. Lastly, impact refers to business impact (product development time, prescriptions, adherence and revenue), patient impact (patient satisfaction and clinical outcomes) and societal impact (health equity and population health), all of which are important to pharma's respective stakeholders. Table 11-1 outlines some specific examples of metrics in each category.

Figure 11-1: Patient-Centric Organizations Adopt Specific Metrics for Activity, Experience and Impact

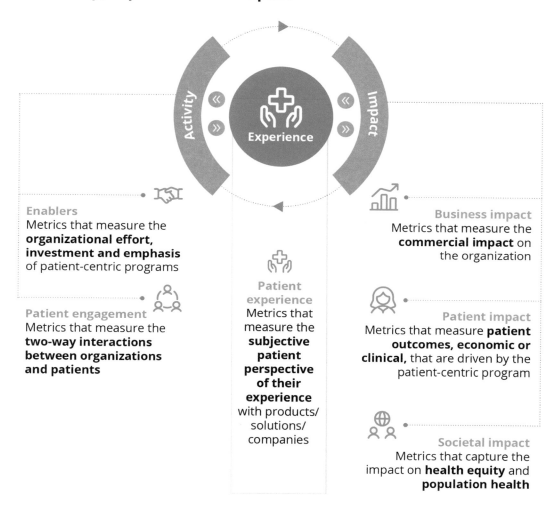

Enablers
Metrics that measure the **organizational effort, investment and emphasis** of patient-centric programs

Patient engagement
Metrics that measure the **two-way interactions between organizations and patients**

Patient experience
Metrics that measure the **subjective patient perspective of their experience** with products/ solutions/ companies

Business impact
Metrics that measure the **commercial impact** on the organization

Patient impact
Metrics that measure **patient outcomes, economic or clinical,** that are driven by the patient-centric program

Societal impact
Metrics that capture the impact on **health equity** and **population health**

Table 11-1: An Integrated Measurement Plan Includes Metrics That Allow for Activity to Be Connected to Experience and Impact

Dimension	Type	Example
Activity	Internal enablers	Budget for patient-centric initiatives, prosocial job characteristics scale, length and number of non-pharma partnerships, clinical trial diversity metrics
	Patient engagement	Web metrics, app usage metrics, program enrollments
Experience	Clinical	Patient-reported outcomes (mood, pain, sleep scores)
	Perceptual	Net Promoter Score (NPS), Quality of Life (QoL), Patient Activation Measure (PAM), Patient Experience Index (PXi)
Impact	Patient	Healthcare resource utilization, healthcare cost, clinical outcomes, QALYs
	Business	TRx, NBRx, therapy switches, adherence on treatment, trial enrollment, trial retention
	Societal	Health equity, overall healthcare costs, population health

Unfortunately, ZS found that most pharma companies fail to connect the dots between activity, experience and impact. Instead, they tend to focus on one dimension at a time. Activity-based measurement is the easiest and most common approach. Over 80% of pharma companies track metrics for their patient-facing promotional activities (including media placements and interaction), patient engagement (with media, websites and other content) and patient service program utilization (such as enrollment and usage of specific solutions). While this is a good start, a critical drawback of focusing solely on activities is that organizations miss many nuances around how, where and why their activities are or are not working to address patient needs and to drive business objectives.

A minority (about 18%) of companies in the ZS study were able to tie some of their activity-based measures to business outcomes. When it comes to tying the patient experience to business outcomes, pharma companies must first determine what constitutes impact. For many, business impact is expressed in terms of revenues or related measures, such as total prescriptions. Others may think of impact in terms of alignment with brand strategic objectives, such as new patient starts or therapy switches. Still others may view impact in terms of market expansion—an increase in the diagnosis rate for a rare disease, for example. Important patient-centric outcomes in the clinical trial setting include trial recruiting rates and retention rates; these are outcomes that can have huge business impact, as moving the needle can make the difference between a completed versus failed trial. Pharma companies are increasingly measuring their own impact on outcomes that benefit both patients and health systems, such as reductions in acute exacerbations, hospitalizations or costs of disease management. As the drivers of value-based contracting agreements between pharma companies and payers, these outcomes are particularly important. Lastly, pharma companies have started to build programs that can address healthcare disparities and combat unequal access to medicine across socioeconomic or demographic lines.

The biggest surprise in the ZS study, however, was that only one in 10 companies was able to rigorously connect its activities to a change in overall patient experience. Patient experience provides the critical link between pharma companies' activities to influence outcomes and their business impact. ZS research conducted with oncologists in 2019 confirmed this: oncologists prescribe 70% more products from companies that they perceive to deliver a positive patient experience than from companies that deliver a negative experience.[4] And companies that create positive experiences have fewer restrictions on customer access and have two to three times stronger digital engagement. We also found that improving the customer and patient experience could drive an incremental $50 million to $75 million per $1 billion in revenue for most oncology companies.

But how can pharma companies measure something as qualitative as patient experience in a consistent and meaningful way? Outside of pharma, benchmarks and indices do exist to measure patient experience, such as the U.S. Centers for Medicare & Medicaid Services (CMS)'s Hospital Consumer Assessment of Healthcare Providers and Systems (HCAHPS), which captures the patient experience in the hospital setting,[5] or customer experience, such as Forrester's Customer Experience Index.[6] To date, pharma lacks a holistic way to measure the patient experience directly from patients, which would help companies understand areas to improve relative to competitors. Measuring against an index can be a key mechanism to inform the pharma industry's patient centricity transformation, enabling companies to hone the ways in which they can improve experiences and outcomes and reduce costs to the healthcare system.

ZS recently worked with patients, caregivers and industry leaders to co-create a Patient Experience Index (PXi), which benchmarks the subjective experience of patients with branded medications, their support services, materials and marketing based on four dimensions:

- The **effectiveness** of the medication and the related programs/materials

- The **effort** required to access and take the medication and to understand the available programs/materials

- The **emotion** elicited from taking the medication or utilizing the programs/materials

- The **expression** of self as a result of taking the medication or engaging with the programs/materials

Figure 11-2 provides a summary view of the PXi showing patients' and caregivers' self-reported ratings of experience with the brands in the study. A relative rating over 1 indicates an above average positive experience, while a rating below 1 indicates a less positive experience. In order to develop the PXi, ZS conducted research with more than 2,000 patients and caregivers across a variety of chronic conditions and demonstrated, unsurprisingly, that drug effectiveness was the most directly related factor to better patient experience.[7] Of course, developing medications with better efficacy takes years of research and many millions of dollars in investment. Assuming a particular drug works to address the disease or condition, the study also identified effort and emotional connection as important factors in driving overall experience.

Figure 11-2: The ZS PXi Provides a Benchmark of Patients' and Caregivers' Self-Reported Experience with Brands

Rank	Brand	N-Size	Indication	Method of Administration	PXi
1	Fasenra	44	Moderate-to-Severe Persistent Asthma	Injection	1.09
2	Xeljanz	129	Rheumatoid Arthritis	Oral	1.02
3	Enbrel	130	Rheumatoid Arthritis	Injection	1.01
4	Humira	153	IBD	Injection	1.01
5	Cimzia	42	Rheumatoid Arthritis	Injection	1.01
6	Trulicity	131	Type 2 Diabetes	Injection	1.01
7	Invokana	86	Type 2 Diabetes	Oral	1.00
8	Jardiance	139	Type 2 Diabetes	Oral	1.00
9	Stelara	98	IBD	1x infusion, followed by maintenance injections	1.00
10	Victoza	110	Type 2 Diabetes	Injection	1.00
11	Nucala	50	Moderate-to-Severe Persistent Asthma	Injection	0.99
12	QVAR RediHaler	167	Moderate-to-Severe Persistent Asthma	Injection	0.99
13	Breo Ellipta	137	Moderate-to-Severe Persistent Asthma	Injection	0.98
14	Entyvio	95	IBD	Injection	0.98
15	Humira	182	Rheumatoid Arthritis	Injection	0.98
16	Olumiant	25	Rheumatoid Arthritis	Oral	0.94

Interestingly, the study highlighted key differences in what drives a good experience based on gender, whether the respondent was answering the survey as a patient or caregiver, and household income (HHI). In symptomatic conditions, female respondents were much more likely to report experiencing symptoms every day in comparison to male respondents (29% compared to 12%), which indicates that there may be perceptual differences related to gender. For patients, making the symptoms feel better (effectiveness) was the most important factor, while caregivers valued experience elements focused on the ease of getting and taking medication, the management of side effects and, ultimately, improving the quality of life (see Figure 11-3). These differences are important to consider when creating content or support.

Figure 11-3: Caregivers Put More Emphasis on Transactional Components of the Patient Experience

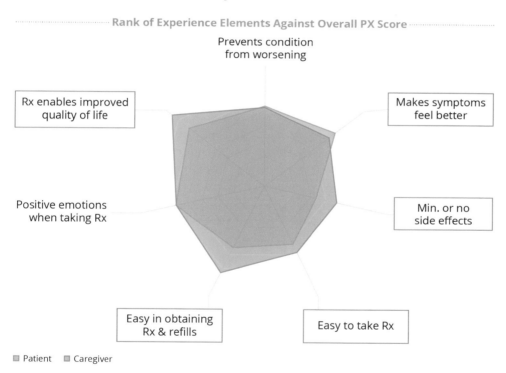

This research also found that individuals with household incomes under $20,000 were half as likely as individuals with household incomes over $100,000 to use patient services or support offered by pharma, which means that those who might benefit most from additional support may not have access to it, were not aware of it, may not have trusted the resources or turned away for other reasons. These are experiences that pharma can directly impact through marketing, education, financial assistance and other services that make the drug easier to obtain and take and that help create an emotional connection between the patient and the brand or company.[8]

The extent to which pharma's actions affect the patient experience depends on the disease state, the brand and individual patient characteristics. As the PXi highlights, pharma companies must listen to diverse patient perspectives to truly appreciate the drivers of patient experience with their specific brands. Once companies understand the drivers, pharma can move forward to better align brand tactics with the desired improvements in the patient experience, ultimately leading to improved health outcomes, business impact and, as numerous studies have pointed out, a reduction in overall healthcare costs. We strongly recommend that pharma companies track the patient experience over time—the earlier in the product life cycle, the better.

Close the Loop with Real-World Data

How can we bring this vision of using metrics, such as those in the PXi, to fruition? The next step is to gather the data needed to assess the impact of patient-centric efforts. Third-party data sources play a critical role here. There has been an explosion in the generation of real-world patient data (RWD) in the healthcare industry over the past decade. Readily available RWD sources, such as insurance claims and electronic medical records (EMRs), give pharma companies a highly detailed view into patients' healthcare resource utilization, clinical history and cost burden. Emerging data sources, like genomics and lab testing data, provide additional layers of clinical detail that companies can use to better pinpoint relevant patient populations or explain (and often predict) health outcomes. Many pharma companies are using these RWD sources to identify areas of greatest unmet patient need—for example, patient groups that exhibit the poorest response to standard-of-care therapies or sub-populations that struggle with medication adherence—and mining that data to inform their actions along the product life cycle. These actions include product development and life cycle management (such as label expansions that align with demonstrated patient needs), clinical trial design (such as identifying sites that serve concentrated populations of prevalent patients) and patient service support design (including co-pay assistance and adherence support). However, even as patient-driven insights provide valuable inputs into pharma's decision-making, RWD alone lacks the explanatory power to quantify the value generated by patient-focused programs.

Recent innovations in the industry have enabled data sources to be linked at the anonymized patient level, which allows for the quantification of causal connections between activity-based measures, patient experience and RWD to show their effects on switches, starts, adherence and clinical outcomes. With RWD providing the "dependent variable," we are then able to determine which activity-based measures and patient experience factors are driving these business impact measures—essentially allowing us to connect the dots between patient centricity activities and business impact.

Pharma organizations can use patient tokenization and data-matching technologies from companies such as HealthVerity, LiveRamp and DataVant to narrow the gaps between patient engagement, behavior, experience and impact. These companies provide algorithms for replacing patient identifiers with a secure, anonymous token. When the same tokenization algorithm has been applied across multiple data sources, it is possible to create a linked data set that appends the information from each input at the token (or anonymized-patient) level. This is the basis for conducting closed-loop measurement. For example, to quantify the impact of a patient service program on medication adherence, two data sources need to be tokenized and linked: patient service participation data and medication utilization data, such as claims. A test-and-control analysis can then determine the change in adherence behavior between program participants compared to non-participants.

As another method for using RWD to measure critical patient-centricity metrics, consider the role of statistics in identifying and understanding the effects of social determinants of health (SDOH). SDOH statistics, which include information on income, demographics, education, employment, food security and access to housing, are an increasingly important component of the data landscape. Data on SDOH is estimated to explain roughly a quarter of individual health outcomes,[9] more than data on healthcare and medication utilization. SDOH sources typically derive from public agencies, which use the data to identify local-level disparities in healthcare access and patient outcomes.

Pharma companies are using SDOH data in several ways. One application is to locate patient sub-populations with the highest unmet needs, often stemming from a lack of healthcare access or affordability. Companies can then develop additional interventions or specialized patient support programs to better serve patients belonging to these subgroups. Another application is to combine SDOH data with other RWD sources to build a comprehensive understanding of the drivers of patient outcomes. For instance, ZS's experience across primary and specialty therapy markets suggests that there are six key factors that explain patient adherence to therapy:

1. Patients' approach to treatment and coping with disease
2. Physician experience in managing patients
3. Product attributes
4. Financial access and reimbursement
5. Pharmacy interventions
6. Social determinants[10]

Being able to link data across these dimensions and build explanatory models of complex patient outcomes, such as medication adherence, are powerful capabilities that allow pharma companies to understand more clearly what they can impact, how they can achieve those impacts and which tactics are best suited to improve outcomes.

Go Beyond the Prescription

With these same rapidly expanding data sources, we can also personalize and optimize services and products for patients to get to the best clinical outcome, lower overall cost of care and learn more deeply about unmet patient needs so we can continue to develop products and solutions to meet them. As discussed in Chapter 9, measuring patient engagement with patient support services and the overall impact on health outcomes and healthcare costs is a great starting point for optimizing the experience for patients. Additionally, tapping into RWD sources beyond common, commercially available RWD data sets (such as scripts, medical claims and electronic health records) could yield insights into the patient that were previously unavailable to pharma. Assessing new and emerging RWD sources (like biomarkers) via partnerships or identifying opportunities to generate new data directly is a critical step in the process of expanding impact measurement.

Partnerships with companies outside of the pharmaceutical industry could yield tremendous value through access to new technologies that capture emerging data on the patient. For example, Apple/Aetna's personalized tracker app captures individual behavior and medical care data,[11] Cityblock/Google's tailored intervention platform generates social circumstances and individual behavior data[12] and Propeller Health's asthma attack prevention sensor uses physical environment data.[13] Through its partnership with healthcare technology company 23andMe, GlaxoSmithKline (GSK) can not only access millions of peoples' genomic data for drug development but also learn from patients' responses to questionnaires about their overall health and experience living with particular ailments.[14] Uncovering insights from partnerships like these will allow pharmaceutical companies to better understand patient need and to deliver a better product.

Continue Listening to Patients

Triangulating across multiple sources of data is needed to connect the lived patient experience to the measurement of impact and outcomes. Qualitative research (as discussed in Chapter 5) allows us to understand and relate to the patient experience by providing context for and lending texture to key moments in patients' lives. We can then overlay insights about patients' motivations, feelings and experiences with detailed behavioral observations from RWD to generate a holistic view of the patient experience, ensuring it doesn't get forgotten amid complex data analytics. The result is a comprehensive patient experience map, which can help pharmaceutical companies prioritize and optimize their decisions and strategies. One client ZS worked with in 2020 did just that, developing a patient experience map to serve as the guiding light for the company's brand team. Mobile ethnography provided an immersive glimpse into patients' lived experience, while data sources allowed the team to quantify how the brand was performing in areas where the company identified opportunities to improve the patients' experience.

Companies can start with patient reported outcomes (PROs), the PXi noted above, or a technique like voice-of-the-patient feedback to understand how various treatments might affect what patients are able to do and the symptoms they experience. For example, a voice-of-the-patient platform is designed to be a longitudinal study that captures individual patient-level feedback through surveys and interviews, and reports it back in real time. Companies typically use PRO instruments in targeted scenarios to design a label for competitive advantage or achieve a certain designation or approval, whereas voice-of-the-patient research has broader applicability and can be used to inform marketing, patient support development, messaging evolution and clinical trial experience. Voice-of-the-patient research is a good example of a mechanism to obtain both quantitative and qualitative insights to measure the patient experience and its impact.

To recap, the first step to link the patient experience to business imperatives is for leadership to endorse placing patient impact at the heart of a measurement-driven culture. The next step is to define meaningful metrics that connect across the three pillars of patient centricity: activity, experience and impact. From there, companies can triangulate different inputs and methodologies to create a complete picture of patients' lived experience, engagement with pharma, healthcare utilization and outcomes. Equipped with these holistic insights, organizations can truly "kill the buzzword" and make patient centricity a genuine driver of business decisions.

Key Takeaways

- For pharma to successfully embody patient centricity, companies should seek to build "virtuous cycles" that link patient centricity activities to experience and impact.

- Companies need to assess impact in multiple ways to reflect the outcomes that pharma's multiple stakeholders—especially patients—value.

- Having the capability to assess and act on patient-centric impact requires committed leadership, the right measurement approach and the right data insights.

- Aligning success measures with patient-oriented outcomes, whether through internal KPIs or external value-based contracts, is critical to sustaining patient centricity.

Acknowledgments

The authors would like to thank the following people for their contributions and input in writing this chapter: Eric Pao, Anna Sato and Sharon Suchotliff.

Endnotes

1. David Waller, "10 Steps to Creating a Data-Driven Culture," Harvard Business Review, February 6, 2020, https://hbr.org/2020/02/10-steps-to-creating-a-data-driven-culture.

2. Hugh Gosling, "Focus on the Patient and Everyone Wins," Reuters Events, April 12, 2017, https://www.reutersevents.com/pharma/commercial/focus-patient-and-everyone-wins; Leigh Householder, "Pfizer: Patients First," Syneos Health Communications, December 31, 2016, https://syneoshealthcommunications.com/blog/pfizer-patients-first.

3. Sharon Suchotliff et al., "The Value of Measuring Patient Experience," ZS, August 10, 2020, https://www.zs.com/insights/the-value-of-measuring-patient-experience.

4. ZS Oncology Customer Experience Report, 2019.

5. Hospital Consumer Assessment of Healthcare Providers and Systems (HCAHPS), "Home Page," last modified August 2, 2021, https://hcahpsonline.org/.

6. Forrester, "CX Index," 2021, https://go.forrester.com/research/cx-index/.

7. Hensley Evans, Lauren Goldenberg and Sharon Suchotliff, "Why Pharma Struggles to Improve Patient Experience," in Vivo, June 17, 2021, https://invivo.pharmaintelligence.informa.com/iv124799/why-pharma-struggles-to-improve-patient-experience.

8. Hensley Evans and Sharon Suchotliff, "The Pharma Industry Needs to Measure Patient Experience from the Patients' Perspectives," STAT, May 10, 2021, https://www.statnews.com/2021/05/10/pharma-industry-measure-patient-experience/.

9. Goinvo, "Determinants of Health," last modified April 14, 2020, https://www.goinvo.com/vision/determinants-of-health/.

10. Albert Whangbo and Vaibhav Bansal, "Mining Insights to Improve Patient Retention on Medication," ZS, June 15, 2021, https://www.zs.com/insights/mining-insights-to-improve-patient-retention-on-medication.

11. Heather Landi, "Aetna Launching New Apple Watch App to Gather Health Data, Reward Healthy Behavior," Fierce Healthcare, January 30, 2019, https://www.fiercehealthcare.com/tech/aetna-launching-new-apple-watch-app-to-gather-health-data-reward-healthy-behavior.

12. Iyah Romm, "Announcing Cityblock: Bringing a New Approach to Urban Health, One Block at a Time," Sidewalk Labs, October 2, 2017, https://www.sidewalklabs.com/insights/announcing-cityblock-bringing-a-new-approach-to-urban-health-one-block-at-a-time.

13. Dave Muoio, "FDA Clears Propeller Health Sensor for Use with AstraZeneca's Symbicort Inhaler," MobiHealthNews, May 26, 2020, https://www.mobihealthnews.com/news/fda-clears-propeller-health-sensor-use-astrazenecas-symbicort-inhaler.

14. Denise Roland, "How Companies Are Using Your DNA to Make New Medicine," The Wall Street Journal, July 22, 2019, https://www.wsj.com/articles/23and-me-glaxo-mine-dna-data-in-hunt-for-new-drugs-11563879881?reflink=share_mobilewebshare.

Chapter 12:
The Future of Patient-Centric Pharma

Hensley Evans

What Are We Aiming for?

We've spent a lot of time in this book talking about how pharma can adopt approaches and business models that are truly patient centric. In each of Chapters 5 through 9, we've provided a variety of examples that illustrate how a focus on the patient not only drives better outcomes for patients but also begets better business results. Going forward, it will be critical for pharma to continue not only developing and commercializing new and better medicines but also creating and delivering outstanding patient experiences. Indeed, patient experience is at the heart of evolving toward a more patient-focused model. Why do we say this?

We know that medical care only accounts for 10 to 20% of overall health, with individual behavior, genetic predisposition, social determinants of health and other factors contributing the rest (see Figure 12-1). As the figure below illustrates, individual behavior is by far the largest driver of overall health outcomes, and medicines alone can't change behavior. Human behavior changes based on our individual experiences—and on what each person thinks, feels and does as a result of those experiences. As we discussed in Chapter 9, pharma organizations are focusing more efforts and strategic thinking on the patient experience—particularly post-Rx—and starting to view patient services and support not as cost centers but as strategic investments. In order to design a patient experience that will have the best possible impact on behavior (both individual and aggregate) and therefore also on health outcomes, we must deeply understand the human perspective and put that perspective at the center of our organizational decision-making. This includes not only how we bring medicines to market but also how we strategize to deliver a better overall experience to the patient.

Figure 12-1: Many Factors Contribute to Overall Health—Medical Care Is Just One Part[1]

Compounding factors include social determinants of health (SDOH) and lifestyle or individual behaviors, areas where the industry has less direct influence

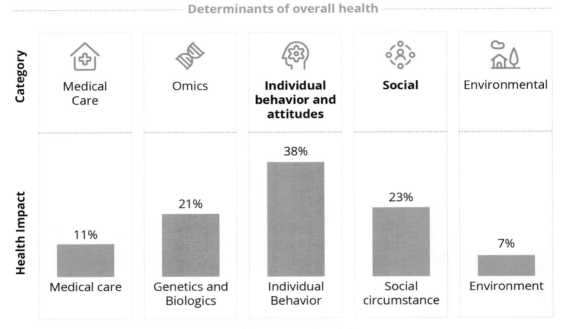

Determinants of overall health

Category				
Medical Care	Omics	**Individual behavior and attitudes**	**Social**	Environmental

Health Impact

- Medical care — 11%
- Genetics and Biologics — 21%
- Individual Behavior — 38%
- Social circumstance — 23%
- Environment — 7%

% Impact on health

In practical terms, making truly meaningful improvements in the overall human health experience boils down to a few concrete challenges for pharma. It means innovating not only better medicines but also improving patient engagement, support and other solutions to improve patient outcomes and also enhance patients' overall experience. It means ensuring affordable and convenient access to healthcare and medicines. It means connecting to people, not just as subjects or even patients but as human beings, and recognizing their social and emotional needs as well as their functional requirements. Accomplishing all of this will require the seamless integration of information across multiple players in the healthcare ecosystem to enable us to get the right information to people at each stage of their healthcare journey. It will require providing consistently available assistance so that people have access to the necessary information, resources and emotional support they need to manage their health. How can pharma best participate to get to this healthier future?

Four Inspirational Ideas for the Future of Pharma

The future evolution of any industry is notoriously difficult to predict (as countless failed businesses would attest). Rather than attempting to gaze into a crystal ball and project one specific direction for patient centricity in pharma, this chapter will instead explore four ideas, inspired by examples outside the industry, for how pharma could help bring a new, healthier world into being:

1. Getting obsessed with understanding people

2. Open-sourcing service innovation

3. Making everything interoperable

4. Using data to reinvent the business model

Getting Obsessed with Understanding People

Delta Airlines was facing a challenge, particularly in Atlanta, the company's largest hub airport in the U.S.[2] Baggage handling and luggage tracking were pain points and were driving decreased overall satisfaction ratings with the airline as a whole. But creating a new tracking system required substantial IT investment as well as physical infrastructure improvements—tunnels, conveyor belts, scanners—that would take years to fully implement. Solving the problem in the short term seemed nearly impossible until Delta uncovered a key insight about the roots of customer dissatisfaction. It turned out that what really bothered people most was idly waiting at the baggage carousel for their luggage, not the total time that elapsed from when they got off the plane to when they got their bags. The company realized that, while getting bags to the carousel faster wasn't possible in the near term, it was possible to delay travelers' arrival at the carousel by updating the algorithm that assigned flights to baggage claims and making the baggage claim further away from the flight gate. Because it took longer for people to walk to the baggage carousel, there was less idle waiting time before the bags came out. People minded the walk much less than they did having to stand around at the carousel, and overall satisfaction increased. Of course, Delta also got to work addressing the infrastructure improvements and now can deliver bags faster to carousels closer to the gate. It's a great example of how frequently in business—including in pharma—it's critical to understand the real problem before trying to solve it.

But how did Delta get to this insight in the first place? First, the company commissioned primary market research and asked customers about their overall experience flying with Delta and what aspects they liked and didn't like, and then it analyzed how different factors contributed to overall satisfaction. Second, Delta analyzed available data about travel time from gate to carousel, baggage delivery times and the correlation with overall satisfaction to understand more deeply what was driving customer ratings. And, finally, the company collected input on a continuous basis from customers in a variety of ways, not only through quick surveys after each flight but through feedback from agents, baggage complaint offices and call centers. Delta was then able to combine information from all of these sources to get to an important insight that drove improvements in customer satisfaction much more quickly and cost-effectively than would otherwise have been possible.

The Delta example reinforces some basic best practices—things we know we should do but that we don't always allot time or resources for in the pharma industry: conducting primary market research with customers (patients), analyzing data, collecting feedback continuously and then using the insights we glean to resolve problems in the patient experience. In pharma's future, our hope is that, in the words of Laurie Meyers, executive director of engagement and experience design at Genentech, "It will be unusual *not* to have involved the patient in the development of the asset or solution." Jeff Bezos famously advised his teams to always have an empty chair at the table to represent the customer in meetings—maybe pharma will take that one step further and actually *have* a patient at the table for key decisions.

It's not enough, though, to get that great insight. Making sure that the insight is then communicated to the right people at the right time is just as important. Intelligence agencies like the CIA receive and catalog thousands of data sources, including satellite feeds, intercepted communications, internet monitoring and news reports from embassies and sources around the world.[3] If the networks within an agency aren't well connected, that makes it difficult for the person who has the information to know exactly who else needs it and when. Especially in an environment where knowledge is disseminated only on a need-to-know basis, important insights often get siloed unintentionally because the person with the information doesn't know how to disperse it to the other people in the network who should have access to it. The 9/11 attacks are an oft-cited example of the terrible consequences of not getting crucial information to the right people. The knowledge required to uncover the plot was present in the counterterrorism community, but, because the information wasn't effectively managed, U.S. intelligence agencies didn't identify the threat until after the tragic events of that day.

However, organizations are increasingly learning how to better manage information. The NATO Information and Knowledge Management (IKM) Program was designed to address a similar information management challenge to that of the CIA—tracking and organizing information coming in from multiple member countries across various departments and programs. NATO has created formal collaboration and resource-sharing sites to store information and make it accessible to everyone who might need it. The organization has also enabled enterprise-level searches of all information based on a standardized taxonomy so that, as new information is added, it is automatically catalogued so as to be easy to search for within the system. Different data have various protection levels, so NATO put in place appropriate governance and processes for individuals within the organization to request or earn access to specific information. Perhaps most importantly, NATO undertook a multi-year process to ensure the cultural adoption of its centralized data and insights repository.

Once an organization has the insights and has established networks to get them to the right people, leadership must enable and incentivize individuals within the organization to act on that information. Ritz Carlton famously empowered all of its frontline employees to solve customer problems by taking immediate action in response to insights gleaned from customers. The company had originally tried to create a standard language and scripts for team members, but this ended up coming across as inauthentic and stilted. Instead, leadership trusted team members to make the right decisions in the moment to address customer issues and wow them with service. Each morning during their daily standup meeting, the leadership team recognized employees who had demonstrated creativity and success in delivering a great customer experience, reinforcing the value of the behavior.

Sven Gierlinger, chief experience officer at Northwell Health, brought his experience from Ritz Carlton to healthcare. From starting each executive meeting with a patient story to improving the administrative processes that can be a source of patient frustration, he has worked to shift the culture of the organization. One simple example is online appointment scheduling. Originally, a patient would go online and request a specific appointment time from a physician, but then most would have to wait for a call back to confirm that the appointment time was available. Their research showed that there was no incentive for the patients to use the online system over just phoning the office and waiting for the office to call them back—they had to wait for a callback in either case. Gierlinger observed: "If you have to call back 60% of the patients, then why do that? The airlines don't do that. Have you gotten a call back when you made an airline reservation to verify your flight?"[4] Of course, in order to make this possible, Northwell had to convince their employees to do something different—physicians had to open up their calendars to the online scheduling system—but with the incentives of increased patient satisfaction, most physicians were willing to do so, especially since patient satisfaction is a key performance metric through which their performance is evaluated.

In pharma, we have to acknowledge that there are barriers—not least compliance concerns—to allowing each employee to make on-the-spot decisions about how to respond to patient needs. However, it's certainly possible to take away one important lesson from this obsession with the customer: Listen to customers and act on insights when we get them! Recently, a ZS client shared a story about a team that had been nominated for an internal patient centricity award. The team had designed a new approach to drug delivery so that patients were able to receive treatment at home (either self-administered or through a visiting nurse service) instead of coming into a physician's office monthly. The client had asked the team if it was a new insight that led to this innovation and heard: "No, we always knew it was an inconvenience for patients to come into the clinic, but, pre-COVID, they were willing to do it anyway. Once the pandemic hit, we were seeing drop-offs increase because patients were reluctant to come into clinical settings." So, the company had gotten the right insight, and it had been communicated to the right people, but the incentives weren't in place to act on it until the company began to experience negative repercussions. We need to empower and incentivize teams to proactively solve problems they see based on patient feedback, and share and celebrate the solutions they innovate. Patient centers of excellence can help by collecting and disseminating examples of successes, but, in the long term, it will be critical to create metrics and incentives at both the individual and team level to ensure distributed accountability for patient centricity.

Futurist Alvin Toffler famously said: "The illiterate of the 21st century will not be those who cannot read and write, but those who cannot learn, unlearn, and relearn."[5] So at the same time that we are learning how to be "patient obsessed," get the right insights, communicate them to the right people and then promptly act on them, we probably have to unlearn a few things. The list might include the belief that HCPs and patients only care about safety and efficacy, that physicians can speak for patients and that patients' experiences are far less important than the effectiveness of the medications they're taking. Although commercial teams in pharma have talked for years about designing the patient experience into the development process, that largely hasn't happened, primarily because many development teams assume that their paramount objective is to prove product efficacy and safety and that marketing can fix any problems with the patient experience later. But this product-centric assumption that product features will carry the day is rapidly becoming outdated. Even in oncology, surveys about the physician experience show that product features account for less than one-third of the overall product perception. While a breakthrough product might carry the day, 90% of new launches are not breakthroughs. The obsession with the patient therefore has to permeate the entire organization and all along the value chain—not just the commercial unit of the organization.

The idea that the experience is just as important as the product itself is a given in many other industries. Look at Ritz Carlton: there are lots of nice hotels around (the product), but the service is what sets the chain apart. A similar approach in pharma would mean that patient-focused drug development (PFDD) would evolve over time to become patient-focused solution development—integrating support and services with the molecule (the product). We need to shift our thinking from focusing only on the drug to focusing on the drug plus the other support and solutions that surround it—just like Ritz Carlton focuses not just on the hotel room but the support and services that customers receive. Data and analytics, direct customer insights, services and solution design, testing and evolution—all of this would be integrated into the R&D process so that, by the time assets are commercially available, organizations would know what services and complementary solutions would drive optimal patient outcomes and experience.

Pharma will need to build in continuous improvement based on customer feedback such that seeking patient input will become the norm throughout the development and commercialization process, rather than episodic market research and response. This will require organizations to become more agile. Companies will need to enable all their constituent teams and units to routinely co-create protocols with patients and use post-trial feedback to optimize both trial design and product support. Organizations will also need to welcome patients as an integral part of commercialization teams, inviting them to review all educational and promotional materials, provide input on product life cycle management and share feedback on the evolution of their healthcare journeys.

During development, patient experience will be a key component of the target product profile (or, as we referred to it in Chapter 5, the target patient value proposition), and development teams will share patient insights uncovered during the development and clinical trial process with the commercial unit. Post-commercialization, marketing teams will collect patient feedback for all touch points and interactions—such as nurse hotlines, patient services, reimbursement support and digital solutions—and use this feedback to streamline and improve these services. Perhaps most critically, pharma organizations will close the loop on the feedback received and communicate with patients about how their perspectives and stated needs became the basis for real and meaningful solutions.

Some of these shifts will require significant cultural adaptation. But there is low-hanging fruit up for grabs here: the insights that are already present within an organization. Many companies have sophisticated analytics and insights units that manage extensive market research, analytics and various forms of patient feedback. But few are really good at managing knowledge and sharing insights across the functional areas of the organization. The creation of a shared knowledge base of patient insights that is both readily searchable and easy to keep up-to-date may sound like a tall order, but natural language processing is making this much simpler to solve. As part of implementing these solutions, organizations will also need to ensure the adoption and celebration of a culture of insight sharing and patient obsession.

Open-Sourcing Service Innovation

When you think about innovative products, chances are you've got one in your pocket or purse as we speak. The evolution of smart phones and Apple's phone-based business model is a fascinating example of open-sourcing innovation. While Apple manufactures the iPhone and the basic operating system (iOS), phones come with only a limited number of pre-installed basic "services" (that is, apps). The vast majority of the apps that users have on their phones are those that users downloaded directly and are not actually Apple creations. The genius of iOS and the App Store is that the open-source platform allows software developers to contribute any app they want. Apple doesn't have to come up with new ideas for how best to use the iPhone—other people do that work instead (although Apple occasionally takes a good idea and builds it with company resources, incorporating it into the pre-installed applications). The App Store has become a curated marketplace, with user reviews, featured apps and ratings that help other users pick which apps they'd like to try. In exchange for giving developers access to this established marketplace, Apple charges a 30% commission on app or in-app purchases. With the iPhone, Apple has focused on product development (we're now on the 12th generation of the iPhone), not the individual services. Apple just operates and optimizes the platform.

Sound familiar? Pharma is great at making medicines—products—but not so great at building or delivering a complete suite of services to allow each individual product user to get the optimal individual results from the product. What if pharma took a page out of Apple's book? What if, instead of trying to excel at beyond-the-pill solutions, we created an open-source platform that would allow others, including associations, health tech companies, payers and providers, to create those solutions in our stead? We could use the deep patient insights we've just talked about to determine which basic services are critical and need to be "pre-installed" with a specific product, focusing on making those discrete services great, while creating room for other actors in the healthcare ecosystem to innovate new services and solutions. In Chapter 9, we highlighted research illustrating that patients often prefer support and solutions from other sources anyway. Customers (patients and maybe HCPs) could then rate and review the solutions so that others can quickly figure out what might help them get to their optimal care experience, and people could select the elements that are relevant to their individual journeys.

One challenge here is the financial model. Apple has millions of iPhone users, so, for developers, it's very appealing to create an app for the App Store, even though that means giving the app away for free. Large numbers of users generate sales or advertising revenue streams, making the tradeoff worth the while. The organizations that are or could be great at building solutions for patients would ask, "What's in it for me?" (the WIIFM). While providers, payers and advocacy organizations may have some shared objectives around helping optimize the care experience, someone will ultimately have to pay for the development of the solutions. In the Apple model, the end user typically either pays directly or accepts advertising in exchange for access to the app. A similar approach would be possible in adapting this model for pharma. More and more consumers are paying for healthcare apps, after all. It's also possible that payers would be willing to defray costs for patients to access solutions that have strong data to demonstrate that they result in better adherence and better outcomes.

Could pharma pay for some of these apps without the payment implying endorsement? If the developer is truly third party, pharma could certainly pay market value. As a possible first step, pharma could create credits that patients could use to pay for applications they choose and use as they like. These credits could even be integrated into existing financial or co-pay support programs. One challenge with this solution is that, unlike Apple, most pharma brands don't have a large volume of patients who leverage the brands' programs or solutions. If developers have to recoup their investments over a few thousand participants, the price per participant will have to be quite high. But, across multiple brands within a company or for larger brands, this could be a viable model.

Creating Interoperability Across the Industry

What if, instead of one company or one brand open-sourcing solutions for patients on its bespoke platform, we could create a standard industry platform for patient services and get a critical mass of organizations to agree to leverage this platform? Suddenly, we would have a much larger volume of patients that could leverage solutions. Many solutions (such as tracking apps, lifestyle support, community connections, scheduling) have applicability across conditions and brands. In fact, many of these solutions would be even more powerful if patients were able to use them for all of their health conditions and medications, rather than separately for each disease or brand. Would it be possible to get so many big organizations to align on an interoperable shared platform?

It was possible for financial services. For decades, almost all banking occurred face-to-face with a teller for simple transactions (like deposits or withdrawals) or in a meeting with a customer service representative for more complicated transactions (like loans or investments). But starting in the 1970s, two important shifts took place. Changing household structures, job markets and evolving cultural norms around customer service led people to start demanding more convenient access to banking services, when and where they wanted them. Banks simply couldn't afford to keep full branches open 18 hours per day and expand to new locations quickly enough to meet these demands. At the same time, technology had advanced to the point where machines could reliably and cost-effectively conduct simple transactions without the need for human intervention. ATMs became a new opportunity to differentiate and provide better service to customers. The data technology was simple: a card with a magnetic stripe allowed the machine to read the individual's account number, and customers verified their identity by entering a personal identification number or PIN. While banks initially installed ATMs at the brand locations themselves, they quickly realized the value of placing ATMs away from existing bank branches.

By the late 1970s, banks realized that their ATMs had tremendous unused capacity and saw opportunities to reduce costs and offer more location options to customers by sharing ATMs. Regional banks formed mutual sharing agreements that allowed their customers to use each other's ATMs for a small transaction fee. In 1981, 10 large regional banks began discussions about how they could collaborate to turn these regional networks into a national one, and, in 1982, they founded Cirrus. The Plus system followed shortly thereafter as a consortium of 34 major banks. By the late 1980s, Cirrus (later acquired by MasterCard) and Plus (which Visa acquired) covered all 50 of the U.S. states. Of course, in order to share machines across the network, participating institutions had to allow other banks' machines real-time access to their data, or at least parts of it (account number, PIN, bank balance and withdrawal limit, among others), while protecting other highly sensitive personal financial data.

These data- and ATM-sharing agreements continued to evolve, and, in 2002, a number of large banks (including Barclay's, Deutsche Bank and Bank of America) founded the Global ATM Alliance, building on the foundation of the now well-established systems the banks had created in the 1980s.[6] The founders of the Global ATM Alliance leveraged the standardized account numbering system that had been created five years earlier (the International Bank Account Number or IBAN). The IBAN system instituted wholly standardized account numbers connecting account information not only within the U.S. but around the world.[7] Today, of course, this backbone that banks innovated in order to share ATMs enables connected apps to aggregate financial information across multiple institutions and to move money and change currencies quickly and easily—all with just the swipe of a finger.

Healthcare is trying to take similar steps toward more data interoperability. As electronic health record (EHR) systems in hospitals and provider networks have proliferated, a key challenge is that the database schemas of these systems vary widely, and they can't connect or talk to each other. Health Level 7 (HL7) is a standards development organization that is seeking to establish a minimum data layer that can be extracted and shared across EHR systems so that, as patients move between providers, there is some means of enabling communication between these incompatible systems. This standard, known as Fast Healthcare Interoperability Resources (FHIR), is in some ways akin to the approach taken by the financial services industry—essentially, it allows hospitals and providers to share a minimum amount of data in a standardized format to facilitate connectivity, without requiring that every company or system adopt the exact same data standards.

If banks and hospitals can create interoperability (while still competing fiercely), then pharma can too. An interoperable, standardized platform would not only allow patients to more conveniently access patient services but would also allow them to much more easily share (or not) their data between apps, providers and support programs. Once patients enroll in any program, they could seamlessly add other programs using the same, consistent data. Anytime they start a new medication, they could incorporate that information into their existing solutions. Pharma could also start to think about how these services and solutions could be more broadly applicable beyond just the commercial side. Could we leverage the same platform and consistent user identification to identify and support patients for clinical trials or to provide feedback and insights to R&D teams on specific conditions or unmet needs to prioritize?

Using Data to Reinvent the Business Model

Creating interoperability would also have another potential benefit for pharma: expanding the availability of data at an individual level, including preferences, behaviors and patterns, beyond the purely medical aspects of someone's life. This could, in turn, create new opportunities for pharma and others in the healthcare system to reimagine how they deliver better outcomes and care experiences in the future.

Netflix is famous for continuously reinventing its business model, leveraging data all along the way. Blockbuster was the undisputed market leader in video rentals when Netflix launched in 1997. But Netflix's founders had realized that, unlike VHS tapes, the compact size and shape of the DVD allowed it to be mailed very efficiently. So, the company started its mail-order business, which, unlike Blockbuster's brick-and-mortar business, relied on an online selection and ordering process.[8] Although DVDs represented only 2% of the home movie market when Netflix launched, penetration quickly grew, which also drove an initial surge of growth for the company. And, because customers managed their mail-order queues online, Netflix quickly started developing a deep data set of people's preferences. One big challenge associated with the mail-order queue was the high demand for new releases and much lower demand for older movies. But Netflix was able to leverage individual preference data to create a recommendation engine that combined title availability with known individual preferences based on genre, actors, and more. This allowed the company to manage its physical inventory much more efficiently and lower the wait times for popular titles. Although Blockbuster eventually joined the online rental market in 2004, it was too late to catch up to Netflix.

A decade in, as broadband internet made streaming large media feasible, leaders at Netflix realized that shifting from physical rental (mailing) to streaming would allow them to make new titles available to all users at the same time (eliminating wait times) and to restructure their subscription model to make it simpler and more affordable. They made it easy to get Netflix on every device, and customers loved the flexibility to watch whatever they wanted, whenever they wanted, wherever they wanted.

The streaming model generated much more usage—and much more data. Initially, Netflix mined the data to generate recommendations, helping customers access more and more content in line with their interests, which ensured long-term customer loyalty. One fascinating experiment Netflix ran during this time was the Netflix prize; the company offered $1 million to anyone who could construct an algorithm to predict users' movie ratings at least 10% better than Netflix's own algorithm.[9] During the contest, Netflix provided participants with a training data set with more than 100 million user ratings from almost half a million users. The contest ran over a three-year period (with progress prizes awarded along the way), and the $1 million prize was awarded in 2009.[10] Netflix canceled subsequent contests due to privacy concerns regarding the data set.

As Netflix got better and better at analytics and predictive modeling, its leaders realized that their data and analytics capabilities could not only predict customers' preferences for existing content but could also accurately forecast the types of new content people would want to watch. Starting in 2013, this allowed them to create their own content based on their models, which turned out to be highly accurate for predicting which shows would be successful with which audiences.[11] Unlike TV networks, Netflix was able to invest in multiple seasons rather than run a pilot, wait for results, then pay more when and if the pilot succeeded.

Inspired by the success of companies like Netflix that have made smart use of data, pharma is already working to leverage data and analytics much more strategically. However, only a limited number of pharma organizations have invested to create a truly integrated view of their consumers and patients by pulling together data from all interactions with their end customers into a single database. Those that have are building a powerful toolset. Through the use of predictive models, pharma companies can identify and recruit diverse clinical trial participants, find and communicate with undiagnosed patients and predict what interventions will best support each person at every stage of the journey. Once these data sets are broad enough, they may enable companies to predict whether new support solutions will be helpful before they are even built! Establishing these integrated data sets is a long-term process and requires a non-trivial investment, but the payoff in both patient experience and business impact is significant.

There is also a huge opportunity for pharma organizations to grow their business by giving others access to their data. Netflix ran into some privacy challenges when it made its 100-million-record data set available to the public; some individuals were able to reverse engineer individual identities in the data set by matching ratings in the Netflix data to ratings on other platforms. But there's a big difference between making data publicly available and sharing data with a limited set of partners. Advocacy groups, patient associations, independent investigators and academic researchers could all bring new insights and expertise to apply to the data. What about offering a prize for those that could most effectively predict interventions that would result in faster clinical trial enrollment, increased long-term medication adherence, lower cost of care or improved overall patient outcomes? Additionally, partnerships with companies that are already using data in similar ways could benefit both pharma and patients. Through collaborations with companies like Science 37, which has an integrated data set that allows for identifying and recruiting patients to participate in trials of new drugs and medical equipment from their homes,[12] pharma could bring the patient to the study rather than bringing the study (via a physician) to the patient.

One final lesson from Netflix: don't assume that tech adoption and channel preferences are static. As pharma moves toward hybrid and digital trial models, digital services and solutions and alternative sites of care for injected/infused therapies will allow flexibility for patients and caregivers to choose the channels that work for them. Pharma will need to understand how patient preferences, technology adoption, and channel use are evolving (for example, from DVDs to streaming, from the web to mobile phones, from email to social media) and adopt strategic approaches that tap into the right channel at the right time. We can't assume that people of a certain demographic don't or won't use a specific channel or technology. Remember those predictions that people would never watch a movie on a tiny iPhone screen? Thirty percent of U.S. households now watch premium video content on their phones every week.[13] Let's catch the wave of digital and data innovation and ride it, like Netflix, rather than getting left high and dry, like Blockbuster.

What Will Have to Change Within Pharma to Enable the Adoption of These Ideas?

In Chapter 4, we discussed why pharma has been talking about patient centricity for so long but changed so little. Perhaps part of the problem is in the language we are using. Pharma organizations are, after all, product manufacturers, and products remain the central drivers of organizations' structures. Asking pharma to replace products with patients at their core may not be practical—or even optimal. However, there is huge, untapped opportunity for pharma to take advantage of patient-*led* approaches and business models to optimize patient experience and outcomes as well as business results. The four ideas above are pulled from customer-*led* models that don't require organizations to step away from their core products or services.

Importantly, these four ideas about the future of pharma are not mutually exclusive, and some aspects of all four strategies are beginning to emerge already. In fact, depending on the specific strategic objectives of various pharma organizations, the future may necessitate a combination of all four. There are some foundational tenets that will enable adoption of some or all of these ideas:

- **Unlearning as we evolve**: Some of the reasons we have not taken these actions yet are the core beliefs that we still cling to—that safety and efficacy are the only important attributes of a medication; that we should seek to "own" the patient in the categories in which we operate; that we cannot partner with the same companies with which we compete.

- **Patient perspective integration**: It will become unusual or surprising not to have diverse and representative patients included in decision-making—and, in order to be at the forefront of this evolution, organizations will need to engage in both highly developed feedback and insights gathering (integrating direct patient engagement and feedback, market research and data analytics) and sophisticated knowledge management to disseminate this perspective.

- **Cross-ecosystem partnership capabilities**: It will be easier and much more common to establish and operate partnerships and consortia between pharma organizations as well as with other health and non-health entities. Stronger partnership capabilities and best practices will enable long-term risk and benefit sharing models over fee-for-service models. Organizations will be partnering regularly with many other organizations in the healthcare ecosystem to address the whole person (including physical health, mental health and general well-being), not just the sick person.

- **Ubiquitous data capture and standardization**: Pharma will need to establish common unique identifiers that protect privacy while also allowing for data connectivity and exchange (with individual permission). Organizations can also share data in order to drive better patient outcomes through collaborative analysis.

- **Analytic prowess**: Organizations that fail to build core capabilities around analytics, including machine learning and AI approaches, will not be able to take full advantage of the data that is already available to them, much less leverage the power of integrated data sets across the ecosystem.

- **Flexible organizational structures that can adapt to changes over time and facilitate work across silos**: There is no perfect organizational structure—but organizations must become more agile and adaptive in order to continue to evolve along with consumer needs and preferences as well as changes in the healthcare system.

Just imagine what the experience of managing illness would be like if we could accomplish these goals! A.C., the manger at a large consumer goods company whose story we shared in Chapter 1, would not have to wait five years to get an accurate diagnosis for stage 4 thymic cancer because deeper patient insights and a connected data ecosystem would allow for the fast(er) identification of rare diseases. The people who participated in the clinical trial for a new type 2 diabetes drug, described in Chapter 6, could stay on the investigational treatment once the trial was completed. Martha, who we introduced in Chapter 7, would recognize much sooner that her symptoms and experiences of pain were cause to see a doctor and that fibromyalgia can be treated. The company producing the insulin for Alec, whose tragic story we recounted in Chapter 1, might have been able to help him with access to the medicine and save his life. You and I would not have to chase our health information. Instead, we could easily understand what's going on with our bodies and seek the care we need. And this is not an unachievable goal, light years away. As we have seen already in other industries (hospitality, retail, tech), giving people a better experience is feasible—and, if we do it right, our business will flourish as well.

Key Takeaways

- We can learn a lot about where the future of patient centricity may go by looking at outside examples: Ritz Carlton for customer obsession; Apple for innovation outsourcing, financial services for interoperability; and Netflix for a data- and analytics-driven business model.

- There are several key tenets that pharma will need to adopt in order to be able to leverage some of these lessons:

  - Unlearning as we evolve

  - Patient perspective integration

  - Cross-ecosystem partnership capabilities

  - Ubiquitous data capture and standardization

- Analytic prowess

- Flexible and adaptable organizational structures

- The end results of pharma adopting these mechanisms for delivering on the promise of patient centricity will not only be better health outcomes but a vastly improved patient care experience.

Acknowledgments

The author would like to thank: Andrew Benzie, Torsten Bernewitz, Gill Hayes, Pratap Khedkar, Pete Masloski, Pete Mehr, Chris Morgan, Joris Silon, Sharon Suchotliff, Bharat Tewarie, Todd Warner and the ZS Patient Centricity Advisory Board members.

Endnotes

1. The percent of health impact was determined using estimated values referenced from eight different organizations, including the WHO (visit https://goinvo.com for a list of organizations). Intervention spending is money spent to address the problem, not total money spent in that area (visit https://goinvo.com for more information).

2. ASP Alumni, "Delta's Baggage Claim Digital Transformation," Harvard Business School Digital Initiative, last modified November 18, 2016, https://digital.hbs.edu/platform-rctom/submission/deltas-baggage-claim-digital-transformation/.

3. James J. Wirtz, "The Sources and Methods of Intelligence Studies," in The Oxford Handbook of National Security Intelligence, ed. Loch K. Johnson (Oxford: Oxford University Press, 2010), 59-70.

4. Jonah Comstock, "Five Tips from Northwell Health for Engaging Health Consumers," MobiHealthNews, May 21, 2019, https://www.mobihealthnews.com/content/north-america/five-tips-northwell-health-engaging-health-consumers.

5. Alvin Toffler, "Future Shock" (New York: Bantam, 1970), 414.

6. "Five Big Banks Form Global ATM Alliance," ATM Marketplace, January 8, 2002, https://www.atmmarketplace.com/news/five-big-banks-form-global-atm-alliance/.

7. Corporate Finance Institute, "International Bank Account Number (IBAN)," accessed October 23, 2021, https://corporatefinanceinstitute.com/resources/knowledge/finance/international-bank-account-number-iban/.

8. Molly Sloan, "Netflix vs Blockbuster – 3 Key Takeaways," Drift, June 1, 2020, https://www.drift.com/blog/netflix-vs-blockbuster/.

9. Casey Johnson, "Netflix Never Used Its $1 million Algorithm Due to Engineering Costs," Wired, April 16, 2012, https://www.wired.com/2012/04/netflix-prize-costs/.

10. Gibson Biddle, "A Brief History of Netflix Personalization (Part Two, from 2007 to 2021)," Ask Gib, May 27, 2021, https://askgib.substack.com/p/a-brief-history-of-netflix-personalization-31d.

11. Blake Morgan, "What Is the Netflix Effect?" Forbes, February 19, 2019, https://www.forbes.com/sites/blakemorgan/2019/02/19/what-is-the-netflix-effect/?sh=3af501e85640.

12. Science 37, "Science 37 and Xperiome Partner to Increase the Efficiency and Speed of Rare Disease Studies for Patients and Providers," PR Newswire, March 11, 2021, https://www.prnewswire.com/news-releases/science-37-and-xperiome-partner-to-increase-the-efficiency-and-speed-of-rare-disease-studies-for-patients-and-providers-301245207.html.

13. Statista, "Devices Used to Watch Online Video Content Weekly Among Viewers in the United States as of July 2020, by Age Group," July 2020, graph, https://www.statista.com/statistics/605628/frequency-video-services-used-by-smarpthone-users-united-states/.

Contributors

Lisa Bance

Lisa is ZS's service line lead and has deep expertise in patient evidence strategy as well as research and development (R&D). Lisa's areas of expertise include registries, observational studies, patient-focused drug development, clinical development and advocacy relationships. In addition to her work with ZS, Lisa has worked in pharmaceutical global marketing (on the client side), pharmaceutical brand advertising, medical education and CRO-based clinical development. Lisa holds a Doctor of Pharmacy degree in radiopharmacy and nuclear medicine and an MBA from the Wharton School of the University of Pennsylvania.

Torsten Bernewitz

Torsten brings over 30 years of experience as a management consultant and business leader, with previous roles in sales, marketing and research. He developed ZS's global change management capability, applying insights from behavioral economics and psychology to increase the success of business transformations. A frequent conference speaker, he teaches for the Kellogg School of Management Executive Education Program at Northwestern University. Torsten holds an MBA from INSEAD, an M.Sc. in economics and geography from Leibniz Universität in Hannover, Germany, and he completed the Digital & Technology Transformation Leadership Program at Harvard Business School.

Hensley Evans

As the leader of ZS's patient and consumer health practice globally, Hensley has worked with clients on a wide range of patient-focused initiatives—from building enterprise-level capabilities to designing programs that address specific patient challenges and support better patient experiences and outcomes. She believes strongly that it's critical to start from a foundation of insights—understanding how and why people make healthcare choices—and that empathy for the whole person is a requirement for success. Hensley has an MBA in finance from the Wharton School of the University of Pennsylvania and a B.A. in economics from Duke University.

Greg Fry

Greg has 15 years of marketing experience, spanning healthcare marketing strategy, insights, tactical execution and measurement. He leverages real-world data to help clients understand and optimize the impact of their patient support services and media investments on real patient health outcomes. Greg holds a B.S. in business management from Bucknell University.

Mary Ann Godwin

Mary Ann serves as the West Coast lead for ZS's strategy and transformation practice area. She brings over 15 years of consulting experience in customer experience design, customer-centric transformations and marketing strategy across multiple clients and therapeutic areas. Mary Ann is a certified ScrumMaster and design thinking expert. She excels at structuring and conducting cross-functional workshops and projects designed to help clients improve their decision-making capabilities and change management using Agile and lean start-up principles.

Sophie Kondor

Sophie is a manager in ZS's strategy and transformation space. She specializes in organizational transformation in the life sciences industry. In this role, she has supported client teams in improving customer centricity and patient centricity by leveraging the Agile methodology. She has designed and facilitated workshops to help clients find purpose and deliver meaningful outcomes. Sophie holds an MBA from Duke's Fuqua School of Business with a certificate in Health Sector Management, as well as a B.A. in psychology from Bucknell University.

Emily Mandell

Emily has 16 years of experience in life sciences marketing and insights, focusing on the voice of the customer and pipeline and launch strategy. She specializes in ensuring life sciences companies amplify the voice of the customer in their decisions to help them bring value to the people they serve. Emily holds a B.A. in business from the University of Wisconsin.

Nikita Reznik

Nikita is part of ZS's medical affairs and research and development (R&D) excellence practice, helping clients in the areas of medical and R&D strategy, patient-centric drug development, analytics and digital transformation. Nikita brings expertise in cross-functional work for R&D, engaging and collaborating with clinical, medical and commercial stakeholders, as well as medical societies and patient advocacy groups, to positively impact patient experience and outcomes in drug development. Nikita brings over 15 years of academic research and consulting experience in healthcare and the life sciences. Nikita holds a Ph.D. from the University of Toronto and an MBA from Columbia University.

Tanya Shepley

Tanya is a member of ZS's patient and consumer health team, which is focused on helping clients build more impactful solutions that improve patients' lives by uncovering how and why patients make healthcare choices. With 17 years of experience in healthcare, Tanya has led multiple lines of business, including developing brand strategies for both direct-to-consumer and healthcare professional audiences. Tanya has worked across a vast array of therapeutic areas in both a U.S. and global capacity. Her experience includes collaborating with clients and their key constituents to co-create patient support service programs.

Sharon Suchotliff

Sharon Suchotliff leads ZS's patient centricity work in the U.S. She brings more than 15 years of marketing communications experience in and outside of healthcare, fused with a background in public health. At ZS, Sharon helps companies develop strategies and build capabilities to further patient centricity and meaningfully incorporate the patient voice into business decisions. Sharon holds a B.S. in public relations from the S.I. Newhouse School of Public Communications at Syracuse University and an Executive MPH from the Mailman School of Public Health at Columbia University.

Victoria Summers

Victoria is the East Coast lead of ZS's patient and consumer health practice, working with clients to bring the patient voice into brand marketing decisions. With 18 years of healthcare marketing experience, she helps clients better understand the effects of their marketing programs and guides the design of optimized solutions. Victoria's areas of expertise include direct-to-consumer strategy and planning, patient experience mapping, patient segmentation and point-of-care marketing. Victoria holds an MBA with honors from Columbia Business School in New York and a B.A. in theatre from the University of Iowa.

Fiona Taylor

As the leader of ZS's global qualitative research practice, Fiona helps clients understand and support their customers through innovative customer insights methodologies. She has expanded ZS's customer insights capabilities by developing innovative qualitative research solutions and building a team of expert researchers. A passionate believer in the importance of improving outcomes through listening to patients and learning from them, Fiona pioneered ZS's patient insight capability, Patient 365. Fiona has over 15 years of experience as a management consultant, with specialization in healthcare marketing strategy and insights. Fiona holds a B.S. with honors in biochemistry, biology and economics from the University of Toronto.

Michael Thomas

As the leader of ZS's global rare disease practice, Michael has supported numerous pharma and biotech companies on their journey to develop and commercialize rare disease therapies and bring hope to underserved patient populations. He brings over 20 years of consulting experience across disciplines, including sales, marketing, technology and operations. With an emphasis on commercial strategies and operations, he has worked to enable the growth of small and mid-size pharmaceutical companies while focusing on bringing the voice of the rare disease patient to pharma. Michael holds an MBA from the Wharton School of the University of Pennsylvania and a B.S. in marketing and logistics from the University of Maryland in College Park.

Albert Whangbo

Albert is one of the leaders of ZS's patient-level data analytics capability, focused on helping life sciences companies make sound decisions through thoughtful research and analysis. He brings 15 years of consulting experience across a wide range of issues, including business development strategy, HEOR and value proposition development, forecasting, sales and marketing resource optimization, and analytics capability building. Albert also leads ZS's real-world data and insights team, a global expertise center that focuses on creating and implementing innovative applications for the rapidly evolving landscape of patient-level data sources. Albert holds a Ph.D. in management science from Stanford University. He also has an M.S. in operations research from Stanford and a B.S. in civil engineering from North Carolina State University.

Index

Symbols

D

E

I

J

K

L

O

P

Z